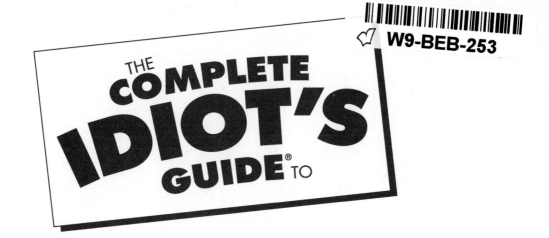

THE

COMPLETE IDIOT'S GUIDE® TO

Sextrology

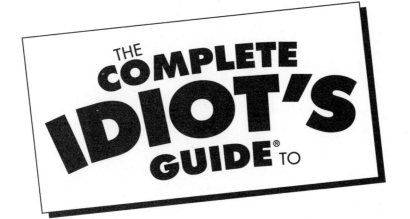

Sextrology

by Megan Skinner

ALPHA

A member of Penguin Group (USA) Inc.

How the stars can guide you to finding the relationship of your dreams.

ALPHA BOOKS

Published by the Penguin Group

Penguin Group (USA) Inc., 375 Hudson Street, New York, New York 10014, U.S.A

Penguin Group (Canada), 90 Eglinton Avenue East, Suite 700, Toronto, Ontario, Canada M4P 2Y3 (a division of Pearson Penguin Canada Inc.)

Penguin Books Ltd., Registered Offices: 80 Strand, London WC2R 0RL, England

Penguin Ireland, 25 St. Stephen's Green, Dublin 2, Ireland (a division of Penguin Books Ltd.)

Penguin Group (Australia), 250 Camberwell Road, Camberwell, Victoria 3124, Australia (a division of Pearson Australia Group Pty. Ltd.)

Penguin Books India Pvt. Ltd., 11 Community Centre, Panchsheel Park, New Delhi—10 017, India

Penguin Group (NZ), 67 Apollo Drive, Rosedale, North Shore, Auckland 1311, New Zealand (a division of Pearson New Zealand Ltd.)

Penguin Books (South Africa) (Pty.) Ltd., 24 Sturdee Avenue, Rosebank, Johannesburg 2196, South Africa

Penguin Books Ltd., Registered Offices: 80 Strand, London WC2R 0RL, England

Copyright © 2008 by Megan Skinner

International Standard Book Number: 978-1-59257-622-7
Library of Congress Catalog Card Number: 2007932631

10   09   08   8   7   6   5   4   3   2   1

Interpretation of the printing code: The rightmost number of the first series of numbers is the year of the book's printing; the rightmost number of the second series of numbers is the number of the book's printing. For example, a printing code of 08-1 shows that the first printing occurred in 2008.

Printed in the United States of America

Note: This publication contains the opinions and ideas of its author. It is intended to provide helpful and informative material on the subject matter covered. It is sold with the understanding that the author and publisher are not engaged in rendering professional services in the book. If the reader requires personal assistance or advice, a competent professional should be consulted.

The author and publisher specifically disclaim any responsibility for any liability, loss, or risk, personal or otherwise, which is incurred as a consequence, directly or indirectly, of the use and application of any of the contents of this book.

Most Alpha books are available at special quantity discounts for bulk purchases for sales promotions, premiums, fund-raising, or educational use. Special books, or book excerpts, can also be created to fit specific needs.

For details, write: Special Markets, Alpha Books, 375 Hudson Street, New York, NY 10014.

Publisher: *Marie Butler-Knight*
Editorial Director: *Mike Sanders*
Managing Editor: *Billy Fields*
Senior Acquisitions Editor: *Paul Dinas*
Development Editor: *Nancy D. Lewis*
Senior Production Editor: *Janette Lynn*
Copy Editor: *Lisanne V. Jensen*

Cartoonist: *Shannon Wheeler*
Cover Designer: *Bill Thomas*
Book Designer: *Trina Wurst*
Indexer: *Tonya Heard*
Layout: *Chad Dressler*
Proofreader: *Mary Hunt*

Contents at a Glance

Appendixes

Contents

Introduction

Sextrology is a fairly new branch of traditional astrology. The practice and understanding of sextrology—how the stars influence your love and sex life—first grabbed the public's attention in the '60s and '70s with the publication of a series of best-selling astrology books by Linda Goodman, most notably: *Sun Signs* and *Love Signs*. For perhaps the first time, astrology became more than a complicated mystical art—or the other extreme, a boilerplate newspaper horoscope. Astrology became comprehensible and personal—it was about you and your relationships. Although tame by today's standards—Goodman's books just hinted at sex—they changed the face of astrology in popular culture and made it inviting and accessible to everyone.

As a young teenager, I discovered a copy of Goodman's *Sun Signs* while babysitting at a neighbor's house. Even then it had the thrill of the illicit ... it was tucked away under their couch! I was immediately hooked. I read all about my astrological sign, my friends' and family's signs, and of course, that of my teenage crush. Goodman's book, along with my copy of *Cosmopolitan* magazine's delightfully fun *Bedside Astrologer*, was my first foray into astrology. This guide follows their tradition while bringing sextrology into the twenty-first century.

The goal of this book is to give you as much information as heavenly possible about the interworkings of your stars and how they affect your relationships and sex life. Sextrology is grounded in the science of astrology. The approach is fun but also informative. We will explore the sexual personalities of each zodiac lover from various astrological viewpoints and give you an idea of how you will interact with one another. We've also included a soul mate section to help you understand your destiny connections.

This book is geared toward helping you better understand your sexual self, be a better lover, and find the relationships of your dreams!

How to Use This Book

Although it is not necessary to have your birth chart to fully utilize this book, it can be helpful. We have provided a list of online astrology services in the appendix at the back of this book. Many offer the service for free or for a very nominal fee.

Part 1, "It's in the Stars," introduces you to basics of sextrology and takes you through the 12 Lovers of the Zodiac by element, Sun sign, and ascendant.

Part 2, "The Moon and Intimacy," explores each of the Moon signs and how they relate to your emotional intimacy and long-term happiness together.

Part 3, "Venus and Mars: Your Sexual Connection," takes you through your Venus and Mars placements, helping you understand your sexual dynamics and relationship compatibility.

Part 4, "Fine-Tuning Your Connection," includes the finer details of sextrology, including your sexual chemistry through the astrological aspects and how the astrological houses reveal what you're likely to experience together.

Part 5, "Soul Mates: Understanding Your Divine Connection," takes sextrology one step further by exploring your soul mate and destiny connections through your star placements.

Extras

In addition to helping you understand and learn more about sextrology, we've included these extras to give you greater insight into your sextrology, to make your journey through the stars even more enjoyable, and to help you avoid potential pitfalls and heartbreaks. These extras are highlighted in the following sidebars:

 Cosmic Lovers

Juicy astrological tidbits about famous lovers: some naughty, some nice! Sexy celebrities and soul mate connections.

 Star Alert!

You'll want to pay attention to these sextrology tips about what to steer clear of in your star connections; they will help you avoid heartbreak.

 Dear Sextrologer ...

To help you better understand your specific sextrology needs, we've included some of the most asked questions in Sextrology.

 Heavenly Relations

Here, you'll get the inside scoop on the stars and how they relate to your love and sex life.

Acknowledgments

The author wishes to thank the following members of her sextrology team who, each in their own way, helped make this book a reality: Cecelia Finnigan, whose sublime editorial skills and finesse were integral to bringing sextrology to life and keeping it on track; C. J. Chaney, for his technical and graphic support, and helpful insight into the male libido; Andrea Hurst, dream agent, friend, and writing helpline; Tiffany Hall and Darcy Pease for their insight and writing support; and last but not least, Divanna Vadree for all of her patience, support, and wise counsel.

This does not mention by name the many friends, family members, clients, and colleagues who were willing to share insight into their own personal sextrology—thank you all!

Trademarks

All terms mentioned in this book that are known to be or are suspected of being trademarks or service marks have been appropriately capitalized. Alpha Books and Penguin Group (USA) Inc. cannot attest to the accuracy of this information. Use of a term in this book should not be regarded as affecting the validity of any trademark or service mark.

Part 1

It's in the Stars

Sextrology is a branch of astrology that focuses specifically on your romantic, sex, and love life. Why are you so attracted to Leos? Why do Capricorns drive you crazy? The stars have the answers if you know how to ask!

Exploring the 12 Lovers of the Zodiac, from impulsive Aries to intuitive Pisces, will reveal each astrological sign's sexual likes and dislikes—as well as what they really, really want in bed!

What Is Sextrology?

In This Chapter

- ◆ Astrology has evolved into a sophisticated science
- ◆ Sextrology explores the sexual dynamics of astrology
- ◆ There are eight essentials to sextrology
- ◆ Sextrology is fun and easy to explore
- ◆ You can be your own sextrologer

Sextrology is similar in nature to love and relationship astrology. It is a branch of astrology that focuses specifically on the attraction potential between the 12 signs of the zodiac. Sextrology takes the astrological love equation one step further by exploring the sexual needs and desires of each astrological sign. Sextrology will help you understand your deepest sexual nature and those of your lover, as well!

The 12 Signs of the Zodiac

Aries	The Impulsive Lover	March 21st–April 20th
Taurus	The Sensual Lover	April 20th–May 21st
Gemini	The Fickle Lover	May 21st–June 22nd
Cancer	The Nurturing Lover	June 22nd–July 23rd
Leo	The Dramatic Lover	July 23rd–August 22nd
Virgo	The Discerning Lover	August 22nd–September 22nd
Libra	The Graceful Lover	September 22nd—October 23rd
Scorpio	The Mysterious Lover	October 23rd–November 22nd
Sagittarius	The Adventurous Lover	November 22nd–December 22nd
Capricorn	The Serious Lover	December 22nd–January 21st
Aquarius	The Elusive Lover	January 21st–February 19th
Pisces	The Intuitive Lover	February 19th–March 21st

The dates for each sign of the zodiac may change within a few days depending on the year.

Dear Sextrologer …

"I am a big fan of astrology! I often check my astrological forecast online and am always amazed at how informative it is. I also check out what's happening for my significant other. Some of my friends, however, think I'm a flake for doing so. Any suggestions?"

Of course you find astrology informative, stargazer. People have used the science of astrology for eons to understand everything from their money and career potential to their love and sex lives! Revel in your brilliance and all that you are learning—about yourself and your partner!

Astrology: Ancient to Modern Times

Since the beginning of humanity, people have gazed into the heavens and wondered about the stars and how these mysterious orbs affected their lives. Granted, in ancient times stargazers were not primarily focused on their dating and sex lives! For the ancients, the science of astrology was used to understand how to survive. How would the planets affect the weather and the crops? Did the stars portend an advantageous birth or a powerful alliance?

Remember what life was like before *Sex and the City* was a cultural phenomenon and modern technologies such as cell phones, text-messaging, and Internet dating were invented. Whereas today astrology is available to everyone, in the ancient world people might have had to travel miles outside their village by foot or horseback to find a skilled star-caster! Although many ancients viewed *astrology* as a form of magic, the ancient astrologers were in fact the educated, wise men and women of their day.

Modern astrologers are still very wise—now perhaps more than ever—because astrologers have a wealth of information available to them that would have been unimaginable to their ancient counterparts. Over the centuries, astrology has developed into a sophisticated science. Today, there are thousands of websites and numerous best-selling books dedicated to astrology, and for good reason: people want to know what their stars have in store for them!

Heavenly Relations _____

Throughout the ages, astrology has been associated with the occult. The word "occult" means secret or mystery. The science of **Astrology** explores the mysteries of life through the knowledge of the stars.

Dear Sextrologer ... _____

"I've dabbled in astrology but would like to get a professional reading. I'm especially interested in my astrological compatibility with my boyfriend. Is there anything I should know about finding a good astrologer?"

Good question! Getting a referral is probably the best way to start, but if you can't do that, there are professional associations for astrologers that will be able to point you in the right direction. Be sure to briefly interview your prospective astrologer in order to get a better idea about his or her background and methodology. It's important to be specific about what you're looking for; that way, you will get the kind of reading you want.

Although many astrologers are self-taught, there are a number of astrology schools and accreditation programs. One of the most reputable is the *American Federation of Astrologers* (AFA)—a worldwide organization that offers accreditation certification and ongoing classes.

As Above, So Below

Astrology calculates the exact positions of the planets and other galactic orbs and their movements through the heavens at a specific moment in time. Mapping the stars at the time of your birth will give you a working and evolving blueprint for your life.

Your astrological chart shows the cosmic patterns that pertain to your life experience—thus: as above, so below. In a spiritual sense, your astrology reflects your soul's journey in this lifetime.

Star Alert! _____

Fate is that which you cannot change. Free will is the exercise of choice and has a large hand in shaping your destiny!

Astrology does not predict the future. It does, however, indicate the potential for certain experiences—some universal in nature and others uniquely personal. Astrology shows the workings of fate in your life, yet free will determines most outcomes. You may share strong astrological affinities with another, but the choices each of you makes ultimately decide the outcome of your experience—individually and together.

Sex and the Stars

Astrology gives many insights into the different elements of life: career, family, children, money, spirituality, and more. Sextrology, however, specifically focuses on your love and sex life. For example:

- ◆ What signs make the best lovers?

- ◆ How can you be a better lover to your partner?

- ◆ What sign is your best sex match?

- ◆ What motivates you to sleep with someone or choose someone to be your lover?

- ◆ Why are you attracted to some signs more than others?

In sextrology, it all boils down to your astrological compatibility. How do you relate to each other in love, romance, and sex? Exploring the dynamics of your star connections can give you important tools for understanding yourself, your lover, and what you really want and need in your relationships and in bed.

Heavenly Relations _____

"You have to kiss a lot of frogs to find your prince—or princess!" Although this old adage may be true, understanding your sextrology can narrow down the process!

Sextrology reveals astrological erogenous zones as well as seduction techniques to keep your lover enthralled. It also describes how your stars align so as to offer you the best possible lovemaking experience! It can also help you determine the probability of whether your connection will be a fleeting sexual encounter or more of a deep and lasting one.

The Eight Essentials of Sextrology

The basics and foundation of sextrology are expressed in the eight essentials. Each essential explores a particular aspect of sextrology, different ways to understand the astrological signs, and the ways in which the signs relate together sexually.

The Eight Essentials of Sextrology

Essential	Theme
1: Elements	Basic sexual energies
2: Qualities	Sexual personality and motivations
3: Sun signs/ascendants	Sexual essence and well-being
4: Moons	Emotional intimacy and sexual needs
5: Venus and Mars	Female and male energies
6: Aspects	Degrees of sexual attraction between signs
7: Houses	Playing fields of experience
8: Moon nodes	Soul mate and destiny connections

Learn these eight essentials, and you will see sexual themes emerge that will help you understand how you and your lover operate. The sections that follow detail how these essentials work.

Essential 1: The Elements

There are four elements in astrology: Fire, Air, Water, and Earth. In sextrology, each element has its own sexual personality that manifests in different ways in each of the astrological signs. The elements reflect an individual's most basic needs and desires. You could think about the elements in this way: they are the energetic foundations from which each sign operates.

The Signs and Their Elements

Fire	Air	Water	Earth
Aries	Gemini	Cancer	Taurus
Leo	Libra	Scorpio	Virgo
Sagittarius	Aquarius	Pisces	Capricorn

The first element is *Fire*. Fire signs—Aries, Leo, and Sagittarius—are outgoing and extremely passionate. They have strong sex drives and do not hesitate to express their needs. They can also be self-involved! Fire types value their independence and need plenty of space to explore the opportunities and adventures that they see everywhere around them. They are most compatible with other Fire signs or with their opposite element, Air.

Star Alert! _____

Fire and Water signs do not easily mix! Fire signs find water to be overly sensitive and too emotional. On the other hand, Water signs find fire sexually overpowering and insensitive to their deeper needs.

Earth and Air signs can be a challenging combination. Earth signs find Air to be sexually detached and too impersonal. Air signs find Earth to be too conservative and limited by their need for security.

The second element is *Air*. Air signs—Gemini, Libra, and Aquarius—are intellectual, individualistic, and curious about life. They require lots of stimuli and are perpetually restless for new forms of self-expression. In the bedroom, air can be a bit detached and at times even seemingly indifferent. Like fire, air signs may have commitment issues! Air signs are most compatible with other air signs or with their opposite element, fire.

The third element is *Water*. Water signs—Cancer, Scorpio, and Pisces—are emotional, intuitive, and security oriented. Romantic and passionate, Water signs seek the sublime in their lovemaking experiences. They have active imaginations and their fantasy lives can spill over into their sexual encounters. Water signs are most compatible with other Water signs or with their opposite element, Earth.

Heavenly Relations _____

Fire and **Air** signs represent male energy, and **Water** and **Earth** signs represent female energy. Male energy is yang energy, which represents the outgoing, aggressive part of human nature. Female energy is the yin principal, representing the receptive, nurturing aspects of human nature.

The fourth element is *Earth*. Earth signs—Taurus, Virgo, and Capricorn—are stable and very practical. They live in the here and now. They seek security, and what's important to them is what's tangible and real. They are earthy and tactile and considered to be the most sensual of all elements! Earth signs are best with other Earth signs or with their opposite element, Water.

Essential 2: The Qualities

The qualities, which are also called modalities, are cardinal, fixed, and mutable. The qualities are the driving force for each astrological sign. They represent what motivates each sign and the way in which each expresses their basic needs and desires. Each quality includes four signs of the zodiac and one element. Every sign of the zodiac has a quality and an element. For example, Aries is Fire and cardinal; Taurus is Earth and fixed.

The Signs and Their Qualities

Cardinal	Fixed	Mutable
Aries	Taurus	Gemini
Libra	Leo	Virgo
Cancer	Scorpio	Sagittarius
Capricorn	Aquarius	Pisces

The first quality is *cardinal.* Cardinal signs are Aries, Cancer, Libra, and Capricorn. This quality is active, aggressive, and forward-moving. Cardinal signs are goal-oriented and highly motivated. They can also be pushy! These signs will go after what they want and will expect you to do the same. Although sometimes bossy, they will inspire you in your own sense of achievement.

The second quality is *fixed.* Fixed signs are Taurus, Leo, Scorpio, and Aquarius. The fixed quality is determined, resilient, and intense. This quality is also extremely stubborn! Fixed signs are determined to maintain status quo and avoid change whenever possible. Although these signs need to be in control and do not like to be challenged, they are always reliable.

The third quality is *mutable.* Mutable signs are Gemini, Virgo, Sagittarius, and Pisces. The mutable quality is flexible and oriented to both exploration and growth. Mutable signs seek opportunities where they will be able to learn and evolve. They thrive on being offered a range of options but can sometimes become overwhelmed by life's many possibilities. Although these signs lack persistence, they are always open to new experiences.

Heavenly Relations

The **elements** (Fire, Air, Earth and Water) and the **qualities** (fixed, mutable and cardinal) are key indicators of the basic sexual themes and motivations for your astrological sign and your lovers!

Essential 3: Sun Signs and Ascendants

In astrology, your Sun represents your true self and unique essence. It also denotes your sense of purpose and well-being. Understanding your Sun sign will help you find the right lover for your heart and spirit. It will also help you discover the best match for your body, because Sun signs also represent the 12 distinct sexual types. Sun signs will also show you how your lover relates to his or her sexual essence. It will give you indications of the shape your passion will take when you come together.

The ascendant, or rising sign, is the astrological sign that was rising over the horizon at the moment of your birth. Ascendants are similar in expression to the Sun —both symbolize how you express yourself to the outside world—but the ascendant more specifically reflects your style of expression and how others will perceive you. Here's a good way to understand the difference between the two: the Sun is your essence, and your ascendant is the attire in which you dress it.

Essential 4: The Moon

Although Sun sign and ascendant compatibility is important to sextrology, your deepest connection can have more to do with how your Moon signs relate. In astrology, the Moon represents your emotions and inner personality. Your Moon is at the root of what motivates you and reflects your deepest needs and desires. We place a lot of emphasis on the Moon sign in sextrology because it relates to your intimacy potential together—and because it also dictates your day-to-day harmony and relationship well-being. Moon signs also reflect how individuals are likely to relate to sexual fidelity, including attitudes toward casual or committed sex.

Star Alert! _____

It's not only the Sun sign that determines relationship compatibility. Your Moon sign and the placements of your Venus and Mars are also important components of your sextrology.

Essential 5: Venus and Mars

Venus and Mars have much to do with your astrological love and sex equation. Venus represents the feminine nature. It is the relationship planet, symbolizing pleasure and beauty and the more romantic aesthetic of love. Mars represents the masculine nature. Mars is the action planet, representing the expression of passion and desire. It is the driving force of our sexual nature.

Venus attracts, and Mars pursues! These planets represent the cosmic dance—okay, here more of a passionate tango—between the male and female energies. By comparing your Venus and Mars with those of your partner, you will better understand and be able to predict your sexual dynamics and compatibility.

Essential 6: The Aspects

The aspects are the different degrees between the astrological signs. In sextrology, the aspects relate to the sexual chemistry between the signs of the zodiac and explore the degrees of sexual heat that you will experience together!

Oppositions	Sexually Sizzling
Conjunctions	Sexually Hot
Trines	Sexually Warm
Sextiles	Sexually Lukewarm
Squares	Sexually Cold
Inconjuncts	Sexually Freezing

The hard aspects are:

◆ Squares: 90 degrees between signs

◆ Inconjuncts: 150 degrees between signs

◆ Oppositions: 180 degrees betweens signs

◆ Conjunctions: 0–5 degrees between signs

Squares and inconjuncts are always difficult and sexually cold! Although conjunctions and oppositions are challenging, they can be quite stimulating and sexually hot!

The soft aspects are:

◆ Sextiles: 60 degrees between signs

◆ Trines: 120 degrees between signs

These aspects are harmonious and sexually very compatible. Sometimes, however, they can be almost too compatible! With this level of ease and comfort, you will need to guard against sexual boredom.

Dear Sextrologer ... _____

"I am a SWF Aquarius and find myself continually attracted to Leo men. This is perplexing, because I find Leos overly dramatic and arrogant! So what gives?"

There's no great mystery to your situation, Aquarius. Leo is your opposite sign. In sextrology, opposites do attract! They also mirror each other's hidden selves. Although opposite-sign relationships can be challenging, they also make stimulating love matches.

Essential 7: The Houses

There are 12 houses in astrology, and each represents a specific area of life. For example, the second house represents money and possessions, and the ninth house spirituality, travel, and higher education.

The houses are important to sextrology because they represent the playing fields in which your relationships will likely unfold. By looking at your astrological houses and where each other's planets fall, you will gain strong indications about what your experience together will be like—and also what you will learn from each other.

Star Alert! _____

In sextrology, the houses you'll want to pay special attention to are: the first, representing the relationship with self; the seventh, representing your relationship with others; and the eighth, which represents deeper intimacy and sexual union.

Universal Astrology Wheel.

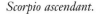

Scorpio ascendant.

The universal astrology wheel shows the 12 astrological houses and the ruling sign for each. Your individual birth chart, based on your day, time, and place of birth, shows your ascendant (or rising) sign and sets up your natal astrology wheel. For example, if you have Scorpio rising, Scorpio will rule your first house; Sagittarius will be the ruler for your second house; Capricorn the third; and so on through each sign of the zodiac.

For more information about getting your birth chart, refer to Appendix B.

 Heavenly Relations

The universal astrology wheel indicates the astrological houses and the natural ruler for each, beginning with Aries on the first house, Taurus on the second house, Gemini on the third house and so on through each house and the 12 signs of the zodiac.

Essential 8: The Nodes of the Moon

The Nodes of the Moon are not planets but astrological points representing karma and destiny. Moon Nodes reflect the soul's evolution and desire for growth in this lifetime. In sextrology, Moon Nodes relate to your soul connections with another. Strong Moon Node connections indicate a soul mate relationship.

Cosmic Lovers

The Bible tells us the story of Adam and Eve, who were lovers facing a mythic choice: knowledge or bliss? In every relationship, choices are always involved. The question is: will you play it safe or choose to grow and evolve?

Keep in mind that although profound, soul mate relationships are not necessarily easy or blissful! In fact, the opposite is often true—because soul mate connections reflect past karma together and ongoing issues that need to be resolved. Ultimately, Moon Nodes indicate mutual growth experiences and the lessons you're meant to learn from each other. (For more info see Chapters 14, 15, and 16.)

Getting Started

If you're feeling a bit overwhelmed by all of the details and elements of sextrology—don't! Exploring your sextrology is like baking a layer cake. First, you mix different ingredients together and then add one layer on top of the next—one at a time! Even seasoned astrologers are always learning and incorporating new information along the way. Sextrology is a serious science, but it's important to have fun and give yourself lots of room to learn and grow in your experience and understanding.

To get started, just take one essential at a time. You can choose between the different essentials and go back and forth as you learn. You might want to first get a feeling for the different signs by looking at their elements and qualities. Then, look at the Sun signs and ascendants, which will give you a lot of information about the sexual essence for each sign. Next, incorporate your Moon sign, your Venus and Mars, your houses and aspects—in no particular order, depending on your interest.

You can also begin to check out your soul mate connections while you're learning other components of sextrology. You will build your understanding of the science as you weave in new pieces along the way.

Getting Your Astrology Birth Chart

Like many elements of modern life, astrology has gone high-tech. In the old days (about 10 years ago!), astrologers drew charts by hand. This process was complicated and involved a great deal of mathematical calculation. Now, we have computers and astrology software to do the work for us—thank heavens!

The new technology is available to amateur and professional astrologers alike. Combined with the wealth of information now available on astrology, the science has become accessible to everyone. Now, you can be your own sextrologer!

Obtaining your astrological chart is easy. Most metaphysical bookstores can create a chart for you, usually for under $10. A number of astrology websites also offer the service for free or for a nominal fee. To get your chart, you will need to know the date, time, and place of your birth. (Note: you do not need your full chart to utilize this book.) We've included some online astrology services in Appendix B to get you started, and you can find all of your planet or other notable star placements by using an *ephemeris*, which you can learn how to read in Appendix C.

Heavenly Relations

An **ephemeris** is a daily listing of planets and their astrological placements by sign and degree.

Dear Sextrologer …

"I want to know more about my astrology, but I'm adopted and don't know my exact time of birth. Can I still get my full birth chart?"

Without your exact time of birth, you cannot calculate your complete astrological chart. Do not despair, however—you can find all of your planets and other notable star placements by using an online ephemeris or by putting your birth data into an astrology website.

The Least You Need to Know

◆ Sextrology explores your love and sex life through the stars.

◆ You can be your own sextrologer!

◆ The eight essentials of sextrology (elements, qualities, Sun signs/ascendants, Moons, Venus and Mars, aspects, houses, and Moon Nodes) will help you to understand your relationship with each astrological sign.

◆ Sextrology also gives important indications about your soul mate connections.

Fire Sun Signs and Ascendants

In This Chapter

- Aries, Leo, and Sagittarius are the Fire signs
- Impulsive Aries, the Ram
- Dramatic Leo, the Lion
- Adventurous Sagittarius, the Archer

Fire signs move fast. They are independent, spontaneous, and extremely passionate. They have very large egos and can also be self-involved. Fire signs really like to get their own way! Optimistic, energetic, and creative, Fire signs are almost always a heck of a lot of fun to be around. This type likes to be on top—in bed and everywhere else! All of these fiery character traits will be amply demonstrated in their romantic relationships—and in the bedroom.

Aries, the Ram: The Impulsive Lover

March 21st–April 20th

Element: Fire

Planetary Ruler: Mars

Quality: Cardinal

Energy: Male

Compatible Signs: Fire and Air

Key Words: Independent, forceful, driven

Color: Red

Gem: Diamond

Erogenous Zones: Head, face, scalp, hair

How to Recognize a Ram: Look out for the Ram's intimidating "power stance." Rams stand tall and hold their heads high—all the better to survey the competition, my dear, and the world that they wish to conquer! They can often be found at their local gym—the watering hole for many Rams—working their biceps, triceps, quads, gluts—and their egos!

Famous Rams: Alec Baldwin, Jennifer Garner, Bette Davis, Warren Beatty, Sarah Jessica Parker, Mariah Carey, Steve McQueen, Marlon Brando

All About Aries

Aries is the first sign of the zodiac, the first Fire sign, and the first sign of spring. If you're sensing a theme here, then you're right on track! Rams like to be first in all that they do. They come first in their own lives and will want to come first in yours, too. The sign of Aries represents beginnings, and Rams are impatient for new opportunities that will propel them forward in life. At the same time, Rams are not good at following through or finishing what they start. Their nature is to set aside the known and move on to the next new thing.

Heavenly Relations

Ruled by Mars (the "action planet"), Rams thrive on physical activity. They are survivors—even warriors at heart. For Aries, it's often them against the world. Rams love to fight the good fight and will always stand up for what they believe in.

Daredevils in life and in love, Rams are risk-takers. They have strong wills and can be very aggressive about getting what they want—and usually, they want it right now! Resourceful and enterprising, Rams are born leaders. They do not hesitate to take charge and are often the first to rush in and save the day.

These impulsive lovers are ruled by their instincts: Rams act first and think later! Rams have fiery emotions; they are easily frustrated and can be quick to anger. Yet, Rams get over their outbursts very quickly and rarely hold a grudge.

Rams are independent and self-reliant. They can take care of themselves, thank you very much! At times, they can be infuriatingly self-confident. They do not like to be controlled and need space to be who they are. At the same time, they will give you the gift of space and the freedom to be yourself and will typically support you in anything you do. Rams can be powerful motivators!

Cosmic Lovers

"Stella!" In his early movie roles, Aries Marlon Brando personifies the raw sexual energy of the Ram.

Dear Sextrologer …

"I'm dating an Aries, and at the beginning of our relationship he couldn't keep his hands off me! Now, it takes a lot to get his attention. Any suggestions?"

After the initial rush of attention, Rams can start to take you for granted very quickly. To renew their interest, you may need to pull back a little. Let him pursue you all over again, and get ready for the sexual fireworks!

Aries in Love and Lust

There's no great mystery about an Aries in love. Rams are honest and open about their feelings, and if an Aries wants to be with you, you will know it—because he or she will tell you. You'll also know it because you will be pursued with a fervent and obvious passion. Rams in love can be relentless! Count on them for constant phone calls and text messages. They may even show up on your doorstep unannounced!

Rams like to conquer new territory. In love, this territory may well be you! They love the thrill of the chase, and they bore very easily. They will expect you to be as spontaneous as they are, and they're never ones to plan ahead.

Rams have strong sex drives and make fearless lovers. They're vigorous and passionate. It's never just sex with an Aries—it's a full-body workout! Male or female, lustful

Rams can be bold about getting you into bed and will do everything they can to sweep you off your feet.

Star Alert!

If your idea of a romantic evening is staying at home and cuddling up together with a DVD, then Aries is not the sign for you. Try mountain climbing, skydiving lessons, or even learning how to fly!

An Aries' bossy side can show up in the bedroom. They like to be in charge and can be impatient about getting their needs met. Once the fires of lovemaking have cooled, however, they may not be quite sure what to do with you! Aries is big on excitement, but snuggling afterward can leave them cold.

Rams are not usually well versed in the finer nuances of lovemaking. Their moves are likely to be very much to the point and outcome-driven! Rams may need some tutoring about what makes you happy and satisfied in bed. On the other hand, they may be very willing to learn!

The Fine Art of Astro-Seduction: Aries

The secret to seducing an Aries is to let them be the pursuers. In the Aries love game, the more unavailable you are the more your Aries will want you! There is nothing sexier to an Aries than confidence. To keep them on their toes (and consequently, in your life), you will need to make it clear that you can take care of yourself and that you can live without them. Game plan: don't call them, let them call you!

The Best and Worst of Aries Lovers

At his or her best, your Aries lover will be a stimulating and passionate love match. Rams can inspire you to possibilities that you've never dreamed of. They can also be strong allies in helping you achieve your greatest desires. Always honest and direct, your Aries lover will not play games with you or lead you on. In the right relationship, Rams are devoted and exciting partners.

Heavenly Relations

Aries turn-ons include: strong bodies and independent minds, intense physicality, experimentation, urgent and athletic sex—and for Rams, one-night stands are not out of the question!

There's no other way to put it: your Aries lover is prone to selfishness. At their worst, Rams are inconsiderate and thoughtless about your needs. They will need to be reminded about you—your needs, your wants, your desires—and then reminded some more. The Aries lesson in life—and in love—is to learn to balance their own needs with the needs of others.

Leo, the Lion: The Dramatic Lover

July 23rd–August 22nd

Element: Fire

Planetary Ruler: The Sun

Quality: Fixed

Energy: Male

Compatible Signs: Fire and Air

Key Words: Creative, loyal, optimistic

Color: Bright gold

Gems: Ruby and peridot

Erogenous Zones: Upper backs, spine

Star Alert!

Fidelity, like loyalty, is important to Lions. The good news is that Leos have great potential for long-term, sustained relationships. The not-so-good news is that Lions can be jealous and territorial. They like to be in control and can be arrogant about their needs.

How to Recognize a Lion: Look for the flamboyant and well-groomed man or woman with an eye on the mirror! Leos often have beautiful, thick heads of hair and long, shapely limbs.

Lions are easily recognized by their natural exuberance and willingness to share every little detail of their lives! You'll learn what's going on in their love lives, who they're dating and why, what they're doing at work, and all about their many personal dramas.

Famous Lions: Mick Jagger, Jennifer Lopez, Robert DeNiro, Madonna, Sean Penn, Martha Stewart, Ben Affleck, Jacqueline Kennedy Onassis

All About Leo

Leos are the true divas of the zodiac! Drama is Leo's calling card, and they cultivate it wherever they go.

Ruled by the Sun—the center of the solar system—Leos love to be the focus of attention. Lions seek out the spotlight and opportunities where they can shine. Vivid and colorful characters, Leos have magnetic personalities—and people want to be part of the Leo experience.

Lions are ambitious by nature. The sign of the Lion rules fame, and Leos have creative personalities and big dreams. They are compelled to share their talents with the world and need to be recognized for their individual gifts and unique contributions.

Dear Sextrologer ...

"I'm a hard-working Leo with a career in business. The problem? I have a secret desire for a career in the performing arts. I have just started taking acting and singing lessons. My husband thinks I'm crazy to even think about pursuing my aspirations. Help!"

Of course you are seeking some form of creative expression—you're a Leo! Let your husband know how important your aspirations are to your sense of wholeness. It probably won't take him long to notice how much sexual drama and spice this will add to your relationship, as well! He may soon be the one who tells you to go for it!

Lions have a talent for making others feel special. They freely offer their royal protection to their favorites, and their princely generosity can be unmatched. At the same time, they will expect you to give them their royal due by making them an integral part of your life. Anything else will be ... well, unacceptable!

Leos are optimists. Their glass is rarely half-empty—it's full of life and ready to spill over! They are brave and courageous and see the best in everyone. Although they can be taken advantage of as a result, they are resilient and will bounce back from defeat. It takes a lot to keep a Leo down!

Leos in Love and Lust

The romance! The passion! The excitement! Leos in love can be dramatic to the extreme. They have big emotions and rarely hesitate to express them. Whatever else is going on in their lives, fulfilling relationships is a primary element of a Leo's happiness.

Heavenly Relations

Leo turn-ons include: play-fighting, toys and props, exhibitionism, videotaping, variety and creative positions, and yes—for Lions—size does matter!

Lion's dating rituals can be extravagant. They are big givers and will shower you with gifts as a way of showing you their affection. Socially adept and always entertaining, these dramatic lovers have immense savoir-faire. Leos in love can be smooth operators and can charm the pants off you—literally!

At the same time, Lions wear their hearts on their sleeves and can be vulnerable in love. They are proud creatures, and despite all their strength and prowess, they tend to be insecure. Their fragile egos make it difficult for them to handle rejection in any form, and their feelings are easily hurt. When not at their best, Lions are overly needy and will want too much of your time and attention.

Leos love a good romp in bed! But first, you can count on them to set the stage. They may choose satin sheets sprinkled with rose petals and plenty of soft candlelight to create the right mood, or they'll pop the cork on some very expensive French bubbly. Sex with a Leo is sure to be a theatrical experience, and they will want to spoil you as much as they want to seduce you! Lions also like to look good, so there will always be some preening involved. Girl Lions might like to dress up in sexy negligées or—roar!—stilettos, while the men will always take time for careful grooming.

Heavenly Relations

Hollywood is a Leo town! It's no coincidence that many of our sexiest and most provocative movie stars are Lions. If you want sexual drama and entertainment, Leo is the one for you.

Once you get past all the external theatrics, you can expect real passion from a Leo. Lions make exciting bed partners. They are fun and playful and can be very creative sexually! Lions are generous bedmates. They aim to please, and the happier you are, the happier they will be.

For all their passionate ways, though, Leos in lust can be vulnerable about their performance. A little flattery, whispered admiration, and even some heartfelt applause will never hurt! In or out of the bedroom, a Lion's pride is always at stake.

Cosmic Lovers

"Material Girl" Madonna is the quintessential Leo! Lions have a passion for flash, a taste for luxury, and a weakness for sexy lingerie.

The Fine Art of Astro-Seduction: Leo

The key to seducing Leos is to make them feel special and appreciated. To achieve this goal, you may need to get creative. Step one: appeal to their romantic natures. Step two: pamper the heck out of them! Step 3: Lions like to have fun, so plan an exciting playdate together. Step four: make them feel like they are the most important person in your life (at least, for the moment!). Game plan: come bearing gifts, and compliment them at every opportunity.

The Best and Worst of Leo Lovers

At his or her best, your Leo lover will be a powerful and positive force in your life. They are great fun, eternal optimists, and big-hearted. Lions are great cheerleaders and will enthusiastically encourage you to do whatever brings you happiness. They are loyal and devoted partners and will stick with you through good times and bad.

At their worst, Leo lovers are self-involved and needy. Although they want to make you happy, they can be inflexible when it comes to their needs. Leos' love of drama can be so extreme that you might find yourself insisting, "Enough already!" Vanity is Leo's downfall and learning humility their lesson in life. Leos must realize that the world does not always revolve around them!

Sagittarius, the Archer: The Adventurous Lover

November 22nd–December 22nd

Element: Fire

Planetary Ruler: Jupiter

Quality: Mutable

Energy: Male

Compatible Signs: Fire and Air

Key Words: Expansive, idealistic, enthusiastic

Color: Purple

Gem: Turquoise

Erogenous Zones: Thighs, hips, butts

How to Recognize an Archer: Archers have a funny way of entering a room. They seem to have the grand "Fire sign" entrance down—head high, chest expanded, forceful gait—but watch! They will clumsily trip over you, themselves, or the carpet, apologize laughingly, and then entertain the crowd with a funny story on their way to the bar or buffet table.

Famous Archers: Brad Pitt, Jane Fonda, Teri Hatcher, Woody Allen, Britney Spears, Bette Midler, Frank Sinatra, Mark Twain

Star Alert!

Gregarious and outgoing, Archers are the life of any party. For Sag, it's, "Let's eat, drink, and be merry, and the heck with tomorrow!"

All About Sagittarius

Sagittarius lives large and has a big appetite for life. For Sag, life is a smorgasbord of tempting opportunities—and the Archer wants the freedom to explore them all! These independent individuals are always on the hunt for new adventures and resent restrictions of any kind. The Archer's motto in life and in love is, "More, more, more!"

The sign of Sagittarius represents the seeker on a quest for truth and higher wisdom. Sagittarians love to learn and travel, and their knowledge is typically obtained through a combination of varied life experiences and formal academic training. Philosophers by nature, Archers strive to understand their purpose in life and sometimes even the very meaning of existence!

The ruling planet for Sagittarius is Jupiter, the biggest orb in the heavens. Archers are big-picture people. They don't worry about details or mundane practicalities—there's too much to do! Sag is versatile and multitalented; yet, these fun-loving gamblers can be irresponsible when it comes to completing tasks or keeping track of their obligations. A great jack-of-all-trades, Sag is nonetheless often the master of none.

Archers have an opinion on just about everything! This sign is not known for its modesty or its tact. Sags are often very intelligent and can be extremely articulate. They have fixed ideas and are passionate about their beliefs. Archers can waver between using their wisdom to inspire others or simply becoming preachy and argumentative.

 Dear Sextrologer ...

"I'm a Sagittarius and recently took the plunge and proposed to my long-time girlfriend. Now, with all the wedding planning—cakes, dresses, floral arrangements—I'm feeling overwhelmed and am starting to get cold feet! What should I do?"

Congratulations on your upcoming marriage, Sag! What you're likely experiencing are two very traditional Sagittarian challenges: commitment phobia and the inability to deal with too many details. Suggestion: let her go ahead and plan the wedding that she's always dreamed of, then relax and enjoy the festivities. And look at it this way—your marriage is going to be a whole new adventure!

Sagittarius in Love and Lust

It's easy to fall in love with flirtatious, fun-loving Sags. It is difficult, however, to capture their hearts. Sagittarius is the sign of the bachelor, and male or female, they are notorious for their fear of commitment. When the game gets too serious, the once-affectionate and funny Sag may turn suddenly grumpy and aloof.

Archers are often uncomfortable with their emotions and can be clumsy when it comes to expressing their feelings. They are more likely to show their affection through actions rather than words. Sags rarely do anything they don't want to, so if they're spending time with you, it's because they really want to!

Sags will love you for your independence and self-sufficiency. No matter how smitten, your Sagittarius lover will need lots of space and plenty of breathing room. They also appreciate honesty, and the more straightforward you are about what you want, the more Sag will appreciate you.

Heavenly Relations

Writer and humorist Mark Twain was a Sag! Archers are born storytellers and will entertain you with stories of their many escapades.

Cosmic Lovers

Sagittarius sex symbol Brad Pitt, like many of this sign, is a gypsy at heart. Archers will search the globe looking for new experiences. Pack your suitcase, and keep your passport handy!

The pursuit of pleasure is always an adventure with Sagittarius. Indoors, outdoors, upstairs, downstairs—name the time and the place, and they'll be there—and all over you! Although your rendezvous with worldly Sag might be at that little French bistro across town, it might also be in London, Rome, or Istanbul! Whatever the location, you're in for an exciting and stimulating lovemaking experience.

Like all Fire signs, Sagittarius has a strong sex drive. Archers are lusty creatures and rarely shy away from exploring new avenues in bed. Sex with Sag is usually hot and passionate, and they make enthusiastic and versatile lovers. They like to have a good time and seldom give tomorrow a second thought.

Sags' love of freedom can apply to their sex lives, as well. Archers don't need to be deeply in love to have sex, nor do they necessarily limit lovemaking to one person. No matter how long your relationship lasts or whether it's over in one night, they will respect you in the morning and genuinely appreciate what you shared together.

The Fine Art of Astro-Seduction: Sagittarius

Seducing a Sagittarius is not difficult: this pleasure-seeker is usually up for a good time. Sags are attracted to outgoing personalities and to people who can make them laugh. Archers also love humanitarians, so you might casually mention your Peace Corps trip to Africa or your work at the local soup kitchen. Top it off with a little flattery, and they're in the bag! Game plan: make your presence known, and go for it!

The Best and Worst of Sagittarian Lovers

Life with Sagittarius will always be an adventure! Archers will expand your world and stimulate you to think in new ways. Buoyant and fun-loving, they will be a positive, motivating force in your life. Your Sag lover may also inspire you to finally purchase that plane ticket and explore that adventure you've always dreamed of. At their best, Sags are wise and intuitive with a wealth of knowledge that they will love to share.

Heavenly Relations

Sag turn-ons: rock-hard bodies, deeply penetrating minds, luxurious foreplay, and decadent food and drink. Paint your body with chocolate, and keep the lights on!

At their worst, Sag lovers are elusive and hard to pin down. Their fear of commitment can become overriding and their romantic feelings short-lived. Brash and opinionated, Sags can make it difficult for you to get a word in edgewise. Archers also may get so caught up in their many activities that they forget to return your phone calls! The Sagittarius lesson in life is to learn to follow through on commitments.

The Least You Need to Know

- ◆ Fire signs are Aries, Leo, and Sagittarius.
- ◆ Impulsive Aries seeks action and bores easily.
- ◆ Dramatic Leo seeks attention and recognition.
- ◆ Adventurous Sag seeks opportunities for growth.

Air Sun Signs and Ascendants

In This Chapter

- Gemini, Libra, and Aquarius are the Air signs
- Fickle Gemini, the Twins
- Graceful Libra, the Scales
- Ambivalent Aquarius, the Water Bearer

Air signs are intellectual, conceptual, and very versatile. They pride themselves on their highly individualistic natures and often live life on their own unique terms. They are idealistic and keep their eyes on the big picture. Much of the most current art and technology are born in the fertile brains of Gemini, Libra, and Aquarius.

Air signs surround themselves with friends who will inspire them intellectually and creatively. Although some may find long-term commitment a challenge, they are always thought-provoking and make inspiring bedmates. And they're voted most likely to sexually experiment!

Gemini, the Twins: The Fickle Lover

May 21st–June 22nd

Element: Air

Planetary Ruler: Mercury

Quality: Mutable

Energy: Male

Compatible Signs: Air and Fire

Key Words: Curious, restless, spontaneous

Color: Yellow

Gems: Alexandrite and agate

Erogenous Zones: Hands, chest, shoulders

How to Recognize a Twin: They're hard not to notice! They will sweep into a room like whirling dervishes of activity. They have wiry physiques and an abundance of nervous energy. Mischievous Twins love to stir the pot to keep things interesting. They will talk on and on, constantly gesturing with their hands to make a point and get your attention.

Famous Twins: Colin Farrell, Nicole Kidman, Mary Kate and Ashley Olsen, Bob Dylan, Angelina Jolie, John F. Kennedy, Johnny Depp

Star Alert!

Twins are notorious gossips, so you may want to think twice before trusting them with your secrets!

All About Gemini

The symbol for Gemini is twins, reflecting the dual nature of this sign. At times, Twins may seem like they have split personalities! One minute they're completely into you and the next they've moved on to someone else or some other new experience. These fickle lovers are easily distracted and continually restless for new excitement. Although pinning their affections down can be frustrating, life with a Gemini will never be boring!

Gemini is ruled by the planet Mercury, which represents the mind and intellect. Twins love to discover new facts—and should guard against becoming information junkies! They can be so caught up in the moment they forget to see the big picture. Twins thrive on variety and are talented multitaskers. They can read the paper, receive a fax, watch CNN, eat a sandwich, and talk to you on their cell phones—all at the same time!

Twins are fun-loving and entertaining. It's no surprise that they are often at the top of everyone's guest list. Extremely friendly, Twins can be social butterflies—happily flitting from one gathering to the next. Gemini is the sign representing communication, and Twins do love to communicate! They have sharp, quick wits and make stimulating conversationalists.

Geminis have so many facets that it can be hard to get to know them, much less understand them. They can be like complicated jigsaw puzzles—or for the more romantically inclined, sublime riddles—just waiting to be solved! Twins' minds are in constant motion, and as a result their personalities may seem to change very abruptly. Expect the unexpected: Twins are true chameleons with the ability to blend easily into many different environments.

 Cosmic Lovers _____

Actor Johnny Depp is a Gemini. This rogue pirate is an elusive charmer and loves to play the bad boy. For Twins, good often equals boring ... and bad is extremely exciting!

Gemini in Love and Lust

Twins like the *idea* of being in love. They are affectionate and can be delightfully romantic in the moment. They can also be quite daring and impulsive when it comes to pursuing the object of their desire. The reality of a sustained connection, however, is often an intimidating proposition. Twins like to keep their relationship options open.

Fun and playful, Twins can be childlike in expressing their affections. They are charming and often have a mischievous twinkle in their eye. For Twins, flirting is an art! Although these lovers make interesting and exciting partners, they quickly lose interest if things become dull. When it comes to emotional intimacy, Twins can be distant and detached. When it comes to remember-

 Star Alert! _____

Sexual fidelity is an issue for this sign. In their pursuit of newness and excitement, they can be sexual players. They may flirt with danger and be irresponsible in their sexual choices.

ing their commitments, they may conveniently develop short-term memory loss! The simple truth: no matter how heartfelt their intentions, Twins have a tendency to be fickle.

Twins are versatile lovers and can be very flexible when it comes to fulfilling your deepest desires. They're curious in life—and in the bedroom! Twins often embrace sexual experimentation. If you enjoy playing sex games, Gemini says: "When do we get started?" If you want to play dress-up or experiment with role-playing, Gemini says: "What do you want me to be?" Whatever your sexual fantasy, Gemini will help you make it real!

Intrigue is a big part of the Gemini sex equation. They will be fascinated not only by your body but by your mind! Talking is an important prelude to sex, and verbal intercourse can really get them going! The fun with Gemini doesn't end with sex, however. They will entertain you with their wit and charm and want to play with you all night long.

Dear Sextrologer …

"I'm dating a Gemini and think that she really digs me. But whenever we go out together, she keeps flirting with other men! When I bring this up, she says that I'm overreacting. Am I insecure, or do I have a right to be concerned?"

Twins are born flirts! It's often their way of expressing their energetic, outgoing natures. Your free-spirited Gemini is unlikely to change, no matter what you say or do. Gauge the strength of his or her affections by how he or she behaves toward and with you. If you need single-minded devotion, find yourself a loving Taurus or Cancer; Gemini is probably not the right Sun sign for you.

The Fine Art of Astro-Seduction: Gemini

The key to seducing Twins is to know that they need to be intrigued. Nothing gets to a Gemini's libido faster than scintillating, sexy conversation. Whisper your sexual fantasies in their ears and tease them with your willingness to play, and you'll have their attention very quickly! Remember, they like variety and don't like to be bored. Game plan: massage their massive mental orbs with interesting conversation spiced with sexual innuendo.

Heavenly Relations

Gemini turn-ons: these cosmic swingers like versatile, imaginative lovers and forbidden fruit—including exhibitionism, teasing, quickies, and kinky, circus-style sex.

The Best and Worst of Gemini Lovers

Life with a Gemini is guaranteed to be a roller-coaster ride with plenty of ups and downs. At their best, Gemini lovers will make you an integral part of their thrill ride. They are fun and stimulating partners and will always keep you on your toes. Twins will teach you to become more spontaneous and flexible and to live your life in the moment.

At their worst, Gemini lovers are undependable and even downright flaky! Their lack of focus can make you nutty, and their need for constant stimulation may drive you to distraction. You may also tire of your Gemini juggling you along with his or her many other interests. At times, you may have to say, "Hello! Remember me?" Their lesson in life and in love is to learn to be consistent.

Libra, The Scales: The Graceful Lover

September 22nd–October 23rd

Element: Air

Planetary Ruler: Venus

Principal: Cardinal

Energy: Male

Compatible Signs: Air and Fire

Key Words: Refined, romantic, diplomatic

Colors: Blue, rose

Gems: Opal and tourmaline

Erogenous Zones: Necks, lower backs

How to Recognize a Scale: Scales are known for their physical beauty. They have good bone structure, long limbs, and lithe walks. Notice their cultured air in all that they do and touch—whether they are arranging their lives in a palace or in a one bedroom apartment—or deciding what ingredients to put into their dinner. Their flair and intelligence will show in every detail.

Famous Scales: Gwyneth Paltrow, Will Smith, Brigitte Bardot, John Lennon, Kate Winslet, Susan Sarandon, Christopher Reeve, F. Scott Fitzgerald

All About Libra

Scales seek the extraordinary in all that they do! Ever-romantic Libra loves nothing more than the experience of being in love and is happiest when in a relationship. Through the inevitable balance that partnerships require, Scales learn the most about themselves. Yet, Scales are no pushovers when it comes to their relationship choices. They can be extremely picky and will seek perfection in their partners and bedmates.

The symbol for Libra is the scales, representing the balance of opposites. Libras have the ability to see both sides of most situations and can make great judges and diplomats. Their decision-making process can be endless, however, and Scales will expend a lot of time and energy weighing and measuring every conceivable option. Once they have made a decision, they will often second-guess themselves. Libra's Achilles' heel is indecision!

Libras tend to be people pleasers. These graceful lovers strive for harmony and are unhappy with chaos or disarray.

Confrontation makes them extremely uncomfortable, and they will take great pains to keep the peace. As a result, Scales often compromise their needs to keep everyone else happy. Most Libras could benefit from assertiveness training! Even when they do manage to stand up for themselves, they will often feel remorseful and apologize profusely.

Like all Air signs, Scales are mentally agile and highly verbal. Scales symbolize justice, and Libras can be righteous in their approach to life. Nothing fires up a Libra's indignation more than unfairness. Scales are lovers rather than fighters, but these fine orators will give you a good debate when it comes to matters of ethical import.

Heavenly Relations

Ruled by Venus, the planet of beauty and pleasure, Libras have a deeply refined aesthetic. Artistic by nature, Scales have a strong sense of style. You will see this trait in their art collections, their beautifully decorated homes, and in the way they present themselves.

Cosmic Lovers

Literary heroine and "wanton sex goddess" Bridget Jones is a likely Libra! The romantically minded Ms. Jones was perpetually frustrated in her pursuit of finding Mr. Right, but even under the most daunting circumstances she never settled for second best.

Libra in Love and Lust

The central focus of Libra's life is the search for the perfect soul. They will often make mental lists outlining their ideal partner's characteristics and personality traits. When the reality doesn't live up to their expectations, Scales can be sorely disappointed. Scales often experience a tug of war between their ideals and the reality of the situation and constantly seek to reconcile the two.

Male or female, Libras in love can be very sweet. When it comes to courtship, they are romantic and old-fashioned. Libra sincerely believes in real dates planned in advance, complete with dinner and dancing or the opera (or some other cultural event). Show up or be ready on time, and be groomed and dressed for the occasion! Although Scales pride themselves in their flexibility, they will consider your tardiness to be a romantic slight. Bad manners or rude behavior will leave them cold.

Libras can be both alluring and sensual while being remote and inaccessible. The resulting combination can be genuinely perplexing! Libras can be quite seductive when they choose and in turn enjoy being seduced. For Libra, seduction is an art. They expect sex to be an exquisite experience; at the same time, however, they are often shy when expressing their sexual needs. They do not like to rush or be rushed into bed and delight in foreplay. Light touching, flirting, and romantic tête-á-têtes can be a very good start. Kissing is also very important to Scales, no matter how long-standing the relationship.

Heavenly Relations

Libra's ruler, Venus, is also known as Aphrodite in Greek mythology. This sexy goddess was a temptress and seductress who enticed both men and gods alike!

Dear Sextrologer ...

"I'm a Libra in love with my husband until death do us part. Yet, honestly, he's a total slob! He would rather veg out in his sweats in front of the TV and watch sports than do anything that I would consider interesting. Help!"

One of your many gifts, Libra, is your ability to compromise. Although you may want a total husband makeover, the reality is that you may have to give a little. Suggestion: plan a sports night together—yes, together—and then a date night for the two of you that focuses on your needs. Make the tradeoff explicit! This should put the much-needed balance back into your relationship.

Star Alert! _____

Here are Libra's seven dating sins: 1) unavailable; 2) uncultured; 3) ill-mannered; 4) cheap; 5) inattentive; 6) ill-dressed; and 7) boring!

Like all Air signs, Libras are intellectually oriented. You will want to stimulate their minds as much as you stimulate their bodies. Reading erotic bedtime stories together could work well in bringing Libra's fantasies to life! Scales are sensitive to the finer nuances of lovemaking and seek beauty in sexual passion. For Libras, pleasure should be slow and lasting.

The Fine Art of Astro-Seduction: Libra

Although Scales are always looking for the mysterious and elusive Mr. or Ms. Right, in order to captivate their interest—and get them into bed—you're going to have to be a class act. The key lies in the presentation: court them faithfully, surround them with beauty, let them know that you admire them, and be sure to respect their deeper sensitivities. Game plan: two tickets to an art show, a romantic dinner, and a copy of the *Kama Sutra*—wrapped in brown paper for discretion, of course!

The Best and Worst of Libra Lovers

At his or her best, your Libra lover is a caring and devoted partner. Scales will appreciate your time and attention and give as much as they receive. Libras love being in a relationship, and they will meet you every step of the way. Intelligent and cultured, Scales will enhance your life with their fine aesthetics, and you will come to respect their sense of ethics and justice as well.

Heavenly Relations _____

Libra turn-ons: sculptured bodies, good grooming, extended foreplay, tongue teasing, love bites, and erotica. Cultured Europeans are also quite nice!

At their worst, your Libra lover is indecisive and passive about his or her needs. Ask Libras what they want you to do—or even where they want to eat dinner—and they are likely to ask what *you* want instead. Insist that they make a decision, and they are capable of vacillating endlessly. This can be frustrating, and you may find yourself growling, "Make up your mind already!" Libra's lesson in life is learning to stick with their decisions.

Aquarius, the Water Bearer: The Ambivalent Lover

January 21st–February 19th

Element: Air

Planetary Ruler: Uranus

Quality: Fixed

Energy: Male

Compatible Signs: Air and Fire

Key Words: Eccentric, inspirational, innovative

Color: Violet

Gem: Amethyst

Erogenous Zones: Legs, knees, ankles

Recognizing a Water Bearer: Attention, fashion police! Water Bearers are often spotted by their very eccentric and often downright wacky choice of outfits. Males may range from a Hugh Hefner smoking jacket and ascot to total nerd attire: stiff white shirts and pocket protectors! Females might wear a hippie skirt and Birkenstocks_ or perhaps even stilettos and a flamboyant boa!

Famous Water Bearers: Oprah Winfrey, John Travolta, Jennifer Aniston, Yoko Ono, Paul Newman, Mikhail Baryshnikov, Ellen DeGeneres, Virginia Woolf

All About Aquarius

Eccentric Aquarius has the mind of a highbrow intellectual and the heart of a freedom-loving hippie! Individuality is the key to their nature, and nothing grieves these free spirits more than complacency or convention. Although Water Bearers present a real challenge when it comes to long-term commitment, they make inspiring friends and bedmates and are always full of surprises!

Ruled by Uranus—often referred to as the earthquake planet—Water Bearers love to shake things up! Original and often ahead of their times, Water Bearers are rebels and rule-breakers. Aquarius will not hesitate to shock! They can wake you up to new ideas and inspire you to possibilities that you never dreamed of. At times, however, you may find their behavior to be unnervingly inappropriate or just plain outlandish!

Water Bearers are innovative thinkers and thrive on intellectual stimulation. They are often well-read on subjects as diverse as politics, quantum physics, and hip-hop music.

Star Alert!

Although many Water Bearers keep the same friends for life, they are essentially loners. As a result, they may come across as distant and detached. It can be hard to know Aquarians on a deep level, and they often have few true intimate relationships.

Water Bearers are often highly critical, and their analytical abilities can cut like a knife. At times, their lofty intellectual standards and innate brilliance may make you feel intellectually inadequate.

Crystals, love beads, energy medicine ... oh my! Many Aquarians are in tune with New-Age practices. They will align your chakras and challenge your traditional beliefs. This sign is highly intuitive and also energetically sensitive. Water Bearers can find peace and happiness in meditation or via other spiritual practices that allow them to commune with their higher selves.

Aquarius in Love and Lust

For independent Aquarius, emotional intimacy is often the final frontier. Their otherworldly intellect in combination with their real need for space can make these ambivalent lovers blow hot and cold. No matter how intrigued they may be with your captivating aura, even Water Bearers in love are likely to be elusive.

Cosmic Lovers

"Make it so!" Star Trek's sexy Enterprise captain Jean-Luc Picard is an Aquarius in mind and sensibility. This cosmic lover adhered to the highest ideals and standards while melting the heart of many a Trekkie!

Aquarius rules the high-tech field, and the Internet is a natural way for them to connect. Water Bearers are often attracted to online dating because it allows them to pursue their romantic options from a distance (and with detachment). It is not usual to meet an Aquarius in dating chat rooms or to get to know them through their personal websites or blogs.

At the beginning of a relationship, Water Bearers can be knights in shining armor. Male or female, this sign loves to rescue and play the hero. Yet, their emotional armor can be thick. Once they have rescued you, they're not quite sure what to do with you! An Aquarius in love will make moves that are sudden and unexpected. They love to surprise, and you will never quite know what to expect!

Dear Sextrologer ...

"I'm an Aquarius and have purposely chosen to be single for a few years. Recently, I started seeing an interesting and exciting man—but I have worked hard for my independence and worry about giving up my freedom. What to do?"

In the right relationship, your partner will give you the space to be independent, to cultivate your talents, and to explore your dreams. Why not wait and see whether this "interesting and exciting man" adds to your life rather than detracts? The right Sun sign pairing could give you all of the emotional and spiritual potential you want—without fencing you in.

At first measure, Aquarius may seem reserved and sexually aloof. Beneath his or her cool exterior, however, often lives an innovative lover. For Aquarius in lust, no rules apply! Behind closed doors, this noble rescuer turns into a real sexual player. Water Bearers are usually open to most sexual experiences—even practices at the outer edges of kink. Aquarius may shock you in the bedroom! Their tastes run the gamut from playful to adventurous and from quirky to hard-core.

One caveat: even in the most lustful circumstances, Aquarius' libido can run hot and cold. In the bedroom, you may encounter the moody, self-involved, and insular aspect of this sign. There may be times when your Water Bearer is sexually distant. Make a move, and you may hear the proverbial, "I have a headache!" Don't worry—these moods pass quickly. Give them space, and they will soon be their old randy selves again.

The Fine Art of Astro-Seduction: Aquarius

It's okay to be sexually aggressive with Aquarius. In fact, Water Bearers enjoy being pursued and will be flattered by your attention. A word of advice, however: keep it casual! These ambivalent lovers will be uncomfortable if you have too many expectations. Nothing turns off Water Bearers more than neediness. Game plan: tell them about the latest Pulitzer–Prize-winning book that you're reading while nonchalantly undressing them!

 Heavenly Relations

Aquarius turn-ons: cyber sex, fantasy, role-reversal, masks, kinky positions, and quirky foreplay. The ultimate sexual experience for Water Bearers is ... no strings attached!

The Best and Worst of Aquarius Lovers

At his or her best, your Aquarius lover will admire your uniqueness and embrace your complexities. Water Bearers will give you the freedom to be your true self and support you in your exploration of your highest aspirations. They will also open your mind to unlimited possibilities. No matter the outcome of your romantic relationship, your Aquarius lover will remain a loyal friend!

At their worst, your Aquarius lover is filled with irritating complexities. One minute they're hot; the next, they're cold. Water Bearers can be emotionally distant and elusive when it comes to commitment. You may also tire of their constant need to intellectualize and play the critic. Aquarius' lesson in life and love is learning to explore their emotions as much as they do their minds.

The Least You Need to Know

- Air signs are Gemini, Libra, and Aquarius.
- Fickle Gemini seeks variety and diversity.
- Graceful Libra seeks the extraordinary.
- Ambivalent Aquarius seeks the freedom to be unique.

Chapter 4

Water Sun Signs and Ascendants

In This Chapter

◆ Cancer, Scorpio, and Pisces are the Water signs

◆ Nurturing Cancer, the Crab

◆ Mysterious Scorpio, the Scorpion

◆ Intuitive Pisces, the Fishes

Water signs are sensitive, emotional, and feeling-oriented. They are also often quite psychic. These are the friends and lovers who will know how you're feeling and what you need sometimes even before *you* will. Water signs are not always in sync with the world, although they are typically very connected to their own necessary rhythms. These lovers have strong emotional needs and will desire a deep connection with you—in and out of the bedroom. Water signs excel at the fine art of romance and seduction!

Cancer, the Crab: The Nurturing Lover

June 22nd–July 23rd

Element: Water

Planetary Ruler: The Moon

Quality: Cardinal

Energy: Female

Compatible Signs: Water and Earth

Key Words: Moody, generous, protective

Color: Silver

Gems: Pearl and moonstone

Erogenous Zones: Stomach, chest, breasts

How to Recognize a Crab: You will find Cancers in all walks of life, but you can pick them out by their odd, sideways walk as they inch in and out of a room: one step forward, one step back. You will also often see them standing with their weight shifted entirely to one leg. Crabs have round, Moon-like faces that reflect their changing moods and emotions. Women have welcoming, curvy, or soft bodies, and Cancer men may have a little extra around the middle.

Cosmic Lovers

Britain's Princess Diana, a Cancer, like many royals before her, sought the counsel of astrologers to help understand her life, relationships, and potential destiny.

Famous Crabs: Pamela Anderson, Tom Cruise, Reese Witherspoon, Robin Williams, Meryl Streep, Tom Hanks, Princess Diana, Harrison Ford

All About Cancer

"Are you feeling down? Come over, I'll cook you dinner. We'll hang out; you'll feel better." Ahh … Cancers are always there when you need them! Crabs are nurturers, first and foremost. Your Cancer lover will be your caring friend, parent, and partner all rolled into one. Cancer is no pushover, however: they can also be stubborn, surprisingly tenacious, and will not stand for being taken advantage of!

The old adage, "Still waters run deep" is an apt description of Crabs. They are private and often have a fear of revealing their deeper selves. Ruled by the Moon—which represents feelings and emotions—these water babies are very sensitive.

Crab's emotions are vast and deep, and their moods can shift with the tides. At times, Cancer's vulnerabilities will cause them to withdraw into their shells to protect themselves.

Crabs are traditionalists in most matters and do not like to step too far outside their comfort zones.

They are also security-oriented, and money is often a central concern. No matter how much they have, Cancers fear that it will never be enough. They like to feel in control and fret about their futures: retirement funds, paying the mortgage, taking care of their parents, and so on. In fact, Cancers tend to worry a lot!

Crabs are deeply rooted and find real fulfillment in their home and family lives. They feel guilty about letting others down and as a result will often take on too much. Crabs have trouble delegating and a difficult time saying, "No!" These nurturing lovers will often neglect their own needs to take care of others.

Star Alert!

Crabs can be pushy and like to play mommy or daddy in their relationships. Get used to hearing, "Honey, is that coat warm enough?" or, "Sweetie, did you remember to pay the credit card bill?"

Heavenly Relations

Cancers are often psychic. Their psychic abilities are especially pronounced during the full Moon, and visions will often come to them in their dreams.

Cancer in Love and Lust

Cancers in love can be extremely possessive. They are very picky when choosing a mate, but once they find the right one, they will never want to let go! Crabs like the security of being in a committed relationship. They will tolerate the dating process and can be social when required. In fact, when Crabs let loose, they can be a lot of fun and will party with the best of them! Crabs are happiest, however, at home with their lover, in their pajamas, and enjoying a good movie and a bottle of vintage red wine.

Cancers have strong biological clocks. And as single Crabs get older, the ticking may become extremely loud! Cancers choose partners who will share their desire to have children and create a family. Crabs want a stable partner to settle down with; one-night stands are not their bag!

Crabs are a classic combination of naughty and nice. On the surface, Crabs may appear to be very wholesome—yet get them in the bedroom, and their naughty sides will come out! Crabs enjoy the carnal aspects of physical intimacy as well as the emotional connection and release. Sex, or lovemaking—the preferred term for Crabs—is important to them. Crabs can get quite cranky without regular nooky!

Cancer is not overly adventurous sexually but is not shy, either! They are passionate and caring lovers. Crabs appreciate romance: nothing too over the top—some John Coltrane, candlelight, and a sensual massage—and you're sure to release their inner passion!

The Fine Art of Astro-Seduction: Cancer

Cancer is looking for a lover with whom they will be able to spend a lifetime. To seduce a Cancer, you'll need to let him or her know that you will be a steady and reliable mate.

Cancers need to feel that you plan to stick around after the lovemaking is done. Telling them about your affection for your family and letting them see that you are good with money is a good start. Game plan: invite them to your own cozy, comforting home … feed them well … and Cancer is yours!

The Best and Worst of Cancer Lovers

At their best, Cancers are loving and supportive partners. Crabs are nonjudgmental and are good listeners who will offer their opinions only when asked. (Okay, sometimes when *not* asked—but only if your love life or career is in serious jeopardy!) They will provide a safe harbor in the midst of all your emotional storms. Crabs are generous to a fault—in life and in the bedroom!

At their worst, Cancer lovers are overly sensitive, emotionally touchy, and overly possessive. At times, their ever-changing moods will be frustrating and their tendency to withdraw perplexing. Crabs' caretaking ways can be controlling. For all their good intentions, they can be excessively needy. Their lesson in life and in love is to learn to balance their needs with the needs of others.

Heavenly Relations

Cancer turn-ons: a healthy 401(k), ice cream, whipped cream ... in fact, any kind of cream (preferably smeared all over the body!). For the ladies, it's all about boxers, not briefs. Cancer men prefer low-cut, bosom-hugging tops.

Dear Sextrologer ...

"I'm a female Cancer and just hit the big 3-0—yet I'm still not married! Many of my girlfriends are having babies, and I'm feeling depressed and left out. I want to have a family but worry that I'll never find my true love. Please advise."

Oh my goodness, Cancer! Thirty and not married! You probably do feel like this is the end of the world. Cancers typically want love, family, and security above all else. Your challenge, dear Cancer, is to be patient. You want and need the right match, not simply a match. Until then, enjoy your friends' little ones—it will be great practice for when you have little ones of your own. And Cancer ... you will.

Scorpio, the Scorpion: The Mysterious Lover

October 23rd–November 22nd

Element: Water

Planetary Ruler: Pluto

Quality: Fixed

Energy: Female

Compatible Signs: Water and Earth

Key Words: Deep, charismatic, sexual

Colors: Burgundy, black

Gems: Topaz, citrine

Erogenous Zones: Inner thighs and genitals

How to Recognize a Scorpion: Scorpions travel incognito—they don't want to be recognized! It won't work, however; you will always be able to spot them by their passion and their fierce presence. You will also know them by their frequently sharp, eagle-like features and deeply penetrating eyes. Their air of wisdom—and of dark knowledge, too, can often be unsettling.

Famous Scorpions: Whoopi Goldberg, Calista Flockhart, Ethan Hawke, Prince Charles, Demi Moore, Julia Roberts, Leonardo DiCaprio, Martin Scorsese, Meg Ryan

All About Scorpio

Scorpio can be described in three words: intense, intense, and more intense! Ruled by Pluto, the planet representing deep transformation, Scorpions will challenge you to think and grow in new ways. These mysterious lovers are enigmas—full of sexual intrigue and nothing short of fascinating!

Heavenly Relations

Although astronomers demoted Pluto from a major to a minor, or dwarf, planet, its significance in astrology has not changed. Pluto still kicks cosmic butt regarding the areas of your life that need to be transformed.

Scorpios are highly charismatic. They can be quite charming when they choose, and their presence can be seductively hypnotic—even spellbinding! Scorpions give off an aura of strength and confidence which—added to their intensity—can be overpowering. Often provocative, Scorpios have sharp tongues and tell it like it is. The Scorpion's stinging words can easily wound, and they may unintentionally hurt your feelings.

Scorpions are uncannily perceptive. They have finely tuned B.S. detectors, and you will find it almost impossible to get anything past them. Scorpios make great detectives and therapists! They look deeply and will want to penetrate your innermost psyche. At times, Scorpios may unnerve you with their ability to read you and know your secrets—even when you don't want to be read!

Fiercely competitive, Scorpions like to win. When they don't get their own way, they can become defiant and aggressive. Scorpions are intelligent and often successful in business. Stealthy and quietly tenacious, Scorpios are great strategists. Much like master chess players, every move they make is calculated … and Scorpions have the next three moves lined up in advance!

Scorpio in Love and Lust

Scorpio in love is one cool customer. It is hard to read these mysterious lovers or know what they really want. Scorpios can be like the proverbial Dr. Jekyll and Mr. Hyde: one minute they are in passionate pursuit, and the next they become cold, distant, and withholding.

Dear Sextrologer ...

"I'm seeing a Scorpio, and she's driving me crazy with her mixed messages. We share a lot in common and have intense conversations about everything from basketball to spirituality—yet I feel like she's always trying to seduce me! Although we have a strong physical connection and the sex is awesome, after the seduction she becomes distant."

You're right. Scorpios often seduce as a way of gaining and keeping the upper hand. The bedroom is their place of power and consequently where they feel most in control. Once she decides to trust you, you will feel the shift from seduction to lovemaking. The sex will still be "awesome," but it will be a coming together rather than a power play.: The Mysterious Lover

Scorpions may seem all-powerful, yet deep down they are actually very sensitive! For Scorpios, knowledge equals power—and as a way of protecting their hearts, they are careful about revealing themselves. Scorpios have a hard time relinquishing control, and you will need to earn their trust before they let you in. They can be territorial and possessive in love, and Scorpions will test you in a variety of ways (including mind games). Although their behavior can be manipulative, it is actually their way of staying safe. Scorpio knows that when he or she falls in love, it's going to be hard and deep.

You should also know that jealous Scorpios do not take sexual or relationship betrayal lightly and will often seek revenge: Hell hath no fury like a Scorpion scorned!

Get ready to breathe! Sex with Scorpio is likely to be pure, raw, and primal passion. It can be all–consuming, and at times they can overwhelm you with the intensity of their desire. Scorpios will expect you to give without pretense in the bedroom. They don't hold back and won't want you to, either. Scorpios can be insistent about fulfilling their sexual needs. It is here that Scorpions often feel free to explore their dark side—just use your imagination!

Cosmic Lovers

James Bond, Batman, and Sherlock Holmes could all be Scorpion lovers. What these dark heroes share in common is a love of mystery and danger.

Some Scorpions engage in sex as a spiritual endeavor. For them, orgasm is not just a sexual release—it's a mystical experience! Scorpios may engage in tantric yoga or other sexual-spiritual disciplines as a way of channeling their higher sexual energies into a spiritual connection with you—and even with the universe!

Because Scorpions are passionate and intense, people often imagine them as the sex maniacs of the zodiac! This perception is rarely true, however. Although Scorpions are highly sexual, they are not necessarily promiscuous. In the right relationship and situation, they will be loyal and monogamous.

Heavenly Relations

Scorpio turn-ons: intrigue, sharp minds and willing bodies, porn, black nail polish, leather (lots of leather!), blindfolds, and acting out sexual fantasies—including pretending that you're a sexy stranger who they just picked up!

The Fine Art of Astro-Seduction: Scorpio

Nothing is sexier to Scorpios than mystery—and strength. Scorpions need lovers who are deeply erotic and not afraid of their own passion. To seduce your Scorpio lover, you will need to intrigue them by showing them your own power. Playing hard to get won't hurt, either: Scorpios love to pursue the unattainable. Game plan: the complete set of *The Matrix* DVDs, a range of sex toys, and a "Do Not Disturb" sign on the bedroom door.

The Best and Worst of Scorpio Lovers

At his or her best, your Scorpion lover will stimulate you to explore your own emotional, sexual, and spiritual nature. Their perceptions can be illuminating and their wisdom profound. One of the most passionate lovers of the zodiac, Scorpio will fill your nights with deep—even mystical—lovemaking. Once they have earned your trust, Scorpions make loyal and loving partners.

At their worst, your Scorpion lover will constantly challenge you and push your emotional buttons. They can be vengeful and often hold a grudge. Their lack of communication can be trying: Scorpio would rather sulk and feel misunderstood than talk about his or her true feelings. Being on the receiving end of the Scorpion's stinging words can be painful and cut deeply.

Pisces, the Fishes: The Intuitive Lover

February 19th–March 21st

Element: Water

Planetary Ruler: Neptune

Quality: Mutable

Energy: Female

Compatible Signs: Water and Earth

Key Words: Compassionate, impressionable, sacrificing

Color: Sea green

Gem: Aquamarine

Erogenous Zones: Feet, foreheads

How to Recognize Fishes: Fishes have dreamy constitutions and will often appear lost in their own space. They will often give you a telling glimpse into their personalities through their choice in footwear. Dainty slippers or hiker boots do not deceive— what you see is what you get! The same cannot be said for fishes in other respects. They have large eyes and long eyelashes, but it is very hard to read their very private souls.

Famous Fishes: Bruce Willis, Drew Barrymore, Spike Lee, Elizabeth Taylor, Sharon Stone, Billy Crystal, Quincy Jones, Albert Einstein

All About Pisces

Pisces are romantic, intuitive, and poetic souls. They have big imaginations and active fantasy lives. Creative and artistic, they are often visionaries. Yet … Pisces would often rather play in the pretty world of fantasy than deal with cold, hard reality. When life doesn't match their idealistic vision, Fishes' rose-colored glasses turn blue and they can descend into escapism and denial.

Heavenly Relations

Ruled by the planet Neptune—the mythological god of the seas—Fishes are psychic sea sponges and tend to absorb everything that's going on around them.

Fishes are not overly ambitious. In fact, they can be downright lazy! They are not driven by material desires, and their motto is: "I go with the flow." Fishes are often called "spacey" because they are not always grounded in real-world, day-to-day practicalities. While they jaunt off to their latest creative venture, they may not have remembered to pay the bills! Fishes are quite happy on an exotic beach, drink in hand, daydreaming about the future.

Star Alert! _____

Pisces are notorious escape artists. Fishes long to transcend ordinary reality and love altered states of awareness—and therefore, should watch out for addictive behaviors.

Like all Water signs, Pisces is feeling-oriented and can be moody. They are generally good-natured, however, and profoundly compassionate. Fishes are deeply empathic and generous with their time and attention. Pisces are the priests or high priestesses of the zodiac, offering their wise and often spiritual counsel and ministering to those in need. These wise old souls are slow to judge. They understand that there is more in this world than most of us will ever know.

Pisces in Love and Lust

Pisces in love seeks enchantment. Think of Cinderella, a likely Pisces, content to sweep cinders and spin romantic fantasies until her prince appeared to sweep her off her feet! Pisces' message is: "Please rescue me from my dreary, mundane reality!" Fishes want all the trappings of deep, romantic love—often the kind that they see in their favorite movies. Yet, unrequited love is a reoccurring theme for Fishes. Pisces in love often set their sights on the unattainable!

Cosmic Lovers _____

Movie star Elizabeth Taylor is very Piscean. Fishes fall in love easily and deeply, but it doesn't always last: this Fish has been married eight times!

Once they find their soul partner, however, Fishes give the gift of unconditional love for as long as their love lasts. Romantic Pisces will write you beautiful poems, compose a love song, or send you romantic e-mails about what is possible for the two of you. They will also make it a priority to attend to your every need. Fishes in love can be attached at the hip! They will sometimes sacrifice their own needs for those of their partners. Therapists have a term for this behavior: co-dependence!

Fishes are very attentive and often experienced lovers. They will expect you to surrender yourself completely … body, mind, and soul. If you are willing to join them, you will likely find lovemaking a sublime, transcendent experience—physically, emotionally, and even spiritually. Their caresses will touch you to your deepest core. Sex with Fishes can even have a healing effect as they soothe your deepest fears and awaken you to previously unknown sexual possibilities.

Dear Sextrologer ...

"I recently met a Pisces online. At first, he was very romantic and thoughtful. Yet, lately I'm feeling like he's becoming less interested. For example, he insists on keeping his profile online even though we've been dating for several months."

Pisces often like the fantasy of romance and relationships more than they like the reality. Take charge of your situation! Insist that if he wants to keep seeing you, he needs to make a commitment and let go of other possibilities. If he won't, you will know that it's time to move on—and you will save yourself much heartache by doing so immediately.

Fishes' sexual fantasy lives would put that of most mortals to shame—and sometimes their sexual histories will, as well! They may ask you to play sex games and can be especially keen on role-playing. Fishes are rarely shocked and will play along with your every fantasy. Yet, there may be times where you feel that your Pisces lover is using sex as an escape or that they're imagining someone else in bed! As with alcohol and drugs, some Fishes will use sex as a way to escape reality.

Heavenly Relations

Pisces turn-ons: voyeurism, mirrors, artistic natures, nude photography, and lots and lots of fantasy. Shoe and foot fetishes are not unheard of!

The Fine Art of Astro-Seduction: Pisces

Fishes are sweet seducers; they have a way of quietly getting under your skin. They love to be seduced themselves and will delight in your romantic attention and the magical spell that you cast. A Pisces' key words are "romance" and "magical." Fishes appreciate the subtle nuances of seduction. Tell them your sorrows, and whisper your dreams in their willing ears. Try reading them love poetry or playing romantic music, and they will willingly fall under your sexual spell. Game plan: soft candlelight, Bach's *St. Matthews Passion*, exotic cocktails—and leave your inhibitions at the door!

The Best and Worst of Pisces Lovers

At their best, Fishes are compassionate, nonjudgmental, and loving. They will bring magic into your daily life, inspire your own creative visions, and encourage you to fulfill your highest dreams. Fishes' abilities to love unconditionally can have a healing effect, and you will flourish under their devoted and caring attention.

At their worst, Pisces lovers are wishy-washy and full of emotional contradictions. They can also be passive-aggressive about expressing their needs. Their need to check out from reality, whatever the form, can be a drag and make you feel less than special. You may also tire of them playing the victim instead of dealing with their problems. Their lesson in life and in love is to learn to ground their dreams in reality.

The Least You Need to Know

- ◆ Water signs are Cancer, Scorpio, and Pisces.
- ◆ Nurturing Cancer seeks long-term security.
- ◆ Mysterious Scorpio seeks intensity.
- ◆ Intuitive Pisces seeks the transcendent.

Earth Sun Signs and Ascendants

In This Chapter

◆ Taurus, Virgo, and Capricorn are the Earth signs

◆ Sensual Taurus, the Bull

◆ Discerning Virgo, the Virgin

◆ Serious Capricorn, the Goat

Earth signs move slowly and don't like to be rushed—which can be very appealing when it comes to sex! When it comes to other areas of life, however, it can be pretty frustrating! Earth signs are stable, practical, and security-minded. They are also (yum!) extremely tactile and sensual lovers. In relationships, Earth signs make great partners and friends; they will stick with you through thick and thin. Earth signs seek long-term relationships where they can settle in and get comfortable.

Taurus, the Bull: The Sensual Lover

April 20th–May 21st

Element: Earth

Planetary Ruler: Venus

Quality: Fixed

Energy: Female

Compatible Signs: Earth and Water

Key Words: Stable, determined, stubborn

Color: Green

Gem: Emerald

Erogenous Zones: Neck and throat

How to Recognize a Bull: Look for the Bull's famous lack of grace as they awkwardly barge into the room. Male Bulls have solid bodies and lots of hair—although not necessarily on their heads! Female Bulls have curvy bodies—a reflection of their Venus influence, which denotes goddess-like beauty.

Both sexes tend toward the lazy, especially when it comes to working out—and their physiques tend to show it.

Famous Bulls: George Clooney, Audrey Hepburn, Cher, Barbra Streisand, Jerry Seinfeld, Michelle Pfeiffer, Jack Nicholson, Uma Thurman, Gary Cooper

All About Taurus

Bulls inhabit their own astrological time zone—in a word, "Slow!" They are conservative in their approach to life and don't like to expend unnecessary energy. Why hurry? Bulls would rather enjoy life. This doesn't mean that they're indifferent to success—far from it! Bulls' determination and perseverance make them likely to outlast their quicker rivals, and they will often win the game … and your affections!

Taurus is an Earth sign and is closely aligned with nature. Bulls often have an affinity for animals big and small, for gardening, organic foods, and even

Star Alert! _____

Although usually patient and reasonable, Bulls don't like to be pushed. Try to get them to do something they don't want to, and you will encounter the Bull's famous stubbornness!

winemaking. Bulls can be decadent when it comes to good food. They are often gourmets and typically enjoy both cooking and eating. No matter their shape or size, Bulls celebrate their bodies and treat them as temples—always worship-worthy! They are often comfortable au natural, and it's not unusual to find them walking around naked—in the privacy of their own homes, of course!

Ruled by Venus—the planet of love and beauty—Bulls tend to surround themselves with nice things. These sensual lovers enjoy spending money and don't hesitate to indulge themselves in the luxury they feel they deserve. For Bulls, enjoying the richness of life often translates to acquiring beautiful possessions—sometimes to the point of excess.

Bulls love to build empires and are usually very successful in business. It is in the company of family and friends, however, where they are the most content. Community is important to Bulls. You will often find them taking a leadership role in supporting and mentoring others—whether at their church, school, or the local YMCA.

Heavenly Relations _____

Bulls are highly musical and often have great voices. They love to sing—whether in the local choir or in the shower—and may play various musical instruments. Their musical tastes tend towards the classical.

Taurus in Love and Lust

For Bulls in love, it's all or nothing. Because they move slowly, it may often seem that they take their time when choosing a potential love mate. In reality, however, Bulls often fall in love at first sight! It's not that Bulls are superficial—in fact, they most certainly aren't—it's that they know that they can trust their instincts. That said, they may take their sweet, Taurean time letting you in on their discovery! Once a Bull has chosen a partner, he or she will prefer to mate for life. Bulls are among the most loyal and devoted lovers of the zodiac.

Stoic Bulls do not fluster easily, nor do they deal well with emotional complications. Too much relationship drama makes Bulls extremely uncomfortable, and they will rarely participate. It is not in the Bull's nature to "talk stuff out," either. In fact, Bulls are not very good at communicating their deeper feelings. But Bulls will accept

Heavenly Relations _____

Taurus turn-ons: deeply penetrating kisses, naked skin on naked skin, lots of touching, scented candles and sensual massages, sleeping in, and breakfast in bed.

you for who you are, without pretense or show, and often without condition. They will expect the same from you.

Dear Sextrologer ... _____

"I'm a divorced male Taurus and part-time parent to two teenage girls. I would like to settle down again but am continually frustrated in my pursuit of Ms. Right. My parenting situation seems to be a turn-off to a lot of the ladies I've been seeing. Any suggestions?"

You've been dating the wrong women, Taurus! There are plenty of women out there who would love to be a part of your family. Look at your prospects' Sun sign. You are most likely to find success and happiness with a woman who loves hearth and home as much as you do. Another Taurus, a Capricorn, or a Cancer would be most likely to embrace you—and your daughters. Your famous perseverance will put you in good stead on your search!

Like all Earth signs, Bulls are very physical. Translation: they like to have sex—and plenty of it! Lusty Bulls are tactile and very sensual. They are also extremely sensitive to all sensory stimuli—taste, hearing, sight, smell, and especially touch. Bulls love both caressing and being caressed. Sex with a Bull is likely to be slow and lingering and will often last through the night! They also like to snuggle afterward as the fires of your lovemaking cool to glowing embers.

Cosmic Lovers _____

Whether male or female, Bulls are typically the strong, silent type. Like sexy Bull George Clooney, their quiet reserve and smoldering sensuality often makes them irresistible!

Although Bulls are passionate in the bedroom, they're usually not interested in anything too sexually adventurous. They may be willing to try some kinkiness every once in a while, but they prefer to stick to comfortable routines. Wonderfully slow and sensuous Taurean sex, however, will show you that these routines can be deeply satisfying!

The Fine Art of Astro-Seduction: Taurus

Bulls do not want to be rushed into bed and enjoy full-out seduction. Allowing them to be slow and deliberate in their pursuit is a big plus. Sensual foreplay and your attention to stimulating each of their senses will also work very well. Game plan: some wine or chocolate for taste; perfume, after-shave, and scented candles for smell; soft music for their sensitive ears; satin sheets and warm naked skin for touch—and the sight of your naked body to fully arouse their libidos.

The Best and Worst of Taurus Lovers

At his or her best, your Taurus lover will be a grounding and stabilizing force in your life. Bulls thrive in strong relationships and are extremely loyal partners. They stick around. Bulls are generous with their time, money, and support. You will have many nights of sensuous lovemaking together … plus lots of snuggling afterward!

At their worst, Bulls can be passive, plodding, and even boring! They can be stubborn and resistant when it comes to talking about their needs. Like the proverbial bull in a china shop, Taurus often lacks finesse when dealing with your deeper feelings. Their lesson in life and in love is to learn to be more sensitive to the needs of others.

Virgo, the Virgin: The Discerning Lover

August 22nd–September 22nd

Element: Earth

Planetary Ruler: Mercury

Quality: Mutable

Energy: Female

Compatible signs: Earth and Water

Key Words: Efficient, exacting, helpful

Color: Blue

Gem: Sapphire

Erogenous Zones: Stomachs, lower backs, and inner thighs

How to Recognize a Virgin: If a stranger offers you a tissue for your runny nose or an aspirin for your headache, you've probably encountered a Virgin! Virgins come well prepared for any emergency. They are meticulous about their appearance, from the scarf that perfectly matches their eye color right down to their perfectly polished shoes! Physically, male Virgins tend toward lean bodies while the females have bodies with lots of curves.

Famous Virgins: Beyoncé, Adam Sandler, Sophia Loren, Keanu Reeves, Greta Garbo, Sean Connery, Ingrid Bergman, Bill Murray, Virginia Madsen

All About Virgo

Virgos desire a well-ordered life. They are notorious perfectionists—and fussbudgets! Virgins can't help themselves: it's their nature to want to dot every "i" and cross every "t." At the same time, they are giving and supportive partners. They want you to succeed and will do their very best to try and help you achieve a well-ordered life, too!

Heavenly Relations

Virgo is the sign of the Virgin, but don't take this term too literally! Virgos have strong sexual natures. The virginal aspect of this sign is Virgo's openness to greater wisdom and life experience.

Ruled by the planet Mercury (which represents the mind), Virgos are highly intellectual and have a need to analyze everything around them. Virgins are brilliant problem solvers. They are the go-to person when it comes to figuring out what to do with your life or how to solve your greatest dilemmas. Beware, however: Virgins can be both critical and judgmental and will get upset if you don't take their counsel seriously!

For all their critical ways, Virgins are sensitive and get their feelings hurt easily. They are kind-hearted souls and have a soft spot for those who are most in need. Virgins find fulfillment in service, and you will often find them volunteering for a local charity. They will roll up their sleeves and work hard with nary a complaint! Yet, there can be martyr-like aspects to their giving ways. Like Mother Theresa—a Virgo—Virgins sometimes have a secret desire to be saints.

Virgins tend to be worriers—whether it's about the fate of Planet Earth or the nutritional value of their lunches! Meticulous to a fault, Virgins will make endless lists as a way of feeling on top of all aspects of their lives. They are practical and usually quite frugal, yet Virgins do enjoy the finer things in life. They have discerning tastes, however, and their indulgences tend toward the useful: top-of-the-line cookware or a new car to replace their well-worn model.

Dear Sextrologer ...

"I'm going out with a Virgo and really, really like her. In fact, I think I'm falling in love! She's sexy, smart, and very organized. And that's the problem—I'm kind of a slob. I'm scared to have her over to my house because it's such a mess. Do you think there's any hope for us?"

Believe it or not, you just may be your Virgo girl's dream come true! Virgos love to fuss over others. In fact, it's often their way of showing love. She may be critical at first, but give her free reign to organize your closets—and this relationship could turn out to be a lasting love match!

Virgo in Love and Lust

In love and in their sexual relationships, Virgos are cautious and extremely particular. These discerning lovers will study every relationship possibility and the consequences of their choices. Expect them to put you through your paces. They may ask you many, many questions about yourself or your actions. At times, you may feel more like you're on a job interview instead of a date! Don't be fooled. Grilling you is often a protective smokescreen behind which Virgos hide their deeper selves and desires. Even when openly committed and in love, Virgins are not overly demonstrative when it comes to expressing their feelings.

Poor Virgos! They are often seen as sexually fussy or even prissy. Although Virgo has a reputation for being uptight, this characteristic rarely applies in the bedroom! Like all Earth signs, they are physically oriented and deeply sensual. They may like to play at being the good girl or boy, but Virgins want nothing more than to surrender to their sexual desires. In fact, when seemingly modest Virgins let go, they can be very passionate!

Star Alert!

Good hygiene, especially in the bedroom, is important to Virgos. Virgins can be hypersensitive about their health and may even flirt with hypochondria.

Cosmic Lovers

Virgins are earth mothers or fathers who want to nurture your deepest desires. If in doubt, look to Virgo Sophia Loren. This earth mother embodies the sensual and loving ways of the Virgin.

Just as Virgos are emotionally cautious, they can be initially reserved about expressing their sexual needs. They often have many secret fantasies about their ideal lover. When these fantasies become reality, however, Virgins can become shy, tongue-tied, and a bit flustered! Through lovemaking, Virgins get out of their minds and into their bodies. In fact, sex is often a way in which Virgins release their abundance of nervous energy. Once comfortable with their partner, Virgo's legendary sexual finesse comes through and they are extremely perceptive lovers.

Dutiful Virgins offer a big payoff in the bedroom. What better combination than a sensual lover and a perfectionist? All of your needs are sure to be fulfilled! For all their complications, Virgins are warm and generous lovers. They are monogamous partners and will not tolerate infidelity.

The Fine Art of Astro-Seduction: Virgo

Although Virgins may not admit it, they really do want to be seduced! Virgins will seldom take the initiative, so it's up to you to play the role of seducer. You will also have to negotiate some of their complications—namely, mixed messages about what they want (on one hand, surrender; on the other hand, a desire to play it safe). Game plan: plan a rendezvous to look at historical documents at the library, don some glasses for added seriousness, and when they least expect it … engage them in a deep and lasting kiss. The rest could be lovemaking history!

The Best and Worst of Virgo Lovers

At his or her best, your Virgo lover will be a giving and loving partner. Virgos will help you fine-tune the details of your life and get you on track with everything from your finances to your healthcare routine. These earth mothers or fathers will cook you chicken soup when you're sick and stick with you through thick and thin. They are also attentive and nurturing lovers!

Heavenly Relations

Virgo turn-ons: discerning minds, monogamy, the missionary position, submissiveness and surrender role-playing, talking about their secret fantasies and desires, and … good hygiene!

At his or her worst, your Virgo lover is a critical nitpicker. Even Virgo's loving ways can be exacting, and you may find yourself rolling your eyes and saying, "Chill out, baby!" Their need to be in control and play it safe can be frustrating, as well. Your Virgo lover may also be overly sensitive, and at times you won't know what to expect. Their lesson in life and love is learning to relax, enjoy, and let go!

Capricorn, the Goat: The Serious Lover

December 22nd–January 21st

Element: Earth

Planetary Ruler: Saturn

Quality: Cardinal

Energy: Male

Compatible Signs: Earth and Water

Key Words: Practical, ambitious, disciplined

Colors: Deep red and brown

Gem: Garnet

Erogenous Zones: Backs, spines and knees

How to Recognize a Goat: Goats naturally command any room with their confident, steady, take-charge attitude. They have lean, hard bodies and strong features. They love to exercise their bodies and their minds: these are the guys or gals reading *The Wall Street Journal* on the treadmill! Even though Goats seemingly have little time for vanity or fussing over their clothing, they can be vain about their appearance—particularly, their bodies. Just don't expect them to admit it!

Famous Goats: Nicolas Cage, Jim Carrey, Diane Keaton, David Bowie, Elvis Presley, Faye Dunaway, Howard Stern, Dolly Parton, Cary Grant

All About Capricorn

Goats are strong and stoic, extremely practical, and take a no-nonsense approach to life. They have "type A" personalities and like to be on top and in control. Although usually reserved—you won't see them dancing on a tabletop anytime soon—they are very sexual creatures and make stable and reliable partners.

The symbol for Capricorn is the goat—a metaphor for climbing his or her mountain slowly and cautiously, one sure-footed or hoofed step at a time. Ambitious Goats are career-minded yet are rarely overnight successes. Goats work hard for their accomplishments. They are goal-oriented and disciplined about achieving their dreams. Their secret weapon—and greatest virtue—is their supreme patience.

Goats are often focused on outward appearances, and their reputation is very important to them. They tend to be conservative by nature and are rarely given to extremes. Goats are often social climbers and like to impress others with their business savvy. Financial security is also a central focus. Goats are frugal—some would even say stingy—and invest very carefully. They will own their own homes, and their possessions—even the ones meant to impress—will be practical rather than frivolous.

 Star Alert!

Capricorn is ruled by Saturn, the planet representing structure and limits. For these serious lovers, there's often little time for fun and frivolity. Capricorns may need reminding that all work and no play can make them very dull Goats indeed!

Capricorns like to play by the rules. Although they can be tough taskmasters, Goats tend to be hardest on themselves. Those born under this sign often have a natural air of authority. Goats are often at their best and thrive in leadership roles. It is here that the Goat's generous nature comes through, especially when it comes to helping and inspiring others to achieve their own goals.

Capricorn in Love and Lust

Pragmatists in life and in love, Goats are not spontaneous lovers. They are also not very romantic! Goats are rarely effusive: they don't gush about their feelings and are not overly demonstrative. Male or female, they will not write you love poems or surprise you with a whirlwind trip to Maui—unless it happens to coincide with a business meeting! Even in love, Goats tend to be emotionally reserved.

Cosmic Lovers

Debonair movie star Cary Grant, like many Goats, may come across as perpetually smooth and in control. Yet Goats, too, have a silly side! Their funny bones are tickled by slapstick comedy, and they also are likely to have a very dry—or even sexually randy—sense of humor.

Heavenly Relations

Capricorn is associated with the hoofed and horned pagan god Pan. It is said that the sounds of Pan's flute cast a spell on humans, making them give in to their most basic needs and desires. Pan-Capricorn reflects the lusty and sexual side of the Goat.

Goats want mates who will share their need for emotional balance and control. They appreciate strength and modesty and those who are serious about their lives and careers. Secretly, however, Goats have an affinity for physical beauty. They also appreciate sexual openness—and even prowess. Although they don't give them out freely, they like compliments and are not immune to flattery. In fact, they will revel in your praise!

Once they have found the right lover, Goats are calm and deliberate in their pursuit. To say that Goats in love are tenacious is an understatement! They go after what they want and are rarely thrown off track by any obstacles—even if the object of their affection is initially indifferent. Goats are traditional in their commitments and enjoy secure partnerships.

In the movie *Working Girl*, Tess McGill asks, "I have a head for business and a bod for sin. Is there anything wrong with that?" She must have been a Capricorn! Once you get a Capricorn in the bedroom, their reserve falls away and the notorious "randy" goat appears. Nothing really shocks a Goat—they've usually been there and done that (literally!). Many Goats have been around the sexual block a time or two and usually bring more than a fair amount of expertise to the bedroom.

Dear Sextrologer ...

"I'm a Capricorn and have worked hard to get to my position as a successful business executive. I'm seeing a man who is less successful than I am, though he's a hard worker—okay, I'll just say it: he's a mechanic! I'm sure that I make more money than he does, and I don't know if my friends will respect his job. Do you think I can be happy in this relationship?"

Tsk tsk, Capricorn. Your typically Goat-like identification with your career and your financial and social standing could be getting in the way of true love. You both work hard, and both of your careers are worthy of respect! Plus, mechanics are usually not only smart but very good with their hands! Take time out from your busy career and give this relationship a chance!

Like all Earth signs, Goats are sensual, tactile, and in tune with their deeper physical senses. Lovemaking with Capricorn tends to be passionate and intensely physical. They will often make it their goal to meet all of your physical desires and will demand that you meet their sexual needs, as well. Goats will bring out the animal in you and encourage you to be yourself and go after want you want in the bedroom. Also, Capricorn's sexual endurance is legendary! Whew! Need we say more?

Heavenly Relations

Capricorn turn-ons: sleek physiques, role-playing, uniforms, executives, doctors, and librarians. For male goats, turn-ons include high-heels, garter belts, and corsets. For female goats, it's starched white shirts and hard, tight bodies underneath.

The Fine Art of Astro-Seduction: Capricorn

Don't be put off by your Goat's serious demeanor. They are very sexual creatures! To get under your Capricorn lover's sometimes tough exterior, entice them with your reserved yet oh-so-barely unrestrained sexuality! Goats love a compliment, especially about their business sense. They will also delight in your dry sense of humor and flirting with randy sexual innuendos. Game plan: schedule a "business meeting" at your home, break out the wine, and meet them buck naked at the door.

The Best and Worst of Capricorn Lovers

At their best, your Capricorn lover will be a stable and supportive partner worthy of your love and respect. They will respect you and encourage you to achieve your personal and career goals. Emotionally balanced, these lovers will ground you with their steady love and fulfill your every sexual need. Once they have committed, Goats usually stick around for life!

At their worst, your Capricorn mate will be emotionally stingy and controlling. They can also be downright stodgy! Your Capricorn lover's need to always want to play by the rules can be a drag, and you may feel ignored by their tireless work ethnic—which can run 24/7. Their lesson in life and in love is to balance work with play.

The Least You Need to Know

 ◆ Earth signs are Taurus, Virgo, and Capricorn.

 ◆ Sensual Taurus seeks comfort and the warmth of family.

 ◆ Discerning Virgo seeks order and security.

 ◆ Serious Capricorn seeks stability and sex.

Chapter 6

Finding Your Heart's Desire: How Your Suns and Ascendants Align

In This Chapter

- ◆ Fire with Fire or Air is sexually in-tune
- ◆ Fire with Earth or Water does not easily mix
- ◆ Water with Water or Earth is sexually sublime
- ◆ Air with Earth or Water can be a challenge

You know your Sun sign; now it's time to see how it aligns with your lover's! Here, we put together each of the signs of the zodiac so that you can see how you are likely to relate together in love, sex, and in your relationship. Understanding how your Sun signs and ascendants match—or not—will help you find the right lover to fulfill your heart's desires (and because each sign has its own individual sexual wants and desires, your physical needs, too!).

These connections are fundamental to your relationship compatibility and will give you important insight into yourself, your lover, and what you are likely to experience together in life—and in the bedroom. You will also be able to determine whether your connection is likely to be fleeting lust or destined longevity!

When Fire Meets Fire

Fire signs together are sexually in sync. At the same time, Fire signs are self-involved—and together they can be highly combustible! Although there's sure to be much passion, too, much fire can burn out quickly. Fire sign relationships may be hard to sustain, and long-term connections depend on your willingness to make some compromises.

Sex is mutually aggressive and urgent with **Aries and Aries** because they are great friends and passionate lovers. Yet, they may butt heads regarding whose needs come first.

Cosmic Lovers _____

Movie-star husband and wife Leo Ben Affleck and Aries Jennifer Garner, like many Fire signs, both share a love of action flicks and playing super-heroes!

Star Alert! _____

Same-sign relationships can work depending on the sign and element. Although sexually on fire, two Aries, two Leos, or two Sags have strong egos and can find themselves competing. The key in these relationships is to be respectful of each other's needs.

For **Aries and Leo,** it's pure animal passion. Although both are fiercely loyal, there will be times when you compete for attention and try to outdo each other.

It's a cosmic love and sex match for **Aries and Sagittarius**—not to mention one big party! You two "get" each other, particularly with respect to your mutual need for independence.

Sexual and relationship drama defines **Leo and Leo.** The sparks fly, but you will both have to check your egos at the bedroom door.

Its lust meets lust for **Leo and Sagittarius.** Neither of you holds back sexually, and there will be fireworks as you willingly explore your wild sides together. This relationship is built to last.

For **Sagittarius and Sagittarius,** sex is enthusiastic, uncomplicated, and basically a whole lot of fun! With both of your busy schedules, however, phone sex may have to suffice!

When Fire Meets Air

Fire and Air signs both seek sexual excitement and opportunities to learn and experiment. These two elements meet each other every step of the way when it comes to fun and creativity in the bedroom. They're also both highly creative when it comes to avoiding commitment! Expect lots of drama as Air fans the flames of Fire's deepest desires.

It's a whirlwind romance for **Aries and Gemini.** You two are sexually in sync when it comes to experimentation and the need for independence. Will it last? Very possibly.

It's love at first sight for **Aries and Libra.** Aries is the sexual aggressor, and romantic Libra loves being pursued. It works—big time!

Sex is wild and exhilarating for **Aries and Aquarius.** Both of you are on a quest for greater sexual freedom and independence. This love match is fated to last.

Leo loves drama, and Gemini is only too happy to bring it on. Desire runs high between **Leo and Gemini.** Together, you two make a dynamic and exciting sexual pair.

Romantic **Leo and Libra** share a love of being in a relationship. You two are happy to fulfill each other's sexual needs. Dare we say, "Destiny?"

Aquarius brings out Leo's sexual kink; Leo ignites Aquarius' hidden fires. Together, **Leo and Aquarius** often find the right relationship balance.

Freedom-loving **Sagittarius and Gemini** are both sexual risk-takers. Your eyes meet across a crowded room—and the rest is history. It's a total cosmic fit.

Sag is intrigued by Libra's sophistication; Libra is enamored by Sag's worldliness. What starts as a hot affair for **Sagittarius and Libra** can become very serious very quickly.

Sagittarius and Aquarius respect each other's need for sexual freedom. This is a cosmic coupling as you two bond over your search for greater meaning in life.

Cosmic Lovers

Sagittarius Brad Pitt and Gemini Angelina Jolie have stars that align well when it comes to sexual excitement and adventure. With both of these commitment-shy signs, however, it's uncertain whether it will last.

When Fire Meets Water

Imagine hot fireworks in the pouring rain and you get a picture of Fire and Water signs together. Fire often finds that Water's sensitive and emotional ways dampen their sexual flame. In turn, Water gets parched with fire's arrogance and lack of emotional nurturing. It takes a lot of patience and understanding to make these combinations work.

Although Aries may temporarily inspire Cancer's naughty side, **Aries and Cancer** together will rarely last. Cancers need more security than Aries is willing to offer.

Sex is "down and dirty" for **Aries and Scorpio.** Yet, it is often over quickly—and so is any potential relationship! Ultimately, you two are both too headstrong for this to work.

Dear Sextrologer ... _____

"I'm an Aries smitten with a Scorpio man. We have a great sexual connection, but we also argue—a lot! I get the feeling that he's competing with me and trying to control our relationship. Should I stay or move on?"

It's true that you are likely to have an intense sexual connection with your Scorpio lover, Aries. You will find however, that *both* of you may be too controlling to make each other truly happy. You like to be in charge and are impatient for results; your Scorpio also likes to feel powerful and in control and takes a lot of time to feel safe and secure. So, move on!

Romantic Pisces says, "Will you love me tomorrow?" Headstrong Aries says, "Who cares ... let's get it on!" **Aries and Pisces** is a sexual washout.

There's little attraction between **Leo and Cancer.** If you two *do* connect, however, you will find yourselves pussyfooting around each other's sensitivities.

Leo and Scorpio are both sexual dynamos. Yet, with both of your strong wills, the question remains—who will survive? Too often, this match is heartbreak history.

Pisces wants more than Leo is willing to offer. Leo thinks that Pisces is wishy-washy and dampens their spirit. **Leo and Pisces** are just not in sync—sexually or otherwise.

Sagittarius is too worldly and adventurous for home-loving Cancer. Together, **Sagittarius and Cancer** don't have much in common. What's worse—neither of you seems to care.

Sagittarius and Scorpio rarely understand each other and don't speak the same language in bed. You might as well be from two different countries—with no dictionary available!

There's little common ground for **Sagittarius and Pisces.** Here, Fire and Water do not mix—in life or in the bedroom.

Pisces is way too sensitive for blunt, adventurous Sag.

Cosmic Lovers _____

Sag Katie Holmes and husband Tom Cruise, a Cancer, make the perfect movie-star couple. Yet, Katie's Sagittarian independence and Cancer Tom's love of home and family is astrologically at odds. Is this relationship a "mission impossible?" Only time will tell!

When Fire Meets Earth

Fire and Earth signs both have strong sexual natures, and together your intense desires can be like a volcanic eruption! But independent Fire thrives on adventure, and conservative Earth likes to play it safe. Although Earth may initially ground Fire's wild and outgoing nature, Fire ultimately scorches Earth's need for security.

Aries says, "Go faster!" Taurus says, "Slow down!"

There may be some initial sexual sparks for **Aries and Taurus,** but ultimately you two are more likely to agitate than ignite.

It's pretty much hopeless for **Aries and Virgo.** Virgo is unnerved by Aries' sexual recklessness; Aries finds Virgo just plain uptight.

Power struggles define the **Aries and Capricorn** relationship. You two are both too headstrong for a good match. Yet—secretively—you both respect each other's sexual drive!

Stubborn meets stubborn with **Leo and Taurus.** Taurus thinks Leo is too overtly "sexy" (translation: smutty). Leo finds Taurus too "natural" (translation: "Bring on the wax job, please!").

The match of **Leo and Virgo** is a cosmic stretch. You two have little in common and no real desire to understand each other. That results in awkward sex—if it happens at all.

Leo and Capricorn are both sexual power players. You both may be initially intrigued with each other, yet Leo is ultimately too overdramatic for respectable, conventional Capricorn.

Heavenly Relations

Although Earth and Fire signs together are not always sexually in sync or lasting, Earth often has great admiration for Fire's passion and leadership abilities. In turn, Fire finds Earth's sexual stamina to be very intriguing.

Sagittarius with Taurus is generally not a good match in the bedroom. Freedom-loving Sag is too to sexually casual and adventurous for loyal, conservative Bulls.

Virgos disapprove of Sag's recklessness. **Sagittarius with Virgo** is a prime example of Fire and Earth not getting along. There's no chemistry—sexual or otherwise.

It's not that you don't like each other; in fact, **Sagittarius and Capricorn** may be excellent friends. It's just that neither of you has any idea what the other needs in bed!

When Air Meets Air

Air signs together are like a cool, refreshing breeze! Intellectually and sexually stimulating, you give each other tons of room to explore all of your sexual needs. At the same time, Air signs often live in their minds and in the realm of possibilities and inspiration; together, your feet may never touch the ground! Ultimately, Air signs together will have to work at sustainability.

Cosmic Lovers

Libra Susan Sarandon and long-time partner Tim Robbins, also a Libra, is an example of a same-sign relationship that works very well. Both of these outspoken Libras have a disdain for unfairness and have worked together politically for universal equality.

It's double the trouble, double the sexual fun for **Gemini and Gemini!** The question for you two players is, "Who's playing whom?" Will it last? Neither of you really care.

Gemini and Libra is a cosmic coupling. Both of you are fascinated by each other's minds! Sex is stimulating, too—if you can stop talking long enough to get it on!

Gemini and Aquarius reach a relationship and sexual high point together. Sex between the two is filled with fantasy and experimentation. In a word, it's otherworldly!

Libra and Libra is a same-sign relationship that works beautifully. The two bond over their shared love of beauty. In bed, it's a mutual admiration society!

A **Libra and Aquarius** match often comes with some tussling. Yet, their sex is harmonious and cosmically in sync. In the end, you two really do "get" each other!

Unpredictable describes **Aquarius and Aquarius.** You two will either last three weeks or a lifetime! Sex is mutually experimental (although a bit detached).

> **Star Alert!** _____
>
> Just as two Fire signs together can burn out quickly, too much Air can become overly stimulated—and poof, it's over!

When Air Meets Water

Air and Water signs can be the hardest astrological combination to work out. Air signs often find Water to be emotionally heavy and limiting to their airy sexual buoyancy. Simply put, Air signs think that Water rains on their parade! On the other hand, Water finds Air a bit perverse and sexually "out there." More often than not, these elements just don't happily mix—in the bedroom or in life.

Gemini and Cancer have wildly divergent needs in the bedroom. Cancer doesn't trust Gemini's tendency toward promiscuity, and Gemini finds Cancer a sexual bore.

Gemini and Scorpio is a case where Air and Water really don't mix—in the bedroom, anyway. Although there may be some initial intrigue between you, it will quickly fall flat.

Quicksilver Gemini likes to skim the surface, and Pisces likes to dive very deep. For **Gemini and Pisces,** the relationship is often over before it gets started.

Extravagant Libra loves to spend while Cancer loves to save. The compromises required for **Libra and Cancer** are often too much to negotiate. Sex? Not so great, either!

Libra and Scorpio have little in common. Libra feels affronted by Scorpio's aggressive need to seduce them; Scorpio has little patience for Libra's obsession with refinement.

Although **Libra and Pisces** are both romantically inclined, Pisces is too sexually passive and dreamy for Libra's need for a significant connection.

> **Heavenly Relations** _____
>
> Sun sign and ascendant compatibility is important, but there are other astrological factors involved in the success of your relationship. Check out the placement of your Moon and Venus and Mars to obtain more information about your full sextrology picture!

Cancer wonders what planet Aquarius is from; Aquarius thinks that Cancer is too needy. It's a cosmic "no-go" for **Aquarius and Cancer.**

Aquarius and Scorpio clash in the bedroom. Both of you can be defiant about getting your needs met and are too inflexible to make a relationship work.

Aquarius and Pisces rarely relate. Pisces struggles with Aquarius' lack of emotional connection and romance; Aquarius finds Pisces too needy.

When Air Meets Earth

In sextrology, the elements of Air and Earth easily extinguish each other. Air feels as if Earth clips their sexual wings and restricts their need to explore all possibilities. In turn, Earth finds Air too sexually wild and not loyal to their need for a lasting commitment. Together, you are not quite sure what to do with each other—and these connections are rarely lasting.

Gemini finds Taurus too conservative; Taurus thinks that Gemini is sexually "out there" and talks too much in bed! It's a cosmic "no-go" for **Gemini and Taurus.**

Dear Sextrologer …

"I'm a Gemini and have been seeing a Taurus for a few months. Although he's a great guy and we have fun together, I'm just not sexually attracted to him. Should I hang in there and hope for the best?"

Sorry, Gemini. You and Taurus are rarely a great match between the sheets. You would be more sexually in tune with another Air sign—a fellow Gemini, a Libra or Aquarius, or a Fire sign such as Aries, Leo, or Sagittarius. Hang onto this great guy as a good friend, but keep looking for a partner that will give you the sexual excitement that you want and deserve!

Gemini and Virgo is not a great love or sex match. You both pretend to tolerate each other, but the reality is … you irritate the heck out of each other!

For **Gemini and Capricorn,** there's little common ground. Although Capricorn would never admit it … Goats *are* intrigued by Gemini's sexual kinkiness!

Libra and Taurus, both ruled by Venus, have a love of beauty and nice things … which could make up for the lack of spark in the bedroom!

Libra and Virgo often make better friends than lovers. You two are both a bit too selective—okay, picky—to make this a sustaining romantic or sexual connection.

Capricorn's brusque nature sends poor Libra spinning into despair. The potential for hurt feelings and misunderstanding will rule your **Libra and Capricorn** relationship.

Taurus resides on planet Earth; Aquarius lives in unknown galaxies. In bed, **Aquarius and Taurus** are a potential disaster zone of mutual misunderstandings. Do not enter!

Virgo likes order; Aquarius thrives on creative chaos. In bed, Virgo is shocked by Aquarius' need to get freaky. **Aquarius and Virgo** together rarely work.

Aquarius and Capricorn enjoy really randy sexual romps in bed. Yet, there's no real connection there—and you may find yourselves avoiding each other in the morning.

Cosmic Lovers _____

Aquarius Sonny Bono and Taurus Cher are the quintessential Air and Earth combination. Although married for many years and endlessly intrigued by each other, grounded diva Cher and oddball Sonny were ultimately seeking different experiences in life.

When Water Meets Water

Water signs together create a sea of tranquility that can lead to sexual heaven! Water signs flow together seamlessly in the bedroom, and sex is often profound, compassionate, and deeply nurturing. Although these connections are often lasting, Water signs together can drown out each other's life spark. You can become so comfortable with each other that you forget to leave the bedroom and go to work!

Cancer with Cancer is almost *too* compatible. You two may get so comfortable with each other that your sexual passion dies. Pass the Ben and Jerry's and the remote control!

Heavenly Relations _____

Water signs can be very psychic. And when two Water signs meet, there can be a feeling of instant or deep recognition.

Dear Sextrologer ... _____

"I'm a Cancer married to a Cancer, and we just celebrated our 10-year anniversary. I feel lucky to have a man in my life who is a loving and supportive partner, yet lately our sex life has become routine! Any suggestions on how to spice up our love life?"

Typically, Cancers are not great when it comes to expressing their emotional or sexual needs. You two need to spend some time communicating about what turns you on in the bedroom. Cancers love the ocean, so take a long weekend together at a romantic bed and breakfast near the water. Then, relax and explore your deepest sexual fantasies together. I bet that you'll quickly find your sexual magic again!

Dream lovers, dream partners: together, **Cancer and Scorpio** are a great love and sex match. This one is destined to last.

Cancer and Pisces, both super-sensitive, find solace in each other's arms. You two bond deeply over nurturing and soulful sex. Together, it's often happily ever after!

Mirror, mirror on the wall: sex is great between **Scorpio and Scorpio**—if you guys don't kill each other first! Watch for power struggles.

Star Alert! _____

"I want to stop the world and be with you!" describes two Water signs together. Water signs have a tendency to dissolve all boundaries and completely merge with their lover—sometimes to the point of obsession and co-dependence.

Scorpio and Pisces is like an instant bolt of sexual lightning. Often it's "Hello, lover! Have I known you before?" Who knows, who cares—together, this relationship is a keeper!

It's a sweet and very romantic dream come true for **Pisces and Pisces.** Sex is sublime and all-consuming. Yet, together you two have a hard time sustaining your fantasies.

When Water Meets Earth

The combination of Water and Earth often makes for lasting relationships. These elements are extremely compatible and have a natural sexual flow. Water nurtures Earth and soothes many of their gruff edges. Earth grounds Water, giving them a safe vessel for exploring their sexual fantasies. Oh, and did we mention that sex together will be sublime?

Sex is superbly yummy for **Cancer and Taurus.** In fact, it's so good that you two may never leave the bedroom! Ultimately, however, someone's got to get up and get those bills paid.

Both practical and security-minded, **Cancer and Virgo** enrich each other's lives. Sex is mutually nurturing, and you can help soothe each other's fear of being left behind.

The balance of opposites works well for **Cancer and Capricorn.** One's the sensitive, nurturing, motherly type and the other the hard-working fatherly type. Together, you're a power couple!

Scorpio and Taurus together are intense and passionate. Although you two may challenge each other when it comes to being in control, this relationship is fated to last.

It's rip-roaring sex for **Scorpio and Virgo.** Scorpio ups Virgo's lust potential. Virgo grounds Scorpio's extreme passion for a potentially lasting relationship!

Both **Scorpio and Capricorn** are sexual power players. Although you two may initially challenge each other, ultimately there's a lot of respect and longevity.

Sex is heavenly for **Pisces and Taurus.** You two know how to push all the right sexual buttons. Plus, Taurus grounds all of Pisces' sexual fantasies.

Cosmic Lovers

Playwright and actor Sam Shepard—a sexy, secretive, and shy Scorpio—and Oscar-winning actress and sexy mother Jessica Lange, a Taurus, are long-time partners. Both are individually intense and together make a passionate love match.

In bed, **Pisces and Virgo** fit together like a dream. In life, the same is true. Watch out, however: both of you have a tendency to look for something better.

Pisces and Capricorn make a sweet pair. Pisces brings out Capricorn's soft side to an unmatched degree, and Capricorn happily grounds Pisces in reality.

When Earth Meets Earth

In most cases, Earth signs together are sexually simpatico. Sex is slow, sensual, and usually quite delicious. Earth signs easily come to feel comfortable and secure together and are faithful and loyal partners. Earths can create dynasties together! Or, you can become so bogged down in your mutual need for security and risk-aversion that you never get anything much done at all!

Dear Sextrologer ...

"I'm a Taurus, and my long-time girlfriend is a Virgo. Although instinctively I feel that we are good matches, she drives me crazy with all of her insecurities. Sometimes I think there is someone else out there for me. What should I do?"

Your initial instincts are right: You and Virgo together are a good match! Even in the best of relationships, however, there's always bound to be some differences. Here's the deal: your Virgo girlfriend is looking for stability, which you can give to her—in spades! In turn, you can benefit from her ability to keep you on your toes, especially when it comes to embracing the finer details of your life. A major plus—you two are both extremely sensual and can help each other explore your deepest sexual needs and desires. So, stay put and let the little things go!

Sex for **Taurus and Taurus** is deeply sensual and lasts all night long. You two will have to guard against getting too lazy and comfortable together that you never get anything done!

Heavenly Relations

The astrological signs represented by land animals tend to be the most overtly sexual. This includes all Earth signs: Taurus the Bull, Capricorn the Goat, and yes ... Virgo the Virgin (the two-footed human animal). Fire signs are similarly sexual: Aries the Ram, Leo the Lion, and Sagittarius the Archer (also known as the centaur ... half man, half horse).

Although there can be some initial obstacles to negotiate, sex is smoldering for **Taurus and Virgo.** Ultimately, you will bring each other peace by making each other feel safe.

Surprise, surprise! Bulls and Goats *do* get along—and how! **Taurus and Capricorn** instinctively know how to please each other sexually. Wait—can you hear wedding bells?

Virgo and Virgo together is a same-sign relationship that can work, if you two can stop nick-picking each other to death! Let go of your perfectionism and feel the love.

Together, **Virgo and Capricorn** make a refined pair. Capricorn grounds Virgo's edginess, and Virgo loves the security that Capricorn offers. Oh, and the sex is pretty much legendary!

Sex is slow and steady for **Capricorn and Capricorn.** You two responsible loners can make each other very happy. Plus, there's lots of mutual respect—and the sex is sublime.

The Least You Need to Know

- Fire signs together are, yes, sexually ablaze!
- Fire and Air fan each other's sexual flames.
- Fire with Earth or Water is always a challenge.
- Air signs together are a compatible and sexually explorative match.
- Air with Earth or Water is sexually difficult.
- Water with Water is sexually deep and profound.
- Water with Earth makes for a long-lasting relationship.
- Earth signs together are sexually—and sensuously in synch.

Part 2

The Moon and Intimacy

The Moon is yin to the Sun's yang. Your Sun sign and ascendant represent your astrological essence and outer personality, but your Moon represents your inner self. Your Moon sign reflects your deepest needs and hidden desires. It also indicates how you will relate to sexual fidelity.

Your Moon sign compatibility reveals how you and your lover will engage in sexual and emotional intimacy and will often determine the long-term happiness of your relationship.

Exploring the cycles of the Moon and its placement in the various signs of the zodiac will let you know when you are most likely to have an exceptional sexual or lovemaking experience!

Going Deep: The Moon Signs

In This Chapter

- ◆ Find your Moon sign
- ◆ Understand your emotional personality and deeper needs
- ◆ Fire Moons need attention and ego-stroking
- ◆ Air Moons need inspiration and excitement
- ◆ Water Moons need nurturing and reassurance
- ◆ Earth Moons need security and resist change

Your Moon sign indicates your inner personality. It represents your emotions, feelings, deeper instincts, and intuitions. The Moon also represents your unconscious: it is the root of much that motivates you and is reflected in your life through your deepest needs, wants, and desires. Simply put: it's what really makes you tick! Your Moon sign also indicates what you really seek in your most intimate relationships.

Dear Sextrologer ...

"My Sun sign is Capricorn, but when I read my horoscope or astrology profile, it never seems to fit. Am I missing something?"

You may find that you relate more to your Moon sign than your Sun sign. Although your Sun sign gives you a lot of information about your astrological makeup, your Moon sign reflects your deeper personality. When checking out your horoscope or astrology profile, look at both your Sun and Moon signs. That way, you'll get a more complete sense of your full astrology picture.

Your Moon: Your Deepest Self

In astrological terms, the Moon revolves in close orbit to the Earth, providing a mirror that reflects the Earth's light. In a sense, your Moon is your astrological Sun's shadow, reflecting your deeper self and inner, unknown mysteries—which are just waiting to be discovered with your lover! The difference between Sun and Moon signs can be subtle but distinct: the Sun's bright light is easier to see and get a handle on, but the Moon's mysteries can challenge you to look deeper and discover unknown territory within yourself.

The Moon symbolizes your source of nurturing and emotional contentment. Because your Moon also represents your sense of home, it indicates where, how, and with whom you feel the most comfortable and secure. The Moon is especially important to your sextrology because it reveals how you will engage in emotional intimacy. Your Moon sign will give you insight into your deeper personality and what and really want and seek in your relationships. The sign of the Moon also indicates how you and your lover are likely to relate to sexual fidelity, including attitudes toward casual or committed sex. For more information see the following table: you may be surprised at what you find!

Moon Signs and Sexual Fidelity

Moons	Casual or Committed?
Fire Moons	
Aries	Casual
Leo	Committed
Sagittarius	Casual
Air Moons	
Gemini	Casual
Libra	Committed
Aquarius	Casual, Committed
Water Moons	
Cancer	Committed
Scorpio	Committed
Pisces	Committed, Casual
Earth Moons	
Taurus	Committed
Virgo	Committed
Capricorn	Casual, Committed

You know your Sun sign because it's based on your birthday! Your Moon sign is also based on your day of birth, but because the Moon changes signs every two to two-and-a-half days, it is more specifically related to your time of birth. To help you find your Moon sign, we've included an online resource guide in Appendix B with different websites that will give you more information.

Fire Moons

Fire Moons are proud, passionate, and sexually assertive. They also tend to be very independent. These Moons are spontaneous and live in the moment; they don't plan ahead and rarely worry about the future. Although Fire Moons can be self-involved, for all of their fiery posturing, deep down they tend to be emotionally insecure. Although they will rarely admit it, they need constant attention! Some ego-stroking—and a little fawning—never hurts and will make these Moons feel desired and secure. In relationships, Fire Moons dominate with their outgoing personalities and strong egos.

Star Alert! _____

Look out! Fire Moons are very aggressive about going after what they want. In relationships, they are usually the pursuer—and this trait applies to both sexes. When they find the object of their desire, nothing stands in their way. Fire Moons will do their very best to sweep you off your feet!

Moon in Aries

Moon in Aries needs to conquer. These proud warriors want and need to be loved. They are more comfortable giving than receiving the love that they truly desire. Moon in Aries is a survivor at heart. Because they feel as if they must always be strong and in control, they often have a hard time being emotionally vulnerable. Instead, they conquer! Moon in Aries likes to be the hero or heroine: they are rescuers and will often put their emotional energy into "saving" others. In a relationship, Moon in Aries is a passionate and encouraging lover—they will support *you* in going after what you want.

Cosmic Lovers _____

Mel Gibson as Scottish hero William Wallace in the Oscar-winning movie *Braveheart* fits Moon in Aries to a T. A warrior with a soft heart and plenty of pride, he was willing to conquer an empire for what he believed in.

These very independent Moons are geared toward casual sex. Moons in Aries like opportunities to explore their sexual and relationship options.

Moon in Leo

Moon in Leo needs devotion. These Moons need to feel important and recognized for their unique talents and abilities. Moon in Leo has a lot of pride and is easily wounded. They were the children who felt hurt for days when they didn't receive enough valentines! Leo Moons are loyal and fiercely protective of their lovers—sometimes overly so. In relationships, Moons in Leo are romantic and very demonstrative when expressing their feelings. They can also be jealous and will expect to be a major priority in your life.

Moon in Leo prefers committed sex. This Moon, however, does like instant gratification. If they're not getting enough attention in their partnerships, they may look for it elsewhere! In the right relationship, they are usually loyal mates.

Dear Sextrologer ... _____

"I'm seeing a woman with a Leo Moon. She's fun and dynamic but also a total diva when it comes to getting what she wants. She blows things completely out of proportion ... what I would consider to be a discussion to her becomes a big argument! I want to keep seeing her but am tiring of all the drama. What should I do?"

It's no secret: Leo Moons *are* drama kings and queens! At the same time, they also have big hearts and are devoted partners. It's a tradeoff, but at least your life with your Leo Moon gal will always be exciting! If you are seeking a less dramatic, theatrical lover, Leo Moon is not the one for you. As they say: if you can't handle the heat—get out of the fire!

Moon in Sagittarius

Moon in Sagittarius needs to explore. Like Huckleberry Finn, Moon in Sag is filled with a childlike love of adventure! This Moon is constantly seeking the next big experience and has a hard time being tied down to one lover. Moons in Sagittarius are often interested in other cultures and don't always feel at home in their own. As a result, they are often emotionally drawn to lovers and relationships from different cultures. In their relationships, Moons in Sagittarius are stimulating partners who will help open up your world to possibilities and adventures you might have secretly dreamed of!

Moon in Sag thrives on new opportunities. For this Moon placement, it's casual sex—definitely!

Heavenly Relations _____

Are you dating your mom? Your Moon sign represents your deeper personality, but it also denotes your early family environment—including your relationship with your mother! It is not unusual to find that your Moon sign will draw you towards partners that reflect this early childhood relationship.

Air Moons

Air Moons are very intellectual. These Moons tend to be more comfortable in their minds than in their feelings and emotions. Air Moons need lots of mental stimulation to stay romantically or sexually interested. They are restless for new experiences and are easily excitable. Air Moons can be emotionally detached and even initially sexually chilly—so these are not the Moons to go to if you're looking for emotional reassurance or cozy comfort! The way to warm them up is to make sure to have many fun and stimulating experiences together. In relationships, Air Moons need to be inspired and never bored!

Moon in Gemini

Moon in Gemini needs to play. This Moon can be childlike emotionally. In fact, Moons in Gemini can be sexual Peter Pans—never wanting to grow up and face tedious adult responsibilities, especially when it comes to long-term commitment. Moon in Gemini is usually a charming and fun-loving partner and is often very witty. Yet, like all Air Moons, they can be emotionally distant. Moon in Gemini does not like arguments and will avoid most emotional confrontations. In fact, this Moon does not like confrontations of any kind. If they're put under too much emotional pressure, these playful lovers are likely to move on to a new relationship.

These Moons have a hard time settling down with one partner. It's casual sex for them—and lots of it!

Cosmic Lovers

Patrician beauty Gwyneth Paltrow is a Libra with a Moon in Gemini. Both Libra and Gemini are Air signs, which is reflected in her high intellect. Whereas Paltrow's Libra Sun shows her refined nature, her Moon in Gemini reflects her more fun-loving and explorative side.

Moon in Libra

Moon in Libra needs to feel inspired. These Moons have a deep love of beauty and culture. They are also very relationship oriented—in fact, it's often their very reason for being! Moon in Libra often falls in love with love and is easily enamored. At the same time, they are very discerning and want only the best from their lovers! With Moon in Libra, it's often all or nothing: either they're totally into you and your relationship or they become disappointed, disillusioned, and emotionally cold.

When in a relationship, for Moon in Libra it's definitely committed sex, thank you very much! Although this Moon desires a committed relationship, they may flirt with casual sex on their road to finding the right partner.

Dear Sextrologer ...

"I'm an interior decorator with my Moon in Libra. I'm very romantic and like to be courted. I have been dating a few different guys but don't feel that they embrace my need for romance or get my refined aesthetic. Am I completely out of line to want more?"

You, Moon in Libra, can be quite picky about what you want—especially when it comes to your relationships. Your profession as an interior designer is a good match for your artistic nature. But, just as your clients won't always have your discerning eye, you cannot expect your boyfriends to always share your need for beauty. They aren't necessarily going to guess how you long for old-fashioned courtship, either. Because your needs are so specific, you have two choices: either be specific and ask for what you need, or save yourself for an old-fashioned gentleman who loves the details of romantic courtship just as much as you do! A man who also has his Moon in Libra, for example, or a Leo or Pisces Moon will likely share your romantic sensibilities.

Moon in Aquarius

Moon in Aquarius needs breathing room. Extremely independent, these Moons do not like to be tied down—and difficulty with emotional intimacy is often an issue. They can have a fear of abandonment and will bury their emotions in intellectual pursuits as a way of feeling safe. Although these Moons can be sexual players, they are usually serial monogamists (and, in their own way, very loyal). Moon in Aquarius has successful long-term relationships. No matter how committed, however, they need lots of space.

Moons in Aquarius often have great relationships with their ex-lovers—unless you have your Moon in another fixed sign such as Leo, Scorpio, or Taurus. In that case, you're likely to be too jealous and territorial to allow it!

For Moon in Aquarius, it's casual sex (unless they're romantically committed). These Moons like to play around but will settle down with one partner if so inspired.

Cosmic Lovers

Taurus Jack Nicholson has his Moon in Aquarius. Nicholson's Sun sign denotes his highly sensual nature and career longevity. His Moon in Aquarius denotes his more eccentric, detached, and "out-there" personality—and his need to stay unattached and single. For this Moon, it can be: "Let's get married but live in separate houses!"

Water Moons

Water Moons base much of their lives on their feelings, intuitions, and emotions. These Moons are sensitive, no question. They are also very nurturing lovers and usually give as much as they receive in their relationships. Generally, Water Moons flourish in committed partnerships because they feel safe and secure—something that Water Moons require. These Moons do not embrace change; in fact, they can be quite stubborn about letting go of the known and embarking on new experiences. For Water Moons, sex is usually deep and profound—at least, that's their preference!

Water Moons are psychically sensitive and in tune with their deeper intuitions. These Moons will often have an uncanny ability to read you—and your deepest nature— sometimes unsettlingly so!

Moon in Cancer

Moon in Cancer needs commitment. These Moons are conditioned for comfort and security and seek the familiar in their lives and relationships. They are extremely sensitive and have many emotional ups and downs. Although big givers, Moons in Cancer are often emotionally introverted and have a hard time expressing their deeper needs. As a result, they can become isolated. In relationships, this Moon is a nurturing lover but can be a bit possessive and even needy. Because these Moons are caretakers by nature, they can be frustrated when it comes to fulfilling their own creative needs.

Without a doubt, Moon in Cancer wants committed sex. These Moons appreciate loyalty and do not play around.

Dear Sextrologer ...

"I have my Moon in Cancer, and as you well know, we Cancers can be moody! There are times when I feel extremely sensitive and find myself getting cranky with those closest to me. I worry about how my moods are affecting my husband. Any suggestions for this sensitive Moon child?"

You are sensitive, but have you ever noticed that your moods are often in sync with the cycles of the Moon? Moon in Cancer needs a lot of time alone and space to reflect or go within, particularly during these sensitive periods. You are a giver, but it is important that you remember that it's okay to take time for yourself without worrying about taking care of everyone else. Give yourself this time, and you and your husband will both be happier.

Moon in Scorpio

Moon in Scorpio needs passion. These Moons can be highly secretive and have difficulty revealing their deeper selves. Moon in Scorpio often has a survivor mentality and needs to feel in control. Like the proverbial elephant, Moon in Scorpio never forgets! This Moon can be vindictive and finds it hard to forgive. Often jealous and possessive, Moon in Scorpio can become emotionally obsessive and go to extremes. In the right relationship, however, they are committed and very passionate partners. They will help you fulfill your deepest sexual needs!

It may be a surprise, but although Scorpio is known for its highly sexual nature, Moon in Scorpio does prefer committed sex. These Moons may explore their sexual options yet are the most satisfied in committed relationships.

 Cosmic Lovers

As Jane Austen's star-crossed lover Mr. Darcy said to his beloved Elizabeth Bennet, "You have bewitched me body and soul." These two passionate lovers, both filled with pride and prejudice—not to mention major trust issues—surely both had their Moons in Scorpio!

Moon in Pisces

Moon in Pisces needs romance. These Moons are highly imaginative and have active fantasy lives. Moon in Pisces may live more in the fantasy of their ideal lover than the reality. Moons in Pisces can be passive-aggressive about expressing their emotional needs and may suffer from inferiority complexes. These Moons often feel like they need to be perfect and have to constantly redeem themselves—especially when it comes to helping others. Moon in Pisces' Achilles heel is guilt! These Moons thrive on romance and lots of emotional attention. They are also giving and sensitive lovers and will fill your life with romance as well.

Moon in Pisces prefers committed sex, but they're flexible! These Moons desire a committed relationship but will be willing to explore casual sex in the process.

Earth Moons

Earth Moons are grounded in the here and now. They are invested in maintaining the status quo and resist change. Earth Moons can be plodders and planners and are not emotionally adventurous. They take life slowly—one day at a time. Earth Moons like committed relationships and are the most stable and reliable of all Moons. They are not big on emotional or sexual drama, yet in a crisis they are proverbial rocks and will support you through thick and thin—and often for better or for worse.

Star Alert! _____

Earth Moons are not the most sensitive creatures on the planet! They tend to be clumsy when expressing their emotions and deeper feelings. They can also be somewhat oblivious when it comes to your needs. If you want something from an Earth Moon, you will need to let them know!

Moon in Taurus

Moon in Taurus needs to feel secure. This Moon is extremely grounded—sometimes so grounded that they forget to look at the bigger picture and refuse to embrace new ideas. Moon in Taurus can become so invested in their need for security that they become emotionally stuck. They often rely on the same and the known. In fact, they can be like ostriches keeping their heads in the sand when it comes to dealing with the deeper needs of their partners. Yet, they are emotionally stable and reliable lovers and will be a strong support system in your life.

For Moon in Taurus, it's committed sex—and happily so! These Moons are deeply sensual but are rarely sexual players. They seek partners who share their desire for long-term commitment.

Dear Sextrologer ... _____

"I'm a female with a Moon in Taurus. I have been single for a long time—too long! I want to have a relationship, but lately my friends tell me that I have become a bit of a frump and need to 'amp up' my style to get back into the relationship game. I admit, I do like my sweatpants and don't put much energy into my dress or style. How far do I need to go?"

It's true that Moon in Taurus loves comfort. You may have gotten a bit *too* comfortable, however! Approach yourself with some of the sensuality—a known Taurus trait—that you have in store for your partner-to-be. You may find that you start to enjoy exploring your beauty, dressing up, and looking good! Be yourself, but consider sprucing yourself up a bit. You will be surprised at how much better you feel! Then, plan a great dinner party for your friends and surprise them with your new look. Have fun, and celebrate yourself and your entrance back into the dating scene!

Moon in Virgo

Moon in Virgo needs to feel secure. These Moons often act like Chicken Littles: they're always waiting for the sky to fall! Moon in Virgo has many emotional fears and likes to play it safe. This Moon thrives on organization and needs everything to be in its proper place. Moons in Virgo are emotionally sensitive and can be shy about expressing their deeper needs. With all of their discerning ways, Moon in Virgo is looking for a partner that will make him or her feel secure. In relationships, this Moon is an extremely supportive and giving partner.

For Moon in Virgo, it's committed sex—absolutely!

These Moons have a strong sexual nature but don't like to play around. They are happiest and feel the most secure in committed relationships.

Although Moons in Virgo are perfectionists, they are also emotionally sensitive and extremely nurturing lovers. Give him or her a little reassurance, and Moon in Virgo is yours—often for a lifetime!

Moon in Capricorn

Moon in Capricorn needs to feel in control. These Moons like to be in charge and are easily frustrated when they don't get their way. Moons in Capricorn are highly invested in how they appear to others. They like to play by the rules and will usually insist on doing things right. At the same time, beneath their often gruff exteriors, Moons in Capricorn are emotionally sensitive and even a bit insecure! This Moon is reliable and will be a supportive (and, perhaps surprisingly, nurturing) partner—especially when it comes to supporting your career aspirations. Moon in Capricorn often marries early and usually for life.

Moon in Capricorn can be a sexual player; yet, when they find their right mate, it's usually a done deal and they rarely stray. Moon in Capricorn is all about either casual and committed sex, depending on their relationship status.

> **Cosmic Lovers**
>
> *Sex and the City's* Sarah Jessica Parker, an Aries, has her Moon in Capricorn. This Moon reflects the hardworking and disciplined element of her nature. It also explains her angular and sinewy body type. For Moon in Capricorn, it's often, "I can eat whatever I want and not gain a pound!"

The Least You Need to Know

◆ Understanding your Moon sign will help you understand your (and your lover's) deepest needs.

◆ Your Moon sign, and your lovers, will give you important indications about how you both relate to sexual fidelity.

◆ Each Moon sign has its own emotional personality.

◆ Fire Moons are aggressive and proud.

◆ Air Moons are intellectual and emotionally chilly.

◆ Water Moons are sensitive and nurturing.

◆ Earth Moons are grounded and need security.

Chapter 8

Moon Compatibility: Your Deepest Connection

In This Chapter

◆ Fire with Fire or Air Moons are emotionally in tune

◆ Fire with Earth or Water Moons ... not so much!

◆ Water with Water or Earth Moons are emotionally compatible

◆ Air with Earth or Water Moons do not make for easy intimacy

As mentioned in Chapter 7, your Moon sign is based on your date of birth. But because the Moon changes signs every two to two-and-a-half days, it is more specifically related to your time of birth. To help you find your Moon sign, we've included an online resource guide in Appendix B with different websites that will give you more information.

Sun sign and ascendant compatibility are important because they reflect your public face and outward life, but it's your Moon sign compatibility that indicates your deepest and most intimate connection. This chapter will describe how your Moons relate together to dictate your day-to-day harmony and relationship well-being.

Fire Moons Together

Fire Moons together make dynamic lovers and partners. Both of you are passionate, determined, assertive—and self-absorbed! On the upside, you have a deeper understanding of each other's impulses, arrogance, drive, and needs. Your sexual desires are also highly in sync. The great challenge for two Fire Moons is learning the humility and generosity that long-term love needs in order to survive and flourish.

"Explosive!" describes **Aries Moons together.** Although the sex has never been better, ultimately you two both have very strong emotional needs and expectations. If this is going to work long-term, you'll both have to make some major compromises.

Together, **Aries and Leo Moons** are a perfect and very sexy match—provided that emotionally distant Moon in Aries never forgets to show his or her devotion and sensitive and proud Moon in Leo learns to not take personally Aries Moon's need for independence.

Aries and Sagittarius Moons are both adventurous and freedom loving, and neither needs a commitment in order to have great sex. You'll make fast friends and hot lovers—but will it last? It might—if you can work through your mutual need for sexual exploration.

Leo Moons together is a guaranteed glam-o-rama drama! If you allow each other to share the spotlight—no small feat—this can be a thrilling match. You both are deeply sensitive, wildly jealous, and generous to a fault—and when you fight, your makeup sex will be sublime!

> **! Star Alert!**
>
> The deal-breaker between Fire Moons is often ego needs and sexual fidelity. Although Fire Moons need lots of room to explore their sexual options, they nonetheless demand their own unique brand of loyalty and commitment.

Together, **Leo and Sagittarius Moons** are tremendous fun. Both are outgoing, sociable, and very sexual. Happy-go-lucky Sag Moon admires Leo's ambition, while sensitive Moon in Leo longs to learn how Sag manages to remain so easygoing! This is a match that could last!

Sagittarius Moons together can be the most fun you can have with clothes on—and even more fun when you don't! You're both outgoing, adventurous, and live in the moment. Whether you find yourselves settling in together long enough to hang your paintings, though, depends on your willingness to—gasp—take the plunge and commit.

Fire and Air Moons Together

Fire and Air Moons could be described as two kids who love to play and explore together! You thrive on excitement, adventure, and—isn't it fun to be a grown up?—stimulating each other's sexual desires. On an emotional level, you both understand each other's need for space and room to grow. Sure, there's going to be some drama as you challenge each other's individuality and need for independence—but the important factor is that you both just "get" each other!

Both **Aries and Gemini Moons** love excitement and the thrill of discovering unknown territory. You understand what it takes to make each other succeed. Together, there is a compatible fire and air synchronicity at work. You two could pull off a lasting connection!

Although emotionally, **Aries and Libra Moons** come from two different planets (Aries: "planet Self"; Libra: "planet Other"), together you give each other a much-needed balance. You will challenge each other, but it may be well worth the effort!

Aries and Aquarius Moons are both sexually explorative and have much in common around their mutual need for independence. Plus, rebellious Moon in Aquarius loves Moon in Aries' need to follow his or her brazen instincts! You two are in tune enough to make it work.

What makes both **Leo and Gemini Moons** tick is a need for excitement (and yes, drama!). You both love to keep things exciting and are provocative in your approach to life. If Gemini Moon can respect Leo Moon's need for loyalty and Leo Moon can embrace Gemini Moon's sexual curiosity—both a big "if"—this could be a divine match.

Leo and Libra Moons love to get busy together—and not only in the bedroom! You both love the finer things in life and are moved by beauty. You will enjoy shopping together or going to an art show or the latest play or opera. You enjoy spending time together and enhance and further develop each other's deeper aesthetic.

 Heavenly Relations

Your Moon sign is a deeper layer of your Sun sign/ascendant, reflecting your emotional needs, your comfort zones, and what makes you feel secure. Your Moon compatibility indicates what both of you are looking for at the deepest levels of intimacy.

Opposites attract for **Leo and Aquarius Moons.** Leo Moon craves devotion; Aquarius Moon wants independence. You may be coming from two different perspectives, but if you can find a way to meet halfway, this could actually work!

Sagittarius and Gemini Moons are both rolling stones, and there's little moss that will gather under either of your feet (or this relationship!). For you, life rarely grows stale. This pair will understand each other's mutual need for intellectual stimulation and emotional freedom.

Cosmic Lovers _____

Gemini supermodel and media entrepreneur Heidi Klum of *Project Runway* fame has her Moon in Gemini—indicating her ability to multitask! Her husband, Virgo musician Seal, has his Moon in Sagittarius. This is a case where opposite Moons attract in cosmic harmony!

Although blunt Moon in Sag rattles Libra Moon's need for decorum, **Sagittarius and Libra Moons** can work. Plus, Moon in Sagittarius is deeply drawn to Moon in Libra's airy refinement. Surprisingly, this match may not be so much of a stretch!

Sagittarius and Aquarius Moons are cosmic brethren—you have many of the same emotional and spiritual needs. Both of you cherish your independence and can give each other space to explore and emotionally develop in your own time and ways!

Dear Sextrologer ... _____

"I'm a Leo with a Leo Moon and Aries ascendant. I'm getting ready to shop for a new boyfriend. What should I look for in potential astrological compatibility?"

Shopping for a lover, eh? You are definitely a Leo! You have a lot of fire in your astrological makeup. What you need is a partner who will be strong and bold enough to meet you every step of the way. A compatible Moon sign for you is either another Fire sign or an Air sign. A boyfriend with an Air Moon would add some balance to your fiery mix while keeping you sexually stimulated—and never bored!

Fire and Water Moons Together

Whereas Fire Moons are all about adventure and discovering new opportunities, Water Moons like to stick with what's comfortable. While Fire Moons long to get out into the world and explore, Water Moons are happiest at home with someone who wants to settle down and snuggle! You will likely challenge each other over deep relationship needs. In the long term, Fire and Water Moons tend to fizzle.

Initially, **Aries and Cancer Moons** may experience a sexual zing—but it's rarely lasting. You two have many different emotional needs and priorities, and in day-to-day life you're both looking for two very different kinds of relationship experiences.

Both **Aries and Scorpio Moons** are dynamic and passionate and will likely feel a strong sexual attraction. Emotionally, however, you two step on each other's toes. Moon in Aries is too brash and rash for Moon in Scorpio's deeper sensitivities.

Aries and Pisces Moons together rarely have what it takes to make the other feel emotionally content, let alone give the other what he or she really needs and deserves. You two will challenge each other around your differences regarding emotional security.

> **Heavenly Relations**
>
> Fire Moons act from instinct: they move quickly and go with their guts. Water Moons are more intuitive and need time to reflect on what they want.

Although both **Leo and Cancer Moons** seek emotional security, they are coming from different perspectives. Moon in Leo values fun and excitement; Moon in Cancer doesn't want drama or conflict. It's hard for you two to get any kind of emotional rhythm going.

Ego clashes describe **Leo and Scorpio Moons** together. Both of you want to be in charge—Moons in Leo through their aggressive need for attention and Moons in Scorpio through their need to control.

Although both **Leo and Pisces Moons** love drama and exploring their active fantasy lives, Moon in Leo's cup is always half full and brimming with opportunities—whereas Pisces Moon's is half empty and wanting more. This pairing is not emotionally in sync.

It's not that **Sagittarius and Cancer Moons** don't respect each other—in fact, both may secretly desire each other's lives. Sag Moon appreciates Cancer Moon's commitment to family, and Cancer Moon secretly thrills to the idea of Sag Moon's adventures. In the day-to-day, however, it doesn't line up!

Perhaps **Sagittarius and Scorpio Moons** meet together in a Tantric Yoga class and feel a bond around their spiritual beliefs. Unfortunately, mutual respect and exciting verbal intercourse does not equal a deep or lasting connection.

Sagittarius and Pisces Moons share a mutual vulnerability and fear of expressing their deeper emotions—although fiery Moon in Sag would never admit it! You two are following two very different approaches to life, and there is too much of an emotional ravine between you to make it work.

Fire and Earth Moons Together

Both Fire and Earth Moons are highly sexual. They also have a deep need to be in control! But whereas Fire Moons want to expand, grow, and explore new horizons, Earth Moons like to play it safe and are happiest maintaining the status quo. You two will face many conflicts when it comes to making each other feel happy and secure. Bottom line: when it comes to your emotional needs, you have very little in common.

Although **Aries and Taurus Moons** may initially spark sexually and even devour each other in bed, it's usually a one-night stand. You both want different things emotionally: Aries Moons want independence, and Taurus Moons value comfort.

Star Alert!

The deal-breaker between Fire and Earth Moons is around who's going to be the alpha dog in the relationship. Both of you like to be in charge!

There's no way around it: **Aries and Virgo Moons** have little in common, emotionally or sexually. As hard as you two may try, there's little room for either of you to get your deeper needs met.

Aries and Capricorn Moons are much alike when it comes to being on top and in control, but Aries Moon's need for boldness and freedom and Capricorn's desire for security don't match. This Moon combination will be an emotional power struggle!

Territorial **Leo and Taurus Moons** will constantly challenge each other around whose needs come first. Moon in Taurus has little patience for Leo Moon's emotional drama; Leo Moon tires of Taurus Moon's need to play it safe.

Leo and Virgo Moons are not a good match—emotionally or sexually. In fact, the general consensus between you two is that you get on each other's nerves! Unless there's some other astrological factor that is very in sync, move on!

Leo and Capricorn Moons understand each other's ambitions and need to get ahead in life. Yet, Moon in Leo needs more attention and devotion than stoic and often emotionally stingy Moon in Capricorn has to offer.

Freewheeling Moon in Sag wants to explore the world; security-oriented Moon in Taurus would rather stay at home. Together, **Sagittarius and Taurus Moons** don't have much in common.

Sagittarius and Virgo Moons make an interesting combination. Virgo Moon worries about lining up the details; Sag Moon has little patience for straight lines. It will be very hard for you to make each other happy.

Both **Sagittarius and Capricorn Moons** are highly sexual. Playful Moon in Sag, however, is too independent for Capricorn's need to be in control every step of the way. Together, you bring out each other's competitive natures!

Heavenly Relations

Your Moon represents your feelings and emotions, but it also rules your intuitive sense. When your Moon signs are in sync, you will often feel a deep, intuitive connection with each other.

Air Moons Together

Air Moons love excitement and exploring their options—in life and in the bedroom! Both of you are intellectual, perpetually curious, and love to play. Together, you are a sexy match! You stimulate each other in all the right places—especially around your mutual need to be inspired. The result is a lot of fun, but both of you will need to dig deeper for emotional substance. Your long-term relationship will depend on it!

Put two **Gemini Moons together** and the result is intense sexual and intellectual stimulation. You two have a lot of fun playing together and are on the same page when it comes to lifestyles. The question is: will you be able to ground your emotional and long-term needs?

So much to do, so little time! **Gemini and Libra Moons** are compatible on many levels, although Libra Moon may have difficulty with Moon in Gemini's need to play around and avoid commitment. Still, you two have so much fun together that this relationship could work!

Gemini and Aquarius Moons are in sync with their need for emotional freedom. Both of you also love to express your opinions! Together, you will converse and debate long into the night. When you finally decide that it's time for bed, you will devour each other physically, as well! Will it last? It just might!

Libra Moons together will vacillate between their many choices and options. What to do? Consider that you are both emotionally in sync and enjoy spending time together. Sexually, you're a happy, erotic mix and have a deep understanding of each other's needs. Enough said?

Libra and Aquarius Moons together often feel a deep intellectual and emotional pull. Although commitment is a big issue for Moon in Aquarius—and Libra Moon will settle for nothing less—you have enough cosmic synchronicity to make it work.

It's a cosmic roll of the dice for **Aquarius Moons together.** You share a universal philosophy: the need to brilliantly inspire others in making the world a better place. Together, however, you'll have to work hard at making a deeper or lasting connection.

Air and Water Moons Together

Air and Water Moons are like oil and water—they really don't mix! While Air Moons seek excitement and intellectual stimulation, Water Moons want the security of the known. It's the difference between Air Moon's philosophy, "I think, therefore I am" and Water Moon's motto, "I feel, therefore I am!" Together, you're just plain out of sync.

There's no other way to say it: **Gemini and Cancer Moons** have little or nothing in common. You two want completely different things in life at every level.

Although **Gemini and Scorpio Moons** feel an initial attraction when they meet, it's rarely lasting. Gemini Moon's need for constant diversion and Scorpio's Moon need to dig deep don't match emotionally.

Star Alert!

The deal-breaker for Air and Water Moons usually has to do with their deeper emotional needs. Air Moons often have a fear of commitment and hesitate to plunge into what they see as Water Moon's deep emotional abyss.

Gemini and Pisces Moons are at complete emotional odds. Moons in Gemini love to challenge their lovers to think differently; Moons in Pisces live for the illusion of perfect love. Together, it's a no go!

No matter how hard they try, **Libra and Cancer Moons** are perplexed by each other's deeper emotional and sexual needs. This Air and Water Moon combination doesn't work—especially at the level of day-to-day life and priorities.

There's so much that doesn't work or emotionally relate between **Libra and Scorpio Moons** that's its hard to find any common ground at all. Okay, you two both love erotica and sexual intrigue—but in your day-to-day life, you have little in common.

Libra and Pisces Moons can be total fools in love! Both of you adore romance and want to find your perfect soul mate. Together, however, what may be attraction at first sight will dissipate as soon as the going gets tough.

Aquarius Moon is a taker; Cancer Moon, a giver. Although this many sound like a perfect match, together **Aquarius and Cancer Moons** have a hard time negotiating very different emotional needs—especially when it comes to long-term security.

Both **Aquarius and Scorpio Moons** are stubborn about what they want. Moon in Aquarius seeks emotional freedom, and Moon in Scorpio wants emotional depth. Together, you're not emotionally in tune— and the sex won't be, either!

Although **Aquarius and Pisces Moons** are both eccentric and "out there" in their own ways, together they don't mix. Moon in Aquarius is too airy and detached for Pisces Moon's need for deeper emotional intimacy.

 Cosmic Lovers

Aquarius movie star Paul Newman has his Moon in Pisces. His wife of many years, actress Joanne Woodward, is a Pisces with her Moon in Aquarius. Their Suns and Moons in each other's signs denote a strong and lasting emotional connection.

Air and Earth Moons Together

Emotionally, Air and Earth Moons are on opposite pages. Earth Moons want security and an emotional commitment; Air Moons are blithe spirits who resist commitment and don't like to be reined in. Together, you will challenge each other to the nth degree. What to do? Invest in couples counseling to get a handle on each other's deeper needs, and then decide whether it's worth the effort!

Rootless Gemini Moon is often perplexed and even a bit intimated by Taurus Moon's stable nature. Grounded Moon in Taurus finds Moon in Gemini to be an emotional flake! **Gemini and Taurus Moons** together have little in common—emotionally or in the bedroom.

Gemini and Virgo Moons are both thinkers and intellectually oriented, yet whereas Moon in Gemini is a thinker/explorer, Moon in Virgo is a thinker/worrier! Together, there's not enough of an emotional foundation to make it work.

Moon in Gemini wants to play and explore; Moon in Capricorn just wants to play it safe. There's little or no emotional connection between **Gemini and Capricorn Moons**. Any sexual heat will be a flash in the pan!

Although both **Libra and Taurus Moons** share a desire for beauty and love to acquire nice things, you're both too stubborn about getting your very different emotional needs met for this match to work long-term.

Libra and Virgo Moons both require perfection, but when you bring them together, it's anything but. Everything becomes either *all* right and wrong or *all* good and bad. You two will emotionally nit-pick each other to distraction!

Moon in Libra loves romance and hanging out; Moon in Capricorn is all about taking care of business. Together, **Libra and Capricorn Moons** will not only challenge each other but also often hurt each other's feelings!

Together, **Aquarius and Taurus Moons** come from such different places and have such different emotional needs that there's not much to engage the two. Eccentric Moon in Aquarius and grounded Moon in Taurus absolutely perplex each other.

Heavenly Relations

Your Moon will often draw to you a lover who reflects your deepest and sometimes hidden unconscious needs! Although it may not always appear so on the surface, there is a desire to explore similar emotional experiences.

Aquarius and Virgo Moons intellectually and emotionally challenge each other—and not in a good way! You both want different things in life and in your relationships. There's not enough emotional common ground to make this relationship work.

Moon in Capricorn dreams of a house with a white picket fence; Moon in Aquarius is seriously considering joining and living in a commune! **Aquarius and Capricorn Moons** have little in common concerning their lifestyle needs.

Water Moons Together

Water Moons together are intuitively and emotionally in sync. You both share a need for security, comfort, and commitment. Together, you will explore your many sexual fantasies. Although you are emotionally and sexually in tune, a Water Moon pairing can drown out each other's individual needs. Water Moons often have boundary issues! The challenge for this pairing is to balance one's own needs with those of a lover.

It's bed, bath, and beyond for **Cancer Moons together!** This pair loves nothing more than home and hearth, delicious food, wine, and bubble baths together! Both can be a bit bossy, but emotionally you are on the same page.

Cancer and Scorpio Moons are so sexually compatible it's almost scary! You both fulfill each other's ideal fantasies—until it comes to your day-to-day life, that is. Fight, make up, fight, make up—it's all good and very hot sexually.

Dear Sextrologer ...

"I'm a Capricorn with my Moon in Pisces. I'm a hard-working guy but also have a desire to explore some of my sexual fantasies with the right woman. Any suggestions?"

You have a conflict between your Sun in Capricorn—hard-working, stoic, and no nonsense—and your very creative and imaginative Moon in Pisces. What you need is a lover with a Moon in an Earth sign—deeply sensual Moon in Taurus would be a good match—or you might look for another Water Moon, such as Moon in Scorpio. The latter would be more than willing to explore your deepest fantasies!

Cancer and Pisces Moons make beautiful music together—in life and in the bedroom! You both "get" each other on a very deep emotional level. In addition, each Moon nurtures the other's sometimes shaky self-esteem. This relationship is sexually hot and meant to last.

It's a cosmic clash of the Titans for **Scorpio Moons together.** Both of you are strong, willful, and determined to get what you want. To make it work, both of you will have to reach very deeply for patience, understanding, and emotional surrender!

Cosmic Lovers

Leo Jennifer Lopez has her Moon in Scorpio. Her husband, Marc Anthony, is a Virgo with a Moon in Cancer. Although their Sun signs conflict, their deeper emotional alignment is in their Water Moons. Scorpio and Cancer can be a stormy match, but they're on the same page when it comes to commitment and deeper intimacy.

Scorpio and Pisces Moons weave an emotional spell that's too sublime to ignore. (So don't!) Although Moon in Scorpio will often kick Moon in Pisces' lazy butt, they really understand each other's creative and spiritual needs.

For imaginative and sensitive **Pisces Moons together,** there's a very deep connection that is soulful, romantic, and emotionally in sync. The sex is otherworldly, but you two have to watch your boundaries—because you run a danger of becoming emotionally merged.

Water with Earth Moons

In most cases, Water and Earth Moons are highly emotionally and sexually in tune. You both nurture each other's needs and desires, and together you provide each other with a much-needed stability. You're also in agreement about the priorities of your day-to-day lives—especially around the question of long-term commitment. Together, you give each other emotional strength.

Heavenly Relations

Water Moons are more in tune with their deepest selves than any other element. The element of water represents feelings, emotions, and unconscious needs. These Moons are in their natural element when it comes to emotions!

Cancer and Taurus Moons are both caretakers in their own ways. Moon in Cancer is a type A nurturer, and Moon in Taurus is a laid-back, one-day-at-a-time caretaker. Together, you give each other emotional balance and enjoy sensual lovemaking!

Notorious fussbudgets **Cancer and Virgo Moons** are in tune emotionally and have the same top priority: getting their lives in order! You two will challenge each other in your approaches to that goal, but ultimately you feed each other emotionally—and your lovemaking is sublime!

Moon in Cancer loves to nurture, and Moon in Capricorn loves to soak it up! Together, **Cancer and Capricorn Moons** balance each other's deepest emotional needs around career, family, and nurturing.

It's stubborn meets stubborn-er with **Scorpio and Taurus Moons!** In bed, you're sexually hot and burn up the sheets—but in day-to-day living, there will be a lot of power struggles over whose needs come first.

Surprisingly, **Scorpio and Virgo Moons** are emotionally in tune, although outsiders would never guess it by the way they nit-pick each other! Yet, this match is very compatible—especially when it comes to understanding and fulfilling each other's sexual desires!

Star Alert!

The deal-breaker between Water and Earth Moons is often around financial security. Both Moons need to feel secure about their bank accounts! If your spending and saving habits don't match, you probably won't, either!

Scorpio and Capricorn Moons are highly compatible. Both of you respect each other's drive and intensity. And what's even more important, you two are strong enough to stand up to each other. This match is sexy and lasting!

Moon in Taurus grounds Pisces Moon's fantasies with its deep sensuality; Pisces Moon offers earthy Moon in Taurus some otherworldly magic; and—wow!—sex has never been better. Together, **Pisces and Taurus Moons** find a mutual emotional accord that plays well together. This is a lasting connection.

Pisces and Virgo Moons are a match made in chicken-soup heaven! Virgo Moon loves to fuss, nurture, and help; Pisces Moon wants all of the above! Although you two will challenge each other about day-to-day details, you have a cosmic balance!

Pisces and Capricorn Moons are sexually compatible and help each other explore their deepest fantasies! Pisces Moon finds Capricorn Moon's gruff but sensitive soul very sexy; Capricorn Moon loves the delicate fantasies that Pisces Moon spins.

Earth Moons Together

Earth Moons are deeply rooted in their need for security and comfort. Together, you make great partners and are in it for the long haul. Both of you want the same things: emotional and financial security and a partner with whom to create a long-term, loving relationship. Although you may sometimes challenge each other regarding who's in charge, you know that you're both in it together—and that's what's important!

Although **Taurus Moons together** are sure to butt horns about who's in charge, ultimately your intent is the same—to create a loving family and community together. Oh, and the super-sensual, earthy sex is awesome!

Taurus and Virgo Moons are emotionally in sync and relate to each other in their day-to-day needs. Although Moon in Taurus doesn't like to be picked at and Moon in Virgo finds Taurus' stubbornness annoying, together they're in it for the long haul.

Taurus and Capricorn Moons have similar emotional goals—to find a steady, loving, long-term partner. Moon in Taurus inspires Capricorn Moon to slow down and enjoy life; Moon in Capricorn inspires Taurus Moon to get things done.

The deeper issue for **Virgo Moons together** is finding the right balance between your sensual needs and your need to feel safe and in control. Although this Moon combination takes work—okay, a lot of work!—if you both relax, you may find an emotional and sexual synchronicity.

In daily life, **Virgo and Capricorn Moons** may conflict over endless fine details. Ultimately, however, they're only details—and you two are in tune with your emotional and long-term needs.

At the end of the day, **Capricorn Moons together** love to come home to each other. Sure, you will give each other a run for each other's money about the right balance between career and family priorities—but hey, you're in this together. And it shows!

The Least You Need to Know

♦ Fire Moons are self-involved and need to respect each other's needs.

♦ Fire and Air Moons love to play and explore together.

♦ Water Moons understand each other's deeper emotional needs.

♦ Water with Earth Moons are emotionally in sync, especially when it comes to commitment and security.

♦ Fire with Earth or Water Moons are not on the same page emotionally.

♦ Air with Earth or Water Moons face many relationship challenges.

Chapter 9

Under the Light of the Silvery Moon

In This Chapter

- The Moon governs our deeper instincts and emotions
- Exploring the sexual energy of the four Moon phases
- When the Moon is in a Fire or Air sign the lunar mood is extroverted and sexually adventurous
- When the Moon is in a Water or Earth sign the lunar mood is sexually introverted and thoughtful.

Exploring the different phases of the Moon will give you important indications about the waxing and waning of your love and sex life. Hint: sex is not necessarily the best during a full moon! Knowing the placement of the Moon in the signs of the zodiac can tell you when lovemaking is likely to be sublime, when to go out and enjoy the pleasures of life and friendships, and when you might just as well stay home and rent a DVD!

Bothered and Bewitched: The Phases of the Moon

The Moon governs our feelings, instincts, and deepest physical needs and desires. Scientists and astrologers alike have studied the ebb and flow of the Moon and how its energy affects human nature. The cycles of the Moon greatly influence our daily lives, dictating our moods, attitudes, and how we will respond to and engage in our relationships and everyday activities.

The four major phases of the Moon have been used for centuries to understand people's deeper motivations and to plan for major events and activities—from the most opportune moment to make a successful business deal to the right time to have sex! Each Moon phase lasts approximately a week, but its influences are the most pronounced during the first few days of each phase. Attuning yourself to the Moon's different phases will give you specific indications of how to best approach your sex and relationship life.

Heavenly Relations

A moon phase begins with the new Moon and ends with the first quarter Moon. A full Moon cycle, in which the Moon completes its full orbit around the Earth, lasts approximately 29 days.

An astrological calendar shows the different phases of the Moon. An ephemeris (daily listing of planets in the signs of the zodiac) or an annual Moon-sign guide will also show both the Moon's phases and its movement through the astrological signs. For more information, you can go online to your favorite astrology website and connect to their daily planetary forecast, which will often show you the phase and placement of the Moon. (For more information on online resources, see Appendix B and C.)

Waxing Moons

The new Moon and first quarter Moon are the waxing, or increasing Moons. The waxing Moon phase represents a time of new beginnings and the desire to explore new possibilities. This is a time of heightened sexual energy. The waxing Moon phase is outgoing and sexually adventurous—the period when we are most likely to act on our most basic instincts. During this Moon phase, conditions are favorable for growth, expansion, and embarking on new endeavors. This is also a time when you are likely to draw toward you people and relationships that will help you move forward in your life!

The New Moon

During the new Moon, there is a strong pull toward starting anew. This is a high-energy phase, and desires run strong. It is also an impulsive time: people feel the need to act on their deepest instincts and are most likely to embark on new relationships. The energy of the new Moon is action-oriented and often sexually aggressive, with little thought given to the consequences.

This phase lends itself to self-involvement! You might find yourself focused on exploring new territory and opening up new possibilities for your life. It is not a time where you will necessarily feel concerned with details, finer nuances, or the deeper needs of others.

Star Alert!

Feelings and sexual instincts are strongest and most intense during new and full Moons.

Dear Sextrologer …

"I impetuously got involved with a man during the new Moon. Now that I know him better, much to my embarrassment I've come to realize that we don't have anything in common! I feel like I was irrational and acting out on my desire for a new relationship. What to do?"

New moon, new man! It's not unusual to start a new relationship during a new Moon phase. This Moon phase is sexually spontaneous and carries with it a desire to explore new opportunities. Sounds like this guy is not the one for you. Let go of your guilt, and move on. During the next new moon, put yourself out there again—you may get luckier in your choice this time!

The First Quarter Moon

The first quarter Moon tends to be a sexually active time. The energy is dynamic, and there is a strong impulse to meet goals and get things done. This Moon also brings out one's more willful nature and the desire to get what one wants—in life and in bed. The getting-to-know-you phase and the sexual honeymoon of the new Moon are over as reality sets in and challenges begin to arise.

This Moon phase represents a time of achievement. Try to be as disciplined as possible as you define and refine your goals and move toward what you want.

Waning Moons

The full and last quarter Moons are the decreasing, or waning Moons. In the waning Moon phase, moods turn more reflective and sexual energies become more introverted. During this phase, there is often a desire for deeper intimacy and sexual connections. The waning Moon phase is a time to build on the foundations of your relationships, to move projects forward, and to master talents. What was started in the waxing phase reaches its natural completion during this lunar period.

The Full Moon

During the full Moon, feelings and instincts are extreme and there is a tendency to overreact. During this time, there is a desire for deeper sexual fulfillment as seeds planted during the waxing phase begin to come to their full fruition.

What has been brewing in your relationship comes to the surface: what's good becomes more wonderful, and what's bad becomes clearer and more pronounced. Major relationship decisions are likely to be made during this Moon phase.

The full Moon is always an intense period! This is a time during which you may be forced to look deeper into yourself in order to decide what you really want and need.

 Heavenly Relations

The terms "moonstruck" and "lunacy" are associated with the full Moon! The full Moon is the time when the Moon's gravitational influence on the Earth is at its strongest, stimulating our unconsciousness needs and primal desires. It is not surprising that hospitals and the police force put on extra staff to deal with this Moon's fallout!

The Last Quarter Moon

With the last quarter Moon comes the need to complete things. This is a nesting period and is sexually introverted and cautious. It is also unlikely to be a good time for starting new relationships—instead, it's a time to regroup and clear out the things in your life that aren't working. During this period, you might find that sex is routine—that you're both just going through the motions. Relationships that aren't working will fade away during this phase. The last quarter Moon is a time to settle in and reflect on what you want in the next moon cycle.

Star Alert!

When the Moon is void-of-course, it is resting before it moves on to the next sign of the zodiac. This Moon transit can last from several hours to half a day. During its void-of-course phase, the Moon is at an energetic low. This is not a good time for starting or finishing tasks or for generally getting much of anything done. Instead, lie low during this time and let nature take its course!

Where's the Moon?

Knowing what astrological sign the transiting Moon is in will help you attune to the mood and feelings of the day—and night! The Moon spends approximately two-and-a-half days in each sign of the zodiac as it moves through a complete moon cycle. Each Moon sign has its own lunar style, mode, and attitude. As the Moon visits each sign, you will feel the sign's energies and its influence on your love and sex life. Understanding the impact of the Moon in each sign will also help you find the most opportune timing for a range of important events and activities.

The Moon and Timing

Activity/Event	Moons
Communication	Gemini, Libra, Sag, Aquarius
Entertaining	Taurus, Gemini, Leo, Libra, Sag
Playing	Fire and Air Moons
Working	Earth Moons
Learning	Gemini, Libra, Virgo, Sag
Romance	Taurus, Leo, Libra, Pisces
Online Dating	Gemini, Aquarius
Getting Married	Taurus, Cancer, Leo, Libra, Pisces
Breaking Up	Aries, Virgo, Scorpio, Aquarius
Fertility	Earth and Water Moons
Health	Earth Moons
Shopping	Leo, Libra, Gemini
New Relationships	Aries, Aquarius, Libra, Capricorn
Reconciling	Taurus, Libra, Capricorn, Pisces
Alone Time	Water Moons
Relationship Building	Earth Moons

Moon in Aries

This Moon represents an impulsive time, and the mood is sexually feisty and adventurous. Moon in Aries brings out your courage: it signals a time to be bold and aggressive about going after what—and whom—you want! You are likely to take risks during this period, and sex is both passionate and spontaneous.

This is not a Moon during which you should expect to get your deeper emotional needs met, nor is it a time to resolve conflicts. Instead, this independent and outgoing Moon is all about exploring new territory. You may start a relationship, but Moon in Aries quickly runs out of steam!

Setting the mood: lots of fiery food—barbecue or spicy Cajun with some ice-cold beer to wash it down—sex out-of-doors, absolutely!

Moon in Taurus

This Moon is all about enjoyment. Even finishing projects or taking care of business can be a pleasure! This Moon indicates a time to value those who are most important to you and commune with what brings you a greater sense of well-being. Moon in Taurus is a good time to stop and smell your proverbial roses! The mood is slow and steady and signals a time to indulge in sensual and luxurious sex. It is not a sexually adventurous time, however; instead, there is a desire for comfort and familiarity. The potential of this Moon almost guarantees great lovemaking!

If you're not in a secure relationship, indulge your sensual nature by pleasuring yourself and giving into your deeper needs.

Setting the mood: a dinner party for friends with whom you can relax and enjoy each other's company. Menu: steak and potatoes or an earthy stew, good wine, and a decadent dessert—the rest will take care of itself!

Moon in Gemini

With this Moon, there is a general restlessness in the air. Under Moon in Gemini, there is a tendency for overstimulation: there can be so much going on that it's hard to focus on love and sex! Instead, you're having fun, multitasking, and flitting from one situation to another. Moon in Gemini is a great time for socializing and connecting with people. Although you may be open to new ideas, it is not a time to get much done!

Under this Moon, there's plenty of sexual curiosity—but new romantic connections tend to be brief and rarely lasting. Moon in Gemini does not have staying power!

Setting the mood: it's time to play! Plan a get-together with your friends; include light finger foods for variety and lots of games (charades, Monopoly, or poker, perhaps?).

Dear Sextrologer ...

"I'm planning my upcoming nuptials and am wondering—are there some Moons that represent a good time for a marriage ceremony?"

You're right! There are certain Moons that indicate a good time for weddings and celebrations of commitment. For more information, see the Moon and Timing table (in the previous section, "Where's the Moon?"). Once you have compared your prospective wedding date and the corresponding Moon sign, also apply your intuitive sense. The combination of your Moon knowledge and your intuition as to the day that feels right will help you pick the perfect time for your marriage ceremony!

Moon in Cancer

This Moon is a time where feelings run high and there is a tendency toward oversensitivity. Generally, Moon in Cancer represents a time when we seek nurturing and want to be at home or to connect with family and friends. Under this Moon, sex can be profound and you may feel psychically in tune with your lover. Expectations abound, however—particularly those of an emotional nature. Watch for squabbles after lovemaking. This is a time to put aside domestic concerns and commune with your lover or your deeper needs.

Setting the mood: perusing the family photo album or watching a video of your latest vacation may give you the sense of nurturing that you seek. Add a little comfort food, and you'll feel like all is well and good with the world—and with each other.

Cosmic Lovers

People born under the sign of Cancer, such as Britain's Princess Diana, are particularly sensitive to the Moon's changing moods and its seductive, magnetic pull!

Moon in Leo

This is a party Moon! Moon in Leo is a time for celebrating, playing, and generally having lots of fun! Physical instincts are heightened during this time, and so are sex drives. Under this moon, there is a desire to take sexual risks and to show off. Moon in Leo brings out the need for attention and pursuing your options. Watch out for getting caught up in the latest flavor-of-the month guy or gal! This is a romantic and very giving Moon, although you will also feel that you need to be appreciated for what you bring to the table. Moon in Leo is very dramatic! If you want to avoid relationship drama, watch your expectations.

Setting the mood: excitement and drama required! A costume party where you can dress up in a stunning outfit and play your favorite fantasy character, plus foods with lots of flavor to match the mood, should fit the bill.

Moon in Virgo

This Moon sets the mood for lots of work and very little play! Moon in Virgo is a time during which you are at your most discriminating and feel the need to analyze every detail of what is going on in your life. Watch out: you can get so caught up in the details that you lose perceptive and forget the bigger picture! Under Moon in Virgo, there's a need to get things done: balancing the checkbook, organizing your closets, returning phone calls, and so on. It is not a time to take sexual chances—you may regret them later. If you can get to the sex, it will be very physical (but will end quickly).

Setting the mood: be sure and fit in some relaxation time! Break out of your normal routine and give yourself a gift—whether it's a sensuous massage, experiencing your favorite foods, or … if you're feeling restless … some bargain hunting!

Moon in Libra

This Moon is very friendly! Moon in Libra is a time during which people are most inclined to compromise and make their partner happy. In fact, it is a great time for makeup sex! Moon in Libra is also a social Moon: it's a time for sharing ideas and having great conversations. This is not a Moon when you should expect to get much done, however! Moon in Libra is more interested in exploring options, especially of a romantic nature, than focusing on details. During this Moon, sex needs to be meaningful. If not, it's better to channel this Moon's abundance of creative energy into redecorating your bedroom.

Setting the mood: this is a time to shop with friends, throw a party, or take in an art show. Menu: exotic foods—pasta with truffle sauce, tender veal with chanterelle mushrooms, and French white wine.

> **Heavenly Relations**
>
> When the Moon is visiting Fire or Air signs, the mood is often very social and there is a desire for fun and sexual play. The Moon in Water or Earth signs, however, usually indicates a quieter time and sex tends to be deeper and more intimate.

Moon in Scorpio

During this Moon, sexual intensity abounds! With Moon in Scorpio, emotions often reach a peak and everyone's feelings are likely to be extreme. This is a time when people want to get to the bottom of things and delve into deep personal mysteries—whether it's researching your genetic lineage, taking time alone to think, or having a heartfelt therapy session! It's also a time during which you may feel the need to get things done and put your life in order.

For Moon in Scorpio, it's all or nothing—no superficial sex. It needs to be profound and meaningful. During this time, misunderstandings are common. Watch out for power struggles over getting your needs met.

Setting the mood: this is a time to roll up your sleeves, dig deeper, and take care of personal business. If you're feeling a sexual urge, order oysters on the half shell—but watch out!

> **Dear Sextrologer ...**
>
> "I tend to get very cranky whenever the Moon is in Scorpio. During this Moon, I feel emotionally agitated and even a bit obsessive. Please—some insight!"
>
> It is not unusual that when the Moon is in Scorpio—or the other Water signs, Cancer and Pisces, one's deeper emotions come to the surface. Because you feel particularly sensitive to this Moon, it might be useful to see how your natal Moon sign relates to Scorpio: for example, if your Moon is in another fixed sign such as Taurus, Leo, or Aquarius, it forms a difficult aspect to the transiting Scorpio Moon and can indicate an especially trying time. Check out your natal Moon to see what's up.

Moon in Sagittarius

The mood for this Moon is sexually outgoing and spontaneous. During Moon in Sagittarius, there is a feeling of restlessness and a desire for new adventures that can translate to sexual experimentation. Sex during this time is often heated, passionate, and exploratory. Socially, this is a time for having fun—yet there can be a tendency toward overindulgence. Watch for a giant hangover the next morning! During Moon in Sag, there is a need for direct and honest communication. Look at this as a time for getting things off your chest. You may also feel inspired to share ideas of a spiritual or political nature.

Setting the mood: a sporting event with friends. Tennis, horse racing, football, archery, and hunting all work well for this moon! Afterward, gather together for some nosh and lots of discussion about the politics of the day.

Star Alert!

Lunar eclipses represent turning points and pivotal moments—universally and personally. Eclipses, like full Moons, tend to be intense times during which deeper issues come to the surface. At the time of a lunar eclipse, get ready for major change or to face deeper parts of yourself.

Moon in Capricorn

This Moon is very businesslike and fueled with discipline. During the day, Moon in Capricorn is a highly productive time with lots of energy for meetings, defining goals, and getting things done. At night, this Moon morphs into a sexual dynamo with the potential for intense lovemaking. Although the sex may initially be geared toward taking care of business, it can turn really hot really fast! Afterward, you'll want to tuck yourself in under the blankets and rest up, because tomorrow will be another busy day!

Setting the mood: forget organizing your business files and instead take time to explore your deepest sexual desires. Plan a buffet dinner for you and your lover—in the bedroom. Finger foods and no silverware!

Cosmic Lovers

Diana, Artemis, and Brigit are all names of Moon goddesses. In ancient times, these goddesses were worshipped for their feminine power and strength—and also for their dynamic sexual prowess!

Moon in Aquarius

This Moon signals an innovative and exploratory time—in life and in the bedroom! During Moon in Aquarius, you may be stimulated to take sexual chances and engage in experimental sex. It is not a time for deep and profound lovemaking, however. This Moon is too restless for deep emotional connections or intimacy. With this Moon, there is often a desire to hang out with friends who share your ideas and beliefs about life and the world. Moon in Aquarius is a very inventive time where you may find yourself filled with new inspiration.

Setting the mood: sushi and good friends are the perfect combination for this highly social and intellectual moon.

Moon in Pisces

This Moon is filled with fantasy and the desire to explore your deepest sensual needs. Moon in Pisces is often a time during which you will feel psychically in tune with your lover and will want to share your secret desires.

This is also a creative Moon and offers much in the way of exploring your artistic talents. During this Moon, you might feel a desire to check out from reality—so watch out for overindulging in addictive substances. Instead, connect to your spiritual, higher nature through meditation or other spiritual activities.

Setting the mood: this Moon begs for romance—candlelight, soft music, dark chocolate—and soulful sex! If you're not in a relationship, this is a time to stay at home and commune with yourself—perhaps by watching your favorite romantic DVD!

The Least You Need to Know

- Waxing Moons are sexually outgoing and aggressive.
- Waning Moons are more sexually introverted.
- The sign of the Moon sets the tone for both day and night.
- Knowing the sign of the Moon will help you gauge the right time for great sex.
- The placement of the Moon can help you plan activities and even major events in your life.

Part  3

Venus and Mars: Your Sexual Connection

Venus and Mars connections explore your sexual compatibility. Although they make no promises about how long the sparks will fly, they will give you key indications about your sexual dynamics together.

Chapter 10

Love and Desire

In This Chapter

- ◆ Venus and Mars connections are all about your sexual chemistry!

- ◆ Venus is the "feminine" aspect of love, representing your deeper sexual and romantic needs

- ◆ Mars is the "masculine" aspect of love, representing your most primal sexual desires

- ◆ Your Venus and Mars placements will help you understand the synergy between your male and female natures

How sexually compatible are you? A vital factor in your sextrology equation is your Venus and Mars connections. This planetary combination represents your relationship and romantic needs and is significant to your sex life! Venus and Mars are the astrological pheromones that attract you to each other and represent how you will ignite each other's sexual desires!

Men Are from Mars and Women Are from Venus?

Well, sort of! What has become a pop-culture phenomenon is actually based in astrology! Astrologers associate Venus and Mars with your male and female energies and how you express them, both within yourself and with others. Venus and Mars are significant to sextrology because they indicate what kind of lover you are looking for in order to completely fulfill your physical, emotional, and sexual desires. We all have a masculine and feminine side to our natures. Your Venus energy represents your feminine energy, symbolizing how you relate to love and romance or the emotional side of sex. Your Mars represents your masculine energy, symbolizing how you relate to your more primal, physical, and sexual desires. When you put them together, they become beauty and the beast—and make one sexy couple!

Heavenly Relations

The placement of Venus in a man's chart is an important predictor of his choice in female partners. A man's Venus also gives insight into his secret romantic desires!

Because Venus and Mars are closely aligned with our male and female energies, we've included a different perspective for women and men. The differences have important sexual and romantic nuances—so pay attention! (For more information on how to find your Venus and Mars placements, see Appendix B.)

Venus: The Feminine Aspect of Love

Venus is the planet symbolizing love, relationships, and pleasure! Your Venus represents what will make you happiest in love and also the type of love you will attract. Your Venus shows how you relate to dating and mating rituals and what you seek in your romantic connections. Do you want a slow-burning love connection, a lover who will sweep you off your feet, a clandestine lover, a torrid, super-hot affair, or someone who just plain worships you?

Star Alert!

Venus represents the feminine side of love, but she's no weakling—far from it! Venus is a powerful archetype of feminine strength and passion. She is, after all, a goddess!

Venus shows not only how you relate to love but also your social connections and material desires. She represents your inner goddess—and yes, it's true for men, as well. She symbolizes the loving and fruitful gifts that you bestow upon others. Venus is a positive and benevolent planet. In fact, she tends to bring out the best in each sign of the zodiac!

Venus in Fire

When you put romantic Venus in the bold, aggressive, and impulsive element of Fire, the result is drama and high expectations. Venus in Fire enjoys change and challenge and has a daredevil approach to romance.

Venus in Aries tempers Aries' bold and fiery moves—but just a bit! Venus in Aries is independent, daring, strong, very passionate, and can be somewhat romantically challenged when it comes to the finer nuances or details.

Women: she is a passionate woman who has a strong sense of what she wants in life and in the bedroom! She appreciates romance and is impulsive in love. But what she really wants is honesty and to know where you stand. In or out, baby!

Men: he is an enthusiastic and impulsive lover. He will wine you, dine you, and sweep you off your feet. He loves to wrap you up in all of his adventures. Unless you have a Venus or Mars in a Fire sign, however, you may have trouble keeping up with endless energy and total directness.

Venus in Leo is dramatic, flirtatious, sexy, and over-the-top! They approach their relationships with passion and are warm, generous, and very romantic partners. They also crave attention and can be vain about their appearances!

Women: bombshell blonde or otherwise! She loves to celebrate her feminine energy and comes dressed for the party! She has a very creative personality and loves to show off. She is also fiercely supportive of her partners—and fiercely possessive, too.

Men: he secretly reads *GQ*, if only to check out his competition! He also likes his lady to look hot. Men with Venus in Leo see their lovers as extensions of themselves in how they appear to the world. Yet, they are also wonderfully loving and generous!

 Cosmic Lovers _____

Jennifer Aniston is an Aquarian with her Venus in Aries. Although her Aquarian Sun can be a little chilly, her Venus in Aries indicates she likes fiery romance.

 Star Alert! _____

Venus in Fire requires lots of ongoing attention. They also—hint, hint—are suckers for compliments. So, keep them coming!

Venus in Sagittarius is extremely fun-loving and devilishly flirtatious! They love to share their adventures with their lovers, especially if it includes traveling to some romantic location together. For all of their love of fun, they are deeply idealistic. Romantically, they're in the moment and tend to shy away from commitment.

Women: broads and dames! Venus in Sag fully embraces her big energy. She will make you laugh, debate you on politics, and outwit you at poker. Regarding romance, she's passionate but likes to keep things fun.

Men: swashbuckling pirates and playboys! His secret desire is to hang out with the Hef at the *Playboy* mansion! He's also worldly and intuitive but can be difficult when it comes time to pin down his affections.

Dear Sextrologer ...

"I'm a female with my Venus in Sag. I often find that I am much more comfortable with men than women. Is there something wrong with me?"

It is not usual for women with their Venus in Sagittarius to find that they relate well to men. So, no ... there's nothing wrong with you! You enjoy male company because they often relate to your independence and your need to not get too emotionally deep! Relax and enjoy yourself!

Venus in Air

For Venus in Air, it's a romance of the mind! They love nothing more than a romantic tête-á-tête in which they can share ideas. Venus in Air represents the more cerebral and refined aesthetic of Venus. This Venus is emotionally objective and likes to keep things light!

Venus in Gemini is a social creature who loves to flirt and enjoys having lots of romantic options. They are fun-loving and very intellectually stimulating, yet their affections can change with the wind!

Women: she can be coquettish and will sweetly entice you with her amazing mind, diverse talents, and her love of sexual play. Women with Venus in Gemini like to have fun and explore their romantic options.

Men: he will engage you in amazing conversations about everything from politics, the latest reality show, or your favorite restaurant! He is a romantic Peter Pan who wants

Wendy to come out and play. When it comes time for commitment, though, he may disappear!

Venus in Libra is truly at home in the very romantic sign of Libra. Venus in Libra represents a love of beauty, kindness, balanced and fair relationships, and an artistic and refined approach to life.

Heavenly Relations

Venus is the planetary ruler for both Libra and Taurus and is most at home in Air or Earth signs.

Women: how many shoes does she own? More than you can count! She loves to shop—not only for the pleasure of owning beautiful things but also because it is an expression of her creative personality. She is often the "hostess with the mostest" and loves to throw amazing dinner parties.

Men: he also enjoys beauty and the finer things in life, which is often reflected in his partners (who are usually very beautiful and refined women!). Secretly, he watches *America's Next Top Designer* on TV and wants to acquire beautiful and classic pieces of art.

Venus in Aquarius is everyone's best friend but can be chilly when it comes to love and romance. They enjoy intellectual foreplay and seek a lover who will share their need to be inspired. They tend to be offbeat and are attracted to romantic relationships that don't follow the rules.

Women: "Dr. Livingston, I presume?" Her female role models: anthropologist Margaret Mead and media maven Oprah Winfrey. Each is an intellectually powerful woman, humanitarian, and pioneer in their fields. For her, intellect equals sexy—and she's looking for the same in her men.

Cosmic Lovers

Princess Grace of Monaco, the former movie star Grace Kelly, was a Scorpio with her Venus in Libra. Her Venus in Libra is visible both in her beauty and in her ability to step gracefully from Hollywood into a European monarchy!

Men: his role models are scientist Stephen Hawking and sci-fi and horror novelist Stephen King! Each is a creative visionary exploring cosmic secrets! He's looking for someone to explore all his intellectually diverse and somewhat eccentric romantic needs.

Venus in Water

Venus in Water has deep emotional and romantic longings. They have a desire to find a true love who will share all of their passionate desires—and their active fantasy lives! They also want a partner who will stick around for the long term.

Star Alert! _____

Venus in Water signs— male and female—get their feelings hurt very easily!

Venus in Cancer loves to nurture their lovers. They have strong romantic needs but often focus on security instead of expressing their most passionate desires. They are deeply sensitive and occasionally moody, but you can count on them being there for the long haul.

Women: she's strong and stoic but also sensitive and emotional. She loves nothing more than to take care of her family and friends. She is often the calm center in her family's emotional storms.

Men: he's also a caretaker. He feels a deep commitment to his family and relishes being able to support them. He's successful at business, yet his secret desire is to be a stay-at-home, daycare daddy! He is very sensitive and needs to be constantly reassured of your love.

Venus in Scorpio is intensely passionate, emotionally stoic, and often has a survivor instinct when it comes to love. They tend to be reserved until they decide that they can trust you. Once they do, they will be extremely loyal.

Cosmic Lovers _____

Capricorn Denzel Washington has his Venus in Scorpio. The combination of his sensual Sun in Capricorn and his intensely sexual Venus in Scorpio makes this movie star and husband a very sexy guy—who is likely to stick with his marriage!

Women: she is a fierce goddess with intense emotional needs. She is mysterious and even secretive and may be initially distant or defensive. Once you earn her trust, however, she is a passionate and very giving partner. But look out—she can be highly jealous and territorial!

Men: he projects a powerful sexual allure. Venus grounds his Scorpion intensity and gives wings to its passion. He's mysterious and maybe even a bit mystical! His secret desire is to find a partner who is willing—and strong enough—to explore the depths of his sexual and emotional desires.

Venus in Pisces is dreamy, romantic, sensitive, and sometimes elusive. Male or female, this Venus is often a romantic fantasy brought to life. At the same time, they can also be needy and may play a victim role when they don't get their romantic and emotional needs met.

Women: most likely to read romance novels! She has a big imagination and loves to explore her fantasy life—sometimes in the comfort of her own home or head! She is also a sweet and nurturing lover. This may get her into trouble, however, because she tends to give more than she receives in love.

Men: most likely to read *Playboy* magazine—and not just for the articles! He seeks a female muse upon whom he can project his romantic and sexual fantasies. He is a creative, imaginative, and extremely giving lover! He is often dreamy and is more likely than most to be passive in love.

Venus in Earth

Venus in Earth loves pleasure and is the most sensual of all Venus placements! They seek comfort in their relationships and are very security oriented. They are also extremely stable, steadfast, and true in love.

Venus in Taurus exhibits the earthy and sensual aspects of Venus. They love comfortable surroundings, good food, good wine, and very sensual (and even decadent) sex! They are loyal in love and in all of their relationships.

Women: a total goddess in every sense of the word! She loves to celebrate all aspects of her strong yet very feminine nature. She desires the finer things in life but is also down-to-earth and quite practical.

Men: a very sensual guy who is always reliable and loves nothing more than to help support and ground his friends and family. This man will want to build you a beautiful home and would be very content preparing hearty dishes together to go with the hearty sex you will be experiencing!

Venus in Virgo is service-oriented and loves to help others. They are directed, dedicated, and like to be in control. When you get past all that, this placement is very sensual and romantic. Venus in Virgo wants to be needed by their lover.

Women: a sexy accountant, perhaps? She is smart, exacting, and knows how to line up the numbers and ledger lines. Underneath her prim exterior, though, there's sexy lingerie just waiting to be discovered!

Men: a sexy doctor, perhaps? He's also very smart, exacting, and loves to help others. His bedside manner is at times a bit direct and even nagging, but he's really all about making you feel better!

Venus in Capricorn lightens up and tends to bring out the best in this often very serious sign. Venus in Capricorn is stable, loyal, and steadfast in love. You can always depend on this Venus. They are also extremely sensual lovers!

Heavenly Relations

The Sun and Moon never go retrograde, but Venus and Mars do! A retrograde planet represents a more internalized or passive expression of the planet and sign.

Women: she loves to work hard and play hard! When it comes to romance, she can be a tough cookie! But don't be fooled. She really wants a lover who will fulfill her deepest desire to have a compassionate and long-term relationship.

Men: although he's a bit clumsy when it comes to romance, he's a dedicated partner and a resourceful lover. His secret desire is to find a woman who is as strong and passionate as he is and who wants to share his deepest sexual needs and desires.

Mars: The Masculine Aspect of Love

Whether you're male or female, your Mars represents the male side of your nature. In mythology, Mars is the god of war—representing your primal energy and the need to conquer in life and in the bedroom. Mars is a warrior, and unlike Venus has little finesse—he's all about the conquest! To get a picture, look at the astrological symbol for Mars—a circle with an arrow pointing out and upward!

Your Mars represents your creative life force that drives you forward and out into the world to make a place for yourself. Sexually, Mars drives your most primal desires. He brings out the most aggressive aspects of each sign of the zodiac!

Cosmic Lovers

The symbol for Mars is what cinema's "International Man of Mystery" Austin Powers wears around his neck connected to a long gold chain! Like Austin Powers, Mars is totally shag-a-delic and seeks to keep its sexual mojo working.

Mars in Fire

When you put fiery Mars in the element of Fire, it becomes extra fiery: bold, passionate, and very aggressive. Mars in Fire goes after what they want and rarely takes time to consider the consequences of their actions. This placement has loads of astrological testosterone, which can be a bit of a test for women with Mars in a Fire sign.

Mars in Aries is a leader, a pioneer, and a mover and shaker in the world. They have strong egos, strong sexual needs, and very little patience! Mars in Aries is reliably direct: what you see is what you get! At the same time, their deepest desire is often to empower and inspire others.

Women: *Xena: Warrior Princess!* Females with Mars in Aries often have a hard time balancing their overtly male energies. She is sexually passionate and often at the forefront of her career, yet she often has a hard time relaxing and enjoying her love connections.

Men: "Me Tarzan, you Jane!" Men with Venus in Aries tend to be overly and overtly male. After conquering the world and having passionate sex, he wants to kick back and watch ESPN. Sexually, he is aggressive and has a hard time appreciating the more exquisite details of sex and romance.

Mars in Leo is passionate and very creative. In fact, many artists and actors have their Mars in Leo! They have a regal and bright presence, and when they walk into the room, everyone notices them! In sex, they like to be on top—and to be appreciated for their sexual prowess.

Women: strong and confident, she doesn't hesitate to put herself out into the world. She's passionate in bed and wants to be desired. She's also compassionate, loyal, and in her own fierce way, quite sweet.

Heavenly Relations

Mars is closely aligned with Pluto. Before Pluto was discovered in the early twentieth century and became the planetary ruler for Scorpio, Mars was the ruler for both Aries and Scorpio. Some of their shared planetary traits are passion, intensity, and strong sexual desires.

Men: he is a powerful, fiery force to be reckoned with. Men with their Mars in Leo know what they want and will never settle for second-best in bed. At the same time, they can be very romantic and want very much to inspire your greatest needs and desires!

Cosmic Lovers _____

Sir Paul McCartney is a Gemini with his Mars in Leo. This former Beatle is not only obviously very creative but a loving and giving sexual partner!

Heavenly Relations _____

Do you think that your girl is all sugar and spice? Think again! The placement of Mars in a woman's chart will tell you a lot about what she really wants in a man at her most primal and uninhibited level!

Mars in Sagittarius is a worldly adventurer who seeks a partner who will share his or her desire for growth and to discover new experiences in life. They often have a gift in teaching and inspiring others to find their own wisdom. In bed, they're very sexual, explorative, and fun!

Women: she's honest, direct, and outspoken—but she doesn't take herself too seriously. In bed, females with Mars in Sag are confident, free, and uninhibited! At the same time, she wants a lover who will not only sexually entice her but also share her desire for excitement and adventure.

Men: he's also honest and outspoken and loves to have fun. He's worldly, intuitive, and wise—and also a sexual player! Adventure is the name of his game! He lives in the fun of the moment and doesn't want to be tied down.

Mars in Air

This Mars is very intellectually oriented and thrives on mental stimulation. Mars in Air signs are idealistic in love and seek nothing short of inspiration in romance. They can also be sexually distant and even emotionally chilly! Their libido can run hot and cold depending on their whims.

Mars in Gemini are sexually light on their feet. Gemini is the sign of the twins—and the fickle lover. When you put aggressive Mars in this sign, it becomes doubly so! Mars in Gemini is often distracted by relationship options and can be a sexual player!

Women: she may seem to be all over the map when it comes to what she wants, but she's no ditz. In fact, she is highly intellectual and often multitalented. Even though she loves to play in the bedroom, she is actually quite discerning about her sexual needs. Keep her interested if you want to keep her sexual attention!

Men: sexually, he's often looking for the next best thing! He's intellectual and has his finger on the pulse of everything going on around him. Sexually, he's a player. If you want long-term fidelity, you'd better hope that his sun or moon is in a very solid and devoted sign!

Dear Sextrologer ...

"I have my Venus in Taurus and my Mars in Gemini. On one hand, I have a very conservative approach to my relationships and desire a long-term commitment. On the other hand, my Mars in Gemini wants to play and explore all options. What to do?"

Your Venus in Taurus' need for security and your Mars in Gemini's desire to play is quite the sextrology conundrum! What to do? You need to honor both parts of your nature. Look for a lover that will both give you the excitement you crave while at the same time relating to your deeper security needs. With some patience, you will find the right love match!

Mars in Libra thrives on meeting new friends and being at the center of society's most important and classiest events. They are choosey in their romantic partners and sexually discerning, as well. They also pride themselves on their sexual finesse!

Women: she exudes a very feminine allure and brings a lot of class to everything she does. She wants a partner who shares her sense of decorum, yet secretly she wants a lover who will bring her erotic fantasies to life! She will want a commitment before going too far, however.

Men: he seeks a balanced partner who shares his love of harmony. He's fun, loyal, and quite romantic but often shies away from getting too emotionally deep. Like his female counterpart, he has a fierce love of truth and fairness and will expect the same from you!

Mars in Aquarius is a rebel—a revolutionary—who loves to defy the norm. They are also often quite brilliant and have the ability to inspire others. They savor their sexual freedom, and their libidos run the gamut from kinky to reserved and from sexually hot to entirely uninterested!

Women: on the surface, she may seem cold—but her deepest desire is to tear off her clothes and give a "cosmic" finger to her higher ups! Will she do it? It doesn't matter—her perspective on life and love is to stir things up! She's very independent and likes to sexually explore her options.

Heavenly Relations

To understand the synergy between your male and female sides, compare your Venus with your Mars. Then, for you and your lover, compare your Venus with their Mars and your Mars with their Venus. For more information about how your Venus and Mars align, see Chapter 11.

Men: he wants to break all the rules and has a hard time conforming. His sexual desire is to have the freedom to be who he is and fully play out all his sexual and often eccentric desires.

Mars in Water

Aggressive and male Mars in the feminine element of Water becomes very emotional and sensitive. The result is either a watering down or deepening of its driving sexual energy. Male or female, Mars in Water tends to internalize feelings and is not always comfortable expressing deeper emotions.

Mars in Cancer desires one perfect lover who will fulfill all of their sexual and security needs! Mars in Cancer is intuitive, moody, and a bit bossy—yet extremely attentive and nurturing partners.

Women: she's emotional and very in tune with her friends, family, and lover. She's an aggressive caretaker—sometimes overly assertive about making sure that you are okay! She knows what she wants and in life and in love but needs to feel comfortable before expressing her deepest sexual needs.

Men: he's a caretaker who often puts his needs on hold for others. His deepest desire is to find a committed partner who will help him realize his dream of home and family. He is sensitive and can be initially shy about revealing his sexual needs.

Star Alert!

Mars in the element of Water can be passive-aggressive about their needs! On the one hand, they want emotional and sexual fulfillment; on the other, they may feel insecure when it comes to expressing their deepest desires.

Mars in Scorpio is one of the planet's most sexually aggressive placements. It is also very competitive! At the same time, this placement can indicate deep wounds around issues of trust. Although Mars in Scorpio may sexually posture and even intimate, this placement is also deeply vulnerable.

Women: she often comes on very strong sexually as a way to knock you off balance and feel in control. She's often a sexy "mama wolf" with an intense desire to protect those closest to her. Sexually, when you earn her trust, she is a very passionate and loyal partner.

Men: his very sexual Mars in the very sexual Scorpio is as sexy as it gets. He's very passionate, yet at the same time a loyal and fiercely loving partner! Like his female counterpart, Venus in Scorpio can be intensely jealous and does not forgive easily!

Mars in Pisces is sensitive, creative, and compassionate. Mars in Pisces is often an over-giver, sometimes to the point of sacrificing his or her own needs for those of a lover. Sexually, Mars in Pisces is drawn to fantasy and romance.

Women: she's whimsical, romantic, and sometimes has her head in the clouds. She's very intuitive and often knows what you want before you do! Sexually, she has a big imagination and will want to explore her erotic fantasies with you.

Men: he's loving, caring, and very romantic. He's artistic and has strong creative desires. He's intuitive, too, and dreams of a lover who will connect with him on a deep level and bring his sexual fantasies to life. He also delights in making his lover feel sexually fulfilled!

Mars in Earth

Sexual Mars in the sensual element of Earth takes the sex equation to a very passionate and physical level. For all of their sexual prowess, however, they are security oriented and don't like to step too far outside their comfort zones. This Mars wants a lover who will commit!

Mars in Taurus is stubborn, resourceful, and very sexual. They have strong physical needs and love to have all of their senses stimulated in lovemaking! They are devoted lovers and often committed to making their partner happy.

Women: she's a sensual and giving lover. Outside the bedroom, she's strong and reliable—and you can always count on her to be there for you, even in the worst of times. She has a head for business but is often happiest spending time with those she cares about the most.

Men: he's a sensual and giving lover who greatly enjoys your physical intimacy together. He's also loyal, caring, and very reliable. Yet, for all of business success, he too desires time to relax and his enjoy his family and friends.

Mars in Virgo is very precise. 7 A.M.: wake up, read the paper. 8:15 A.M.: work out. Noon: balance the checkbook during lunch. 4 P.M.: mocha latté break. 6 P.M.: make dinner. 7 P.M. and beyond: have great sex!

Women: she's organized, ambitious, and all business on the surface. She loves to help others and thrives on getting things done. Yet, she secretly desires a lover who will entice her to break all of her rules and make a long-term commitment.

Men: he's successful at business and also very organized. If in doubt, check out his sock drawer! He's a grounded, very sensual lover but also somewhat shy. He seeks a partner who will embrace his exacting nature and wants to share a lifetime together.

Cosmic Lovers

Oscar-winning actress Hilary Swank is a Leo with her Mars in Virgo, showing that she is passionate, sensual, and very organized!

Mars in Capricorn has a strong work ethic. They are goal-oriented and thrive on achievement. When out of balance, they are more engaged in their careers then their personal lives! They are committed, dependable, and highly sexual.

Women: she is a high-powered career gal, efficient, and very capable. What she really desires is a committed partner who is as strong and powerful as she is. She wants nothing more than to share her sexual and intimate life with someone who will stick around.

Men: he's career driven, and the women in his life complain about not having enough time with him! He's seeking a balance between his work and his need for a loving and supportive partner who is as highly sexual as he is.

The Least You Need to Know

- ◆ Venus or Mars in Fire are independent and sexually bold.

- ◆ Venus or Mars in Air are more cerebral about their sexual needs and desires.

- ◆ Venus or Mars in Water are romantic, sensitive, and have strong emotional and sexual needs.

- ◆ Venus or Mars in Earth are very sensual and don't like to stray too far from their comfort zones.

- ◆ Comparing your Venus and Mars will give you great insight into your sexual compatibility.

Talking About Sex: Venus and Mars Together

In This Chapter

- Venus and Mars connections determine your sexual dynamics together

- Compare your Venus and Mars with your lover's

- Fire and Air signs combine for lots of sexual heat

- Water and Earth signs combine for a deep and often lasting sexual connection

- Fire combined with Water and Earth signs can be a sexual washout

- Air combined with Water and Earth signs indicates sexual challenges

Although Sun/ascendant and Moon compatibility are important to your day-to-day relationships and to your emotional intimacy, it is your Venus and Mars connections that most define your sexual compatibility. Venus and Mars represent the cosmic and timeless dance between men and women and the male and female energies in each of us. To gain a deeper understanding of the sexual dynamics of your relationship, you will want to see how your Venus and Mars align.

As you will see in this chapter, although you and your partner may connect on other planetary levels, an incompatible Venus and Mars can indicate very different sexual needs and desires—and an unfulfilling sex life!

Venus and Mars Together

In mythology, Venus—the goddess of love and beauty—and Mars—the god of war—had a grand love affair! The result was a lot of steamy sex—and some titanic male and female power struggles! Your male and female energies are reflected in your sextrology through the placement of your Venus and Mars. Venus represents the feminine aspect of love and desire, symbolizing your romantic, giving, and receptive nature.

Mars represents the masculine aspect of desire—the aggressive, outgoing, and very primal part of your sexual nature.

Heavenly Relations

As with all of the signs and planets, Fire is the most compatible with Fire and Air and vice-versa. Fire or Air with Earth and Water signs indicates a more challenging connection. For Venus and Mars connections, this specifically applies to your sexual and relationship needs.

You can find the placement of your and your lover's Venus and Mars by either using an online ephemeris or your astrology charts. (For more information, see Appendix B.) You will want to compare your Venus with his or her Mars and your Mars with his or her Venus to see how you relate together in love, relationships, and sexual desires!

As we learned in Chapter 10, Venus and Mars in each of the different signs and elements each have their own very distinct needs. Here's a quick overview:

Cosmic Lovers

Domestic diva Martha Stewart, a Leo, has her Venus in Virgo and her Mars in Aries. A cosmic matchmaker might advise her to find a lover with his Venus in Leo—to be strong enough to stand up to her bold Aries Mars—and a Mars in another Earth sign, like sensual Taurus, who would share her love of beauty and material possessions.

Venus and Mars in the Signs of the Zodiac

Signs	Venus	Mars

Fire signs: passionate, freedom-loving, and very sexual!

Aries	Independent	Bold
Leo	Dramatic	Passionate
Sagittarius	Playful	Adventurous

Air signs: inspiring and sexually experimental.

Gemini	Versatile	Intellectual
Libra	Creative	Righteous
Aquarius	Inspired	Rebellious

Water signs: emotionally sensitive and sexually deep.

Cancer	Intuitive	Nurturing
Scorpio	Passionate	Intense
Pisces	Romantic	Imaginative

Earth signs: hard-working and very, very sensual.

Taurus	Sensuous	Earthy
Virgo	Giving	Exacting
Capricorn	Stoic	Driven

Venus and Mars in Fire

To say that Venus and Mars in the Fire signs are sexually compatible is an understatement! Both Venus and Mars in Fire are passionate and sexually outgoing. Both are also extremely independent and need lots of room to explore their sexual and relationship options. Together, they are dynamic, adventurous, fun-loving, and very passionate!

At the same time, Fire with Fire can also be extremely combustible! Venus and Mars in Fire signs need to watch out for ego clashes, especially regarding whose needs come first in the bedroom!

Sexpectations: to have as much great sex as possible! Neither of you holds back when it involves getting your needs met!

Star Alert! _____

Diva alert! Venus and Mars in the same Fire signs are sexually compatible but also have strong and sometimes competing sexual desires. For example, Venus and Mars in Leo are passionate, loyal, and also very territorial! These Venus and Mars both need to feel like they come first in the relationship.

The following list includes all of the Fire Venus and Mars combinations:

Venus/Mars Aries

Venus Aries/Mars Leo; Venus Leo/Mars Aries

Venus Aries/Mars Sagittarius; Venus Sagittarius/Mars Aries

Venus/Mars Leo

Venus Leo/Mars Sagittarius; Venus Sagittarius/Mars Leo

Venus/Mars Sagittarius

Venus and Mars in Fire and Air

Venus and Mars in Fire and Air signs combine in an exciting roller-coaster ride of sex and passion. Inspiring and sexually experimental Air stimulates passionate and outgoing Fire to reach new heights of sexual exploration and delight! Both Fire and Air are independent and get bored easily: they both live in the thrill and passion of the moment. For Venus and Mars in Fire and Air, it's an enticing dance of give and take in order to make each other feel sexually inspired and fulfilled.

Venus and Mars in the opposite elements—Fire and Air or Water and Earth—often have the greatest sexual accord!

Sexpectations: passion, adventure, and a very stimulating sexual connection.

The following list includes all of the Fire and Air Venus and Mars combinations:

Venus Aries/Mars Gemini; Venus Gemini/Mars Aries

Venus Aries/Mars Libra; Venus Libra/Mars Aries

Venus Aries/Mars Aquarius; Venus Aquarius/Mars Aries

Venus Leo/Mars Gemini; Venus Gemini/Mars Leo

Venus Leo/Mars Libra; Venus Libra/Mars Leo

Venus Leo/Mars Aquarius; Venus Aquarius/Mars Leo

Venus Sagittarius/Mars Gemini; Venus Gemini/Mars Sagittarius

Venus Sagittarius/Mars Libra; Venus Libra/Mars Sagittarius

Venus Sagittarius/Mars Aquarius; Venus Aquarius/Mars Sagittarius

 Dear Sextrologer …

"My wife and I have been married for 10 years. Although I love her dearly, lately our sex life has become stale. She has her Venus in Libra and her Mars in Aquarius. I have my Venus in Leo and my Mars in Sagittarius. Any suggestions on how to spice things up?"

Your wife has both her Venus and Mars in Air signs, showing that she has a curious nature and likes excitement. At the same time, depending on their ever-changing moods and libidos, Air signs can be a bit sexually detached. You have both your Venus and Mars in Fire signs, signifying that you need lots of passion and your own share of excitement! Diagnosis: your Venus and Mars are actually very sexually in sync. You need to spend some quality time together away from your busy daily lives—work, family, chores—and get to know each other again sexually! Keep in mind that her occasional detachment isn't permanent and that you will delight and entice her with sexual role-play. Hint: your wife's Venus in Libra also loves romance.

Venus and Mars in Fire and Water

Fire and Water Venus and Mars combine together in an awkward sexual dance! Fire is bold, aggressive, and all about conquering—and getting sexual needs met. Water is emotional, intuitive, and wants a deep and lasting connection. Venus and Mars in Water have a hard time expressing their deeper sexual and emotional needs. Venus and Mars in Fire don't relate to the deeper sensitivities of love and romance. Together, it's one step forward and two steps back! Sexually, Air and Water don't have much in common.

 Star Alert!

Fire and Water Venus and Mars have a hard time mixing in the bedroom! For example, a Venus or Mars in adventurous and sexually independent Sagittarius combined with a Venus or Mars in emotional and security-oriented Cancer has very different sexual and relationship needs.

Sexpectations: hope for a compatible Sun or Moon sign connection—otherwise, there won't be much sexual satisfaction going on!

The following list includes all of the Fire and Water Venus and Mars combinations:

Venus Aries/Mars Cancer; Venus Cancer/Mars Aries

Venus Aries/Mars Scorpio; Venus Scorpio/Mars Aries

Venus Aries/Mars Pisces; Venus Pisces/Mars Aries

Venus Leo/Mars Cancer; Venus Cancer/Mars Leo

Venus Leo/Mars Scorpio; Venus Scorpio/Mars Leo

Venus Leo/Mars Pisces; Venus Pisces/Mars Leo

Venus Sagittarius/Mars Cancer; Venus Cancer/Mars Sagittarius

Venus Sagittarius/Mars Scorpio; Venus Scorpio/Mars Sagittarius

Venus Sagittarius/Mars Pisces; Venus Pisces/Mars Sagittarius

Venus and Mars in Fire and Earth

Planets in the elements of Earth and Fire often extinguish each other's deeper needs and desires—and it's especially so for Venus and Mars! Venus and Mars in Fire are aggressive and move fast. Bold and adventurous, they need lots of space and freedom. Venus and Mars in Earth move slowly: they like to take time to fully explore their relationships and sexual connections. Although both Earth and Fire are highly passionate, in a Venus and Mars connection they ultimately have very different sexual needs and desires.

Sexpectations: you may initially sexually spark—but it will quickly grow old.

The following list includes all of the Fire and Earth Venus and Mars combinations:

Venus Aries/Mars Taurus; Venus Taurus/Mars Aries

Venus Aries/Mars Virgo; Venus Virgo/Mars Aries

Venus Aries/Mars Capricorn; Venus Capricorn/Mars Aries

Venus Leo/Mars Taurus; Venus Taurus/Mars Leo

Venus Leo/Mars Virgo; Venus Virgo/Mars Leo

Venus Leo/Mars Capricorn; Venus Capricorn/Mars Leo

Venus Sagittarius/Mars Taurus; Venus Taurus/Mars Sagittarius

Venus Sagittarius/Mars Virgo; Venus Virgo/Mars Sagittarius

Venus Sagittarius/Mars Capricorn; Venus Capricorn/Mars Sagittarius

 Dear Sextrologer ...

"I'm seeing a man with his Venus in Aries and his Mars in Taurus. I also have my Venus in Aries, and my Mars is in Capricorn. At the beginning of the relationship, we seemed to have a great sexual connection—but lately I'm beginning to wonder how compatible we really are. What do you think?"

"P.S. We also seem to fight a lot!"

Although Venus and Mars in the elements of Fire and Earth may experience an initial sexual connection, in day-to-day living you both have greatly different lifestyle and sexual needs—hence the fighting! A man with his Venus in Water would give you the emotional and sexual fulfillment that your Mars in Capricorn wants and deserves. Also, a Mars in an Air sign would add some sexual intrigue and balance your fiery Venus in Aries. Time to move on and get more of what you need!

Venus and Mars in Air

Excitement is the name of the game for Venus and Mars in Air signs! Both Venus and Mars in the Air signs are intellectual, independent, and need to be inspired. Sexually, the sky is the limit! At the same time, Air signs can be sexually detached, and Venus and Mars in Air need lots of space to explore their many ideas and interests. Venus and Mars in Air often combine together in a compatible—and unique—way! Air signs pride themselves on their individuality and together often give each other the room they both need to grow and evolve.

Together, Venus and Mars in the Air signs are on the same page with respect to their sexual needs. Yet, Air signs can be fickle when it comes to love and romance! Together, Venus and Mars in Air want the freedom to explore their sexual needs and desires.

Sexpectations: to inspire each other to reach entirely new levels of sexual fun, intrigue, and excitement!

Cosmic Lovers _____

Virgo Lance Armstrong of Tour de France fame has his Venus in Libra and his Mars in Aquarius—both Air signs. His Venus in Libra indicates a romantic yet highly discerning lover. His Mars in Aquarius also shows a detached and freedom-loving approach to sex and relationships. This airy Venus and Mars combination indicates that he can be a real heartbreaker!

The following list includes all of the Air Venus and Mars combinations:

> Venus/Mars Gemini

> Venus Gemini/Mars Libra; Venus Libra/Mars Gemini

> Venus Gemini/Mars Aquarius; Venus Aquarius/Mars Gemini

> Venus/Mars Libra

> Venus Libra/Mars Aquarius; Venus Aquarius/Mars Libra

> Venus/Mars Aquarius

Venus and Mars in Air and Water

Venus and Mars in Air and Water signs have great difficulty finding their sexual grove. Venus and Mars in Air are independent, like lots of space, and need to be constantly inspired. Venus and Mars in Water are highly sensitive, emotional, and live in their inner lives and fantasies. Together, this Venus and Mars combination may initially spark each other's sexual fantasies—but any intrigue will likely turn to disappointment for Water and irritation for Air! Air and Water have two very different sexual needs for feeling comfortable together in the bedroom.

Sexpectations: your sexual fantasies together will likely be short-lived. In reality, there's little sexual compatibility for these Venus and Mars combinations.

The following list includes all of the Venus and Mars Air and Water combinations:

> Venus Gemini/Mars Cancer; Venus Cancer/Mars Gemini

> Venus Gemini/Mars Scorpio; Venus Scorpio/Mars Gemini

> Venus Gemini/Mars Pisces; Venus Pisces/Mars Gemini

Venus Libra/Mars Cancer; Venus Cancer/Mars Libra

Venus Libra/Mars Scorpio; Venus Scorpio/Mars Libra

Venus Libra/Mars Pisces; Venus Pisces/Mars Libra

Venus Aquarius/Mars Cancer; Venus Cancer/Mars Aquarius

Venus Aquarius/Mars Scorpio; Venus Scorpio/Mars Aquarius

Venus Aquarius/Mars Pisces; Venus Pisces/Mars Aquarius

 Cosmic Lovers

Senator Hillary Rodham Clinton, a Scorpio, also has her Venus in Scorpio and her Mars in Aries. Her husband and former U.S. President Bill Clinton, a Leo, has both his Venus and Mars in the super-friendly sign of Libra! Hillary's Venus in Aries is in the opposite sign of Bill's Venus and Mars in Libra—indicating a deep, sexually stimulating, and lasting connection. Her Sun and Venus in Scorpio, however, are in a challenging aspect to his Leo Sun, indicating power struggles! Life will never be boring for these two!

Venus and Mars in Air and Earth

Remember your high school prom? A time where you wanted nothing more than to find just the right date to go to the dance with? Well ... Venus and Mars in Air and Earth signs are last-minute and totally incompatible dance partners! If you have your Venus or Mars in Air, you were probably the one out on the dance floor happily flitting from one partner to the next! If you have your Venus or Mars in Earth, you were probably sitting on the sidelines wondering how the heck you got there. Together, Air and Earth Venus and Mars have little in common and very different sexual needs and expectations.

Sexpectations: minimal at best!

The following list includes all of the Air and Earth Venus and Mars combinations:

Venus Gemini/Mars Taurus; Venus Taurus/Mars Gemini

Venus Gemini/Mars Virgo; Venus Virgo/Mars Gemini

Venus Gemini/Mars Capricorn; Venus Capricorn/Mars Gemini

Venus Libra/Mars Taurus; Venus Taurus/Mars Libra

Star Alert!

Venus and Mars in Air and Earth signs are rarely on the same page in their sexual and relationship needs. For example, a Venus in pragmatic and practical Taurus and a Mars in free-wheeling and sexually explorative Gemini don't really have much in common sexually!

Venus Libra/Mars Virgo; Venus Virgo/Mars Libra

Venus Libra/Mars Capricorn; Venus Capricorn/Mars Libra

Venus Aquarius/Mars Taurus; Venus Taurus/Mars Aquarius

Venus Aquarius/Mars Virgo; Venus Virgo/Mars Aquarius

Venus Aquarius/Mars Capricorn; Venus Capricorn/Mars Aquarius

Venus and Mars in Water

Together, a Venus and Mars in Water combine in a luxuriously slow-moving and very romantic waltz! This Venus and Mars combination loves spending time with each other and exploring their sexual fantasies. Both Venus and Mars in Water are sensitive and highly emotional: they like to feel emotionally safe in their sexual connections. And when they do, they will often open up and willingly share their very romantic and deeply sensual natures. Venus and Mars in Water are both nurturing and are highly compatible in their sexual and long-term relationship needs.

Sexpectations: a deeply emotional and sexually fulfilling connection!

The following list includes all of the Water Venus and Mars combinations:

Venus/Mars Cancer

Venus Cancer/Mars Scorpio; Venus Scorpio/Mars Cancer

Venus Cancer/Mars Pisces; Venus Pisces/Mars Cancer

Venus/Mars Scorpio

Venus Scorpio/Mars Pisces; Venus Pisces/Mars Scorpio

Venus/Mars Pisces

Dear Sextrologer ... _____

"My boyfriend has both his Mars and Venus in Scorpio. There are times when I get overwhelmed by his intensity—especially sexually. Any suggestions?"

Scorpio has an intense emotional and sexual depth. When combined in both Mars and Venus, it can be doubly so. You didn't mention the sign of your Venus or Mars, but no matter their placement, you will definitely need to define your boundaries and not hesitate to be clear about what works for you in your sexual—and emotional—life. Passion is fantastic—unless it becomes overbearing!

Venus and Mars in Water and Earth

This Venus and Mars connection offers a sexy and very passionate tango! Venus and Mars in Water bring the romance, fantasy, and nurturing that Earth loves. Earth provides the sensuality and sustaining security that Water wants to experience. Together, this Venus and Mars instinctively know what the other wants and needs in the bedroom.

For Venus and Mars in Water and Earth, sex is passionate and sensual! And a big bonus—they're compatible in their day-to-day relationship needs, as well! Venus and Mars in Water and Earth combine for a deep and often lasting sexual connection.

Sexpectations: very high! Your Venus and Mars align on so many levels—and yes, the sex is fantastic!

The following list includes all of the Water and Earth Venus and Mars combinations:

Venus Cancer/Mars Taurus; Venus Taurus/Mars Cancer

Venus Cancer/Mars Virgo; Venus Virgo/Mars Cancer

Venus Cancer/Mars Capricorn; Venus Capricorn/Mars Cancer

Venus Scorpio/Mars Taurus; Venus Taurus/Mars Scorpio

Venus Scorpio/Mars Virgo; Venus Virgo/Mars Scorpio

Venus Scorpio/Mars Capricorn; Venus Capricorn/Mars Scorpio

Venus Pisces/Mars Taurus; Venus Taurus/Mars Pisces

Venus Pisces/Mars Virgo; Venus Virgo/Mars Pisces

Venus Pisces/Mars Capricorn; Venus Capricorn/Mars Pisces

Dear Sextrologer ... _____

"I have both my Venus and Mars in Capricorn. My partner has his Venus in Taurus and his Mars in Pisces. Do you think we make a good sexual match?"

You do—and in spades! Your Venus in Capricorn is highly compatible with his Mars in Taurus. His Mars in Pisces loves to fulfill all of your Mars in Capricorn's sexual fantasies! Together, you have a great sexual and cosmic accord with lasting possibilities.

Venus and Mars in Earth

Together, sensual Venus and Mars in Earth are very sexually compatible. They also have great long-term relationship potential! These Venus and Mars are both on the same page regarding love, sex, desire ... and the all-important Earth component: long-term security! Although there will be times when Venus and Mars in Earth butt heads over whose needs come first, any differences will usually be resolved quickly. Plus, a few clashes make this Venus and Mars connection all the more sexually hot and stimulating!

Sexpectations: the earth moves in this very sensual and physical connection that is likely to last.

The following list includes all of the Earth Venus and Mars combinations:

Star Alert! _____

Although Venus and Mars in Earth signs are sexually in sync, there will be times when each of these very stubborn Venus and Mars wants to feel in control of the relationship.

Venus/Mars Taurus

Venus Taurus/Mars Virgo; Venus Virgo/Mars Taurus

Venus Taurus/Mars Capricorn; Venus Capricorn/Mars Taurus

Venus/Mars Virgo

Venus Virgo/Mars Capricorn; Venus Virgo/Mars Capricorn

Venus/Mars Capricorn

The Least You Need to Know

- Venus and Mars indicate how you will relate together sexually

- Venus and Mars in the signs and elements have different sexpectations.

- Venus is the romantic and receptive aspect of love and relationships; Mars is the aggressive and primal aspect of love and desire.

- Venus and Mars in Fire or in Air are sexually very in sync.

- Venus and Mars in Fire and Water tend to extinguish each other's sexual needs.

- Venus and Mars in Fire and Earth don't have much in common sexually.

- Venus and Mars in Air and Earth or Water don't relate well together in life or in the bedroom.

Part 4

Fine-Tuning Your Connection

Now that you have mastered the basics of sextrology, you can fine-tune your love and sex connections. By exploring your planetary aspects and the astrological houses, you will gain a broader picture of the details of your relationship on a wide range of fronts. This is the nitty-gritty of sextrology!

Chapter 12

Is It Hot in Here? The Aspects

In This Chapter

- ◆ Aspects are the degrees between the astrological signs
- ◆ Each aspect represents a different degree of sexual heat
- ◆ Understanding your aspects is not rocket science!
- ◆ Oppositions, conjunctions, and trines are the most sexually hot
- ◆ Sextiles, squares, and inconjuncts are sexually cooler
- ◆ The aspects worksheet will help you explore your aspects together

The aspects between the signs of the zodiac will tell you a lot about the sexual chemistry between you and your lover. Will you be sizzling, hot, warm, lukewarm, cold, or freezing? To find out whether you are destined to burn out or whether you'll be able to sustain a long-term sexual connection, look to your aspects!

Understanding Your Aspects

The geometrical relationship, or degrees, between the different signs of the zodiac are called *aspects*. In sextrology, the aspects between your planets represent your sexual degrees of heat together! Aspects form different angles between the signs of the zodiac that greatly influence your relationships and the desire for different kinds of sexual experiences.

The complete astrology wheel, like a full circle, is 360 degrees. An astrology wheel incorporates each sign of the zodiac, and each sign encompasses 30 of the 360 degrees. A good way to understand your aspects is by looking at the number of signs between each. For example, conjunctions are usually in the same sign, 0 to 5 degrees apart, and trines are 120 degrees or four signs apart.

Heavenly Relations _____

If exploring your **aspects** makes you feel like you're in high school geometry class all over again, don't despair! It's true that the astrological aspects relate to elements of geometry—degrees, squares, triangles, and such—but here, you just need to know the basics. No compass or slide rule required!

There are easy or favorable aspects and hard or challenging ones. Although in astrology, favorable and compatible aspects are usually in sync—when it comes to your sextrology, the dynamics are somewhat different! In sextrology, the easy aspects don't have the same sexual zing that the hard aspects do!

The most powerful and intense aspects are oppositions, conjunctions, trines, and squares. These aspects sexually challenge each other—for better or for worse! The more moderate or weaker aspects are sextiles and inconjuncts, and they are sexually much cooler.

Dear Sextrologer ... _____

"I want to know more about how my aspects relate to my husband's. How do I find out more?"

Your astrology charts or an ephemeris will give you the specific degrees and aspects for all of your planets. Have fun exploring your degrees of heat together!

The Aspects

Oppositions	180 degrees between signs
Conjunctions	0–5 degrees between signs
Trines	120 degrees between signs
Sextiles	60 degrees between signs
Squares	90 degrees between signs
Inconjuncts	150 degrees between signs

For an aspect to have significance, it needs to be plus or minus 5 degrees. Wider aspects—a greater number of degrees apart—are weaker and have much less impact.

Heavenly Relations _____

Aspects have an orb of influence that describes the proximity between two planets. A good way to think about orbs is: the smaller the orb (or number of degrees), the more powerful the effect of the aspect!

Oppositions (180 Degrees Between Signs): Sizzling!

Key Words: stimulating, thrilling, passionate

Oppositions are easy to remember: they are the pairings between the opposite signs of the zodiac! Each sign of the zodiac has an opposite or polar sign: Aries/Libra, Taurus/Scorpio, Gemini/Sagittarius, Cancer/Capricorn, Leo/Aquarius, and Virgo/Pisces.

Are you and your lover opposites? Lucky you! Oppositions are sexually sizzling because they represent opposite yet mutually agreeable sexual desires. Here, opposites attract—and in a big way! Although you are coming from two different perspectives, they are two sides of the same cosmic coin! Oppositions represent challenges, but they are often sexually exciting and very stimulating. Together, you are one hot, sexy match.

In the long term, you have a balance that works. Planets in opposition stimulate each other to learn and grow in new ways. At the same time, oppositions can make each other feel sexually and emotionally raw as you force each other to explore your deepest needs and desires. Although at times you may confront and even intimidate each other, once again the friction—and even the occasional hint of danger—is sexually hot and stimulating!

Oppositions usually have an intensely sexual relationship, even as time goes by and other couples' fires cool. Your sexual relationship is often the glue that binds the two of you, where you feel the most in tune. Makeup sex will be a frequent, important, and very hot conclusion to your many skirmishes! A suggestion, however: when things get too intense, know when it's time to pull back a little. Relax—your oppositional partner is totally into you and not likely to go anywhere anytime soon!

Cosmic Lovers _____

Catherine Zeta-Jones and her husband Michael Douglas are both Libras, born on the same day—25 years apart! The conjunction between their Suns reflects a similar approach to life—and a passionate and very sexy relationship.

Sexy: the combination of a mutual balance and challenge is an enticing sexual combination.

Not so sexy: coming from two different perspectives can sometimes be a drag and emotionally draining!

Conjunctions (0–5 Degrees Between Signs): Hot

Key Words: intense, competitive, passionate

Conjunctions are usually in the same sign, although you can have a conjunction with the previous or next sign of the zodiac. For example, a Gemini at 2 degrees and a Taurus at 29 degrees—or Scorpio at 29 degrees and a Sagittarius at 3 degrees—still make a conjunction. This kind of conjunction typically has less weight or impact than a same-sign conjunction.

Heavenly Relations

Once you've checked out the aspects for you and your lover's Sun/ascendant, be sure to do the same for your Moon, Venus, and Mars! For more information about your sexual compatibility, see the aspects worksheet at the end of this chapter.

Star Alert!

Although conjunctions tend to be very sexy, they are also intense and can burn out! The long-term potential for conjunctions often depends on the element. Fire and Air conjunctions tend to burn out more quickly; Water and Earth conjunctions tend to have more staying power.

Conjunctions are an intense and often sexually competitive combination—which is why they are so darn hot! Together, you offer cosmic mirrors that reflect each other's strongest sexual needs and desires. Although there will be times when you rival each other over who comes first, you have a heartfelt connection. Together, there is a mutual desire to get know each other and explore future opportunities. You also have many shared interests and are on the same page regarding lifestyle concerns.

When you put same signs together, there is both a greater mutual accord and some sexy competition! Sometimes you can be so much alike that you drive each other a little crazy! It's not always easy to remember where you start and your partner leaves off. Conjunctions offer the best and the worst in relationships. On one hand, you really like and understand each other—but on the other hand, you are likely to compete over whose needs come first.

Conjunctions also love to play and have fun together, especially in the bedroom! You both give each other the freedom to be who you are and to be sexually uninhibited!

Sexy: having a strong, instinctual understanding of each other's needs ignites you two sexually. It's like coming home!

Not so sexy: having so much in common can bring out the worst in each other!

Trines (120 Degrees Between Signs): Warm

Key Words: supportive, enjoyable, romantic

Trines are 120 degrees or four signs apart. Trines always fall in the same element. For example, Fire signs trine each other (Aries, Leo, and Sagittarius); Air signs trine each other (Gemini, Libra and Aquarius); Earth signs trine each other (Taurus, Virgo, and Capricorn); and Water signs trine each other (Cancer, Scorpio, and Pisces.)

Trines are one of the easiest relationship aspects and are sexually warm. A trine between your signs represents a strong degree of cosmic harmony. You are highly in tune on many levels: emotionally, sexually, and in your relationship and lifestyle needs. A trine between your planets signifies the gifts that you bring to each other. Sun trines offer the gift of allowing each other to be who they are; Moon trines result in unconditional emotional support; and Venus and Mars trines result in a deeper understanding of each other's sexual needs!

There's also sure to be plenty of romance, because you both love to celebrate your time together and find it easy to make each other happy! You even have cute nicknames for each other: Sweetie, Babycakes, Stud –Muffin, or heaven forbid—Cutie Patootie! (You fill in the blank!)

On a sexual level, trines are very compatible. At times, however, you may feel so compatible—you both come from the same place and want the same things—that it can get a little boring! Watch out for taking each other for granted! With trines, there is a need to keep things interesting and spice things up in the bedroom. Suggestion: exploring your hidden sexual fantasies together could add some much-needed intrigue and excitement to your routine.

Sexy: you two have a deep, natural knowledge of each other's sexual needs. You know how to make each other feel both at home and alive in the bedroom!

Not so sexy: you know each other so well that your day-to-day sex life can get a little … well … dull.

Heavenly Relations

"Are you feeling lucky?" Lovers with trines usually feel extremely lucky to have found each other. You feel blessed to be together!

Cosmic Lovers

American sweetheart Sandra Bullock is a Leo. Her husband, bad-boy Jesse James, is an Aries. Together, their Leo and Aries Suns form a trine, indicating a comfortable and sexually compatible relationship that has long-term potential!

Sextiles (60 Degrees Between Signs): Lukewarm

Key Words: easy, compatible, dull

Sextiles are 60 degrees or two signs apart. For example, Leo is sextile Libra, and Capricorn is sextile Pisces.

Sextiles are a favorable aspect representing a cosmic sexual and relationship harmony. Yet, sextiles can be so easy and so compatible that they can become sexually boring—which is why sextiles are only sexually lukewarm! Although there's a mutual attraction and sexual synchronicity at work between you two, it is easy to become stagnant and rely on your comfort zones.

Sexually, you understand each other's sexual drives and desires—perhaps too much! A suggestion for reigniting your sexual heat is to do something completely outside your normal relationship parameters. For example, take a trip together and go somewhere you have never been before. Call your travel agent immediately and book a vacation retreat where you can explore each other in a whole new way! How about sex in Paris, a view of the Eiffel Tower, French chocolates, and champagne? Or perhaps sex on the beach in Hawaii? Okay, reality check: maybe it's just a weekend at your lake cabin away from the inlaws. Whatever—it works!

Sexy: you are emotionally compatible and know how to make each other sexually tick.

Not so sexy: been there, done that! For sextiles, it's often the same old routine!

Dear Sextrologer …

"My boyfriend and I have a number of trines and sextiles together: his Sun in Virgo trines my Capricorn Sun; my Pisces Moon sextiles his Moon in Capricorn. What does this mean for our long-term sexual compatibility?"

Both trines and sextiles are compatible aspects. Your planets also fall in Water and Earth signs—again, very compatible. Your astrological compatibility means that you are in sync and have long-term potential together! However, with all of your trines and sextiles, you will have to work at keeping your sexual spark alive!

Squares (90 Degrees Between Signs): Cold

Key Words: intense, challenging, power struggles

Squares are 90 degrees or three signs apart. Squares fall to the three astrological qualities: fixed, cardinal, and mutable. For example, in the fixed quality, Taurus squares Leo and Aquarius; in the cardinal quality, Aries squares Cancer and Capricorn; and in the mutable quality, Gemini squares Virgo and Pisces.

Star Alert! _____

Squares between you and your lover indicate heartache! There are often too many sexual and emotional challenges to make each other happy!

A square between your planets is considered to be very challenging—and not in a good way! Squares represent emotional difficulties and limited day-to-day compatibility. Squares bring out passionate and intense arguments … even all-out fights!

Together, you two compete and collide with each other. The result is a lot of tension and many, many power struggles. Although you may stimulate each other, again, it's not in a good way! Squares can become quickly tedious and even dysfunctional as you challenge each other about what's really important.

Squares may have an initial sexual spark, but it usually burns out quickly—leaving you both sexually cold! Squares force a degree of personal growth in both of you, but you may need to ask yourself whether it has to be this hard? A suggestion is to either learn to give your lover lots of space to do things his or her own way or consider the fact that it might not be meant to be!

Sexy: friction can be very sexy—or at least, for awhile! Squares may sexually spark with each other, but it rarely lasts.

Not so sexy: constantly being challenged—in life and in the bedroom—grows old very quickly!

Inconjuncts (150 Degrees Between Signs): Freezing

Key Words: disjointed, confused, painful

Inconjuncts, also called quincunxes, are 150 degrees between signs. Inconjuncts are the opposite sign plus or minus one sign. For example, Aries is inconjunct Scorpio and Virgo, and Aquarius is inconjunct Virgo and Cancer.

Dear Sextrologer ...

"I'm an Aquarius with my Moon in Taurus. I'm seeing a Scorpio man with his Moon in Leo. Our sex life is phenomenal, but now after being together for three months, I'm realizing that our dates are usually just about the sex! When I bring this up, he changes the subject! I want more and am starting to have serious doubts. What should I do?"

The abundance of fixed signs between you two—Aquarius, Taurus, Leo, and Scorpio—indicate major astrological squares! As hot as your sexual connection may be, sorry to say, you two would have to negotiate some pretty hard challenges to make your relationship work. (And when it comes to deeper intimacy, obviously your Scorpio has some major trust issues!) Enjoy the present—but be ready to cut your losses and move on!

Inconjuncts are so sexually cold ... they're freezing! This aspect represents connections that are not in sync on any level—in life, in relationships, or sexually. The result can be a lot frustration and confusion when it comes to knowing how to make each other happy. You don't understand each other, and you will find it very hard to reach any common ground.

Star Alert!

Of all the aspects, inconjuncts are the most difficult on the relationship front. A number of inconjuncts together is a red flag that you are not cosmically or sexually in tune!

Sexually and emotionally, inconjuncts have enormous potential for hurt feelings! There's sure to be lots of miscommunication as you misread each other's needs. You're both going to struggle with what you truly desire in this relationship.

Sexy: not so much!

Not so sexy: Brr! You have little or no sexual chemistry.

The Aspects Worksheet

This worksheet will help you understand the aspects between you and your lover. You will likely find that you have a combination of different aspects, but use this guide to see which ones have the most prominence. For example, two or more of a particular aspect will have special significance in your sexual compatibility.

Remember the Planets?

Sun:	Your personality and ego
Ascendant:	The face you present to the world
Moon:	Your inner self and emotions
Venus:	Your attitude towards love, romance, and pleasure
Mars:	Your approach toward sex and passion

The aspects between your different planets can be very revealing! Sun/ascendant and Moon aspects are important because they reflect your physical, emotional, and day-to-day needs. Aspects between your Venus and Mars, however, often have the most influence on your sexual chemistry together!

Cosmic Lovers _____

Scorpio movie star and sexy mom Demi Moore has her Moon in Taurus. Her actor/producer husband Ashton Kutcher has both his Sun and Moon in Aquarius. Together and individually, they have significant squares in their charts. When it comes to long-term happiness together, the number of squares between them indicates challenges to come!

Comparing your aspects together is very revealing about your sexual and relationship compatibility. Start with your Sun/ascendant and then move on to your Moon, Venus, and Mars. The more aspects you have together, the deeper the connections—whether it's hot or cold!

Together, we have ___ oppositions. Oppositions are sexually sizzling and indicate a desire to learn and grow together—sexually and in your day-to-day relationship.

Together, we have ___ conjunctions. Conjunctions are sexually hot. They indicate that you are like-minded but also competitive over your sexual needs.

Together, we have ___ trines. Trines are sexually warm. They indicate easy relationships that are in sexual harmony.

Together, we have ___ sextiles. Sextiles are sexually lukewarm and indicate a mutual sexual accord—but in the long term can become dull … even boring!

Together, we have ____ squares. Squares are sexually cold and indicate a challenging connection (lots of quarreling!).

Together, we have ___ inconjuncts. Inconjuncts are sexually freezing and indicate little in common—sexually or other otherwise!

Dear Sextrologer ... _____

"Help! I compared my aspects to my boyfriend's, and we don't have many! What does this mean?"

Few or no aspects between you and your boyfriend is not a good sign when it comes to your sexual connections or day-to-day intimacy. However, one significant aspect—especially an opposition or conjunction—around your Moons, for example, could be enough to giving you sexual staying power.

The Least You Need to Know

- Oppositions (180 degrees between signs) are sexually sizzling.

- Conjunctions (0–5 degrees between signs) are sexually hot.

- Trines (120 degrees between signs) are sexually warm.

- Sextiles (60 degrees between signs) are sexually lukewarm.

- Squares (90 degrees between signs) are sexually cold.

- Inconjuncts (150 degrees between signs) are sexually freezing.

13

The Houses: Where It All Happens

In This Chapter

◆ Astrological houses are the playing fields of experience

◆ Each house represents a specific area of life

◆ Each house has a ruling astrological sign and planet

◆ Planets in your various houses place emphasis upon the experience of the house

◆ Your ascendant sets the stage for your life experiences

◆ Planets in each other's houses will stimulate your experience of the house in whole new ways

Whereas the planets show *what* is happening and the signs show *how* it is happening, the houses show *where* it is happening! In sextrology, the houses relate to the areas of life where your relationship will play out. Into which of each other's houses do your planets fall? This chapter sets the stage.

All the World's a Stage: The 12 Houses

An astrology chart is a pie wheel divided into 12 sections, or houses. The houses are the stages where the different acts of your life's drama will unfold. Each of the astrological houses encompasses a different area of your life experience. For example, the second house represents how you relate to money and possessions, and your seventh house governs how you will experience the significant relationships and partners in your life.

Dear Sextrologer ...

"Help! When looking at my chart, I'm noticing that there are a number of houses where I don't have any planets! Does this mean I'm missing something?"

Don't panic—you're not missing anything! Just because you don't have planets in a house doesn't change the meaning of the house. The sign on the cusp of the house determines the type of experience you will have of the house—no matter whether you have planets there or not! The more planets you have in a house, however, the more time and attention you will be inclined to give to the matters of that house.

Cusps and Rising Signs

Each house has a sign that rules it. The start of every house is called a cusp. The astrological sign on the cusp of a house brings the energies of the sign to the experience of the house. In an astrology chart, Virgo—discerning, practical, and particular—on the cusp of the second house of money and security, for example, operates quite differently than, say, Gemini—diverse, versatile, and fickle—on the second house! Each of your cusp rulers will define your experience of the house.

Heavenly Relations

A cusp represents the start of an astrological house. In the universal astrology wheel, the first house cusp is ruled by Aries; the second, Taurus; and so on. Your rising sign—the sign on the cusp of your first house–will determine your following house cusps. If you have Sagittarius rising, then you will likely have Capricorn on your second house and so on.

Your rising sign, or ascendant, is the sign on the cusp of your first house and begins your astrology chart. Your rising sign is notable, not only because it is the sign that sets up your astrological chart but also because it indicates your predominant attitude toward all of your life experiences.

The 12 Houses of the Zodiac

House	Natural Ruler	Area of Experience
First	Aries/Mars	The self
Second	Taurus/Venus	Money, possessions, self-worth
Third	Gemini/Mercury	Communication, learning
Fourth	Cancer/Moon	Roots, family, home
Fifth	Leo/Sun	Fun, creativity, romance
Sixth	Virgo/Mercury	Health, work, service
Seventh	Libra/Venus	Relationships, partnerships
Eighth	Scorpio/Pluto	Sex, transformation, shared resources
Ninth	Sagittarius/Jupiter	Travel, higher education, philosophy
Tenth	Capricorn/Saturn	Status, career
Eleventh	Aquarius/Uranus	Friendships, aspirations
Twelfth	Pisces/Neptune	Unconscious, dreams, intuition

Significant Houses

In sextrology, all of the houses are important—but the first, seventh, and eighth houses have special significance. The first and seventh houses represent the balance between self and relationship. Planets and the sign on the cusp of these houses indicate how each of you is likely to navigate this balance. The eighth house, representing sex and transformation, is often the place where there is the potential for a deeper or greater intimacy.

Sun, Moon, Venus, and Mars!

Each of the sextrology planets—the Sun, Moon, Venus, and Mars—brings the energies of the individual planets to the experience of the house:

◆ **Sun:** the house of your Sun is where you shine! It is the area of life where you feel most compelled to express yourself.

◆ **Moon:** the house of your Moon represents your emotional base. It is the area of life where you feel the most at home and comfortable.

◆ **Venus:** the house of your Venus is where you seek pleasure, enjoyment, and romance. It signifies the area of life that you most love to experience.

◆ **Mars:** the house of your Mars is where you are the most driven. It is the area of life where you feel compelled to get ahead and conquer new life experiences.

 Heavenly Relations

> Your natal chart shows where all the planets were at the moment of your birth. It never changes. The current movements of the planets and where they fall in your chart are called transits. Transiting planets, much like the placement of your lover's planets, will stimulate the energies of the houses in which they fall.

Comparing Your Charts

By comparing your astrological chart with your lover's and noting where your planets fall in each other's houses, you will gain a lot of insight into the playing fields where your relationship will unfold. The houses indicate the areas of life where you will likely stimulate each other. You will either find a mutual accord, or—depending on the signs and planets—will challenge each other to explore the experiences of the house in an entirely new way!

An astrology software program will give you your chart comparisons. Or, you can overlay both of your charts and find out the location of each of your planets in each other's houses. For more information about how to get your chart, see Appendix B.

Exploring Your Houses

A good way to understand each of the houses is not only by their ruling signs and planets but also by their elements: Fire, Air, Water, and Earth.

The Houses, Elements, and Energies

Element Houses	Energies
Fire 1st, 5th, 9th	Dynamic, outgoing, experiential
Air 3rd, 7th, 11th	Intellectual, inspirational, relationship-oriented
Water 4th, 8th, 12th	Emotional, sensitive, deep, psychic
Earth 2nd, 6th, 10th	Practical, tangible, security-oriented

Ascendants: Your Outer Persona

Your ascendant, or rising sign, governs your outer personality, appearance, and physical attributes. It represents your self-image and often how others see you. It is how you present yourself to the world.

The ascendant is the exact degree of the zodiac sign that was rising over the eastern horizon at the time of your birth. As we learned before, your ascendant represents the beginning of your astrology chart. It sets the stage and is a significant indicator of your predominant attitude and approach toward life:

- **Rams rising:** Aries on the ascendant sets the stage for a bold, aggressive, and impulsive approach to life.

- **Bulls rising:** a Taurus ascendant sets the stage for a conservative, practical, and steady approach to life.

- **Twins rising:** Gemini on the ascendant sets the stage for an open, versatile, and exploratory attitude toward life.

- **Crabs rising:** a Cancer ascendant sets the stage for an emotional, practical, and nurturing approach to life.

Star Alert!

An ascendant changes signs every two hours. To find the precise degree of your rising sign, you will need to know the exact time of your birth.

Heavenly Relations

Rising signs share the same physical characteristics of the Sun signs—only here, they are more apparent because your ascendant shows how you present yourself to the world. For example, Aries rising often has a strong and muscular frame—and a big head! Cancer rising, ruled by the Moon, often has a very expressive moon face that gives away deeper feelings and emotions.

◆ **Lions rising:** Leo on the ascendant sets the stage for a dramatic, powerful, and very expressive approach to life.

◆ **Virgins rising:** Virgo on the ascendant sets the stage for a logical, highly particular, and discerning attitude toward life.

◆ **Scales rising:** a Libra ascendant sets the stage for a refined, fair, and balanced approach to life.

◆ **Scorpions rising:** a Scorpio ascendant sets the stage for an intense, dramatic, and profound approach to life.

◆ **Archers rising:** Sagittarius on the ascendant sets the stage for an outgoing, explorative, and expansive attitude toward life.

◆ **Goats rising:** a Capricorn ascendant sets the stage for a practical, ambitious, and directed approach to life.

◆ **Water bearers rising:** Aquarius on the ascendant sets the stage for an intellectual, inspirational, rebellious, and often eccentric attitude toward life.

◆ **Fishes rising:** a Pisces ascendant sets the stage for an intuitive, creative, and romantic approach to life.

Star Alert!

Scorpio ascendants can be very mysterious! They are often self-protective and even elusive when it comes to sharing their deeper feelings.

Dear Sextrologer ...

"My partner and I have opposite rising signs: I have a Virgo ascendant, and he has a Pisces ascendant. What does this mean for our relationship?"

Opposite rising signs are significant in sextrology because they usually rule each other's seventh house of relationships. Although opposite rising signs indicate that you approach your life in opposite ways, you will likely find that you give each other a lot of balance. You are likely learning a lot from one another as far as how you engage with yourself—and in your relationships.

The First House: It's All About You!

"Me first!" is an apt description for the first house. This house represents self-awareness, personal power, and your ego. Ruled by bold, fiery, and outgoing Aries, the first house shows how you move forward in life. It is in the first house where we are compelled to follow our basic instincts and put them into action.

The first house represents new beginnings and the desire to explore new opportunities in life. The first house tends to bring out the impulsive and more aggressive side of the sign and planets involved. They give no indication, however, about whether you will follow through and bring your desires to fruition!

Planets in each other's first houses indicate an important and mutual synchronicity, especially around your individual purposes in life. At the same time, depending on the signs and planets, your first-house planets can also be somewhat competitive with each other—especially regarding whose needs come first in your relationship!

The Second House: Feeling Secure

The second house is called "the house of values." It represents income, possessions, and personal resources. Ruled by practical and earthy Taurus, this house describes the way in which you relate to security. On a deeper level, the second house represents your sense of self-worth (or, in other words, the ways in which you value yourself!).

Depending on the sign and planets, in the second house you will find that you either have a natural talent for making money or possibly the other extreme—you may feel challenged in this area! Either way, second-house planets like to feel comfortable, enjoy material possessions, and feel secure in all aspects of life.

Planets in each other's second house indicate a shared desire for financial and material security. You are likely to support each other in your mutual need to feel secure. Don't limit this to matters of money, however; it is also true when it comes to valuing each other's contributions to your relationship.

 Star Alert!

"Show me the money!" Planets in each other's second houses often stimulate each other's deeper security needs, including the person who is in charge of your bigger financial picture.

The Third House: Can We Talk?

This house governs the workings of the mind. Ruled by Gemini, it represents your intellectual process, your learning experiences, and how you communicate your knowledge to others. Planets in the third house indicate a deep love of learning. Your third house includes a wide diversity of intellectual interests, yet depending on the signs and planets, they can become scattered and lack focus! For planets in the third house, it can often be difficult to focus on one direction or expression!

Your planets in each other's third house indicate an intellectual synchronicity—and a mutual desire to share your thoughts, ideas, and inspirations with each other.

You two will love to talk and talk, although there's also a danger that you may try to outdo each other with your intellectual prowess!

The Fourth House: Your Roots

The fourth house represents your roots. Ruled by Cancer, this house governs home and family. Planets in the fourth house indicate a deep connection with your family of origin and also with your greater ancestral clan. This house symbolizes your emotional base and the foundation of your inner security. The fourth house reflects your desire to feel at home and comfortable in your life—and with yourself. It also indicates a deep need to feel fully connected to those you love the most.

Planets in each other's fourth house indicate a shared emotional foundation. This is a comfortable and often very nurturing relationship. You will likely find that you will relate to each other's deepest emotional needs.

 Cosmic Lovers

Movie star Marlon Brando had both his Aries Sun and Moon in the fourth house. Although his charismatic Aries Sun and Moon showed in his brave, brash, and pioneering approach to life—because they were in his fourth house, this outgoing adventurer was tempered by a longing for home, family, and inner security.

The Fifth House: Expressing Yourself

The fifth house governs our self-expression. This mode of self-expression comes in different forms, depending on the sign and planets in this house. Naturally ruled by fiery and dramatic Leo, the fifth house represents our creative instincts and a love of excitement, new projects, and new love affairs! This is a romantic and fun-loving house. Yet, because the fifth house represents speculation and gambling, it is also the place where you are most likely to take big romantic risks!

Planets in each other's fifth house indicate a very romantic connection! Whether you will experience a long-term relationship will depend on your signs and planets, however. Whatever your future potential, when your planets are in each other's fifth houses, you are sure to find lots of fun, romance, and excitement while it lasts!

> **Heavenly Relations** _____
>
> Remember, the sign on the cusp of each house determines your experience of the house. For example, if you have serious and hard-working Capricorn on your fifth-house cusp, it indicates that you have a more practical approach to creativity and romance. If you have romantic Libra on your fifth-house cusp, you are more likely to fully embrace the more creative and romantic elements of this house.

Sixth House: Working Toward Fulfillment

The sixth house represents health, work, and service. How do these elements go together? The idea here is that if you're not happy in your work or service, it won't contribute to your health and well-being as it should! This house is the one in which we seek a balance between body, mind, and spirit that will offer us the most fulfilling life experience.

"How can I help?" describes the sixth house. Ruled by Virgo, this house is very service-oriented. Planets in the sixth house indicate that you have a strong desire to make a contribution to others and the world. The sixth house is also very health conscious—sometimes overly so! Planets in this house indicate that we need to keep an eye on tendencies to succumb to Virgo's perfectionism and become overly exacting about the details of life—whatever form they may take.

Planets in each other's sixth houses indicate that you enjoy making each other's lives better! Although you can be hard on each other (and yes, even quite critical), you do have a real desire to support each other in fulfilling your life purposes.

Seventh House: It's All About Us!

Your seventh house governs your significant relationships, joint ventures, and partnerships. Notice that we didn't mention love here! Ruled by romantic Libra, while the seventh house is the house that drives you to seek a fulfilling relationship, it is also the house in which you learn about the balance and inner workings of your day-to-day relationships.

Cosmic Lovers _____

"I got you, Babe!" is not only a popular karaoke song—it also defined Cher and husband Sonny Bono's relationship! Taurus Cher has a Capricorn Moon in her seventh house, indicating that she is a loyal and supportive partner ... whoever her partner may be at the time.

Planets in the seventh house represent the timeless, universal dance between yourself and others. This is where we learn when to give and compromise and when to push for what we want and need. Ultimately, the seventh house represents the desire for balance and harmony in your all of your relationships.

Planets in each other's seventh houses indicate a significant connection. You will often find that you are mirrors reflecting each other's relationship desires. Together, you are likely to find that you have much to learn from each other—and are greatly inspired to do so!

Dear Sextrologer ... _____

"I have a number of planets in my seventh house, including both my Moon and Venus. What does this mean?"

Planets in your seventh house, especially a Moon (symbolizing your inner emotions) and Venus (symbolizing your attitude toward love), indicate that you are very relationship-oriented! Your Moon indicates the desire for a deep and emotional connection in your relationships. Your Venus also says that you want lots of romance! Also, remember that the sign of your Moon and Venus and the cusp of your seventh house will give you more information about the way in which you express your relationship needs.

Eighth House: What's Sex Got to Do with It?

The eighth house represents not only sex but also transformation and shared resources. Traditionally, the eighth house is the house of death and rebirth, symbolizing the desire for a deeper and more profound meaning in life. Planets in the eighth house often have a mystical and spiritual bent. You want to explore and understand the greater mysteries of life!

In the eighth house, we seek transformative experiences—which may include sex! In the eighth house, one's sexual desires tend toward deep, meaningful, and even spiritually enlightening sexual experiences!

Planets in each other's eighth houses represent a significant, deep, and even life-altering connection. At the same time, your eighth-house planets indicate that you may push each other's emotional buttons. Depending on the sign and planets, you may run into power struggles. One way or another, you two will likely transform each other's lives!

Heavenly Relations

Although the seventh house represents relationships, it is in the eighth house where you will determine whether you are likely to commit to the next, deeper levels of your relationship!

Ninth House: Understanding the World

The ninth house represents higher education, foreign travel, religion, politics, legal matters, publishing, advertising, and–your inlaws! Whew! This is an active, diverse, and expansive house. Ruled by Sagittarius, the ninth house is where we expand into a greater perspective and understanding of our experience in the world.

Your ninth house represents the development of your higher mind. Here, we are compelled toward a desire for a bigger, spiritual, and adventurous experience in life. Planets in the ninth house say, "I want to experience it all!"

Planets in each other's ninth houses represent a shared love and interest in different cultures, politics, religion, and spirituality. Together, you will likely inspire each other to expand your awareness of life and the world!

Heavenly Relations

You can have more than one sign in a house. Houses with two or more signs are called intercepted houses. This means that the sign on the cusp of the house was in a later degree, so it also encompasses the next astrological sign (or signs). The sign at the cusp of the house, however, is usually the most significant.

Tenth House: Building Your Reputation

The tenth house represents your profession, reputation, and public image. This house has much to do with your career identity. Ruled by Capricorn, it is the place where you are driven to succeed professionally and to share your talents with the world. It is also the house where you demand to be respected!

Cosmic Lovers

Emperor Napoleon Bonaparte had his Leo Sun in his tenth house, indicating both an extremely driven nature and a very large ego! Although this is obviously an extreme example, when planets are out of balance in the tenth house, they can become overly driven and even dictatorial!

The tenth house is a hard-working house. Here, success can be hard-earned. Yet—depending on the sign and planets involved—in the tenth house, we are nonetheless compelled to stick to our guns and make our deep desire for professional success work. Planets in your tenth house can also indicate an overemphasis on one's work life and career, however!

Planets in each other's tenth houses indicate a desire to explore the balance between your working and home lives. When in sync, planets in each other tenth houses indicate that you will share and support each other's day-to-day needs.

Eleventh House: You've Got to Have Friends!

The eleventh house represents friends, shared creativity, and cooperative efforts. Ruled by Aquarius, it also relates to what inspires you. In the eleventh house, we explore our hopes and wishes for the future. It is in the eleventh house where we are the most stimulated toward achieving our highest aspirations. Often, these aspirations relate to making a difference in the world— in your own unique way!

This house represents a desire to find community and friends with whom you can come together and share common goals. Sometimes these goals involve a greater or humanitarian purpose, and sometimes the goal is just to commune and relate with others in whole new way.

Planets in each other's eleventh houses indicate that you share the same dreams and aspirations. You two can support each other in making your dreams real!

Dear Sextrologer ...

"My boyfriend has his Sun and Mars in my eleventh house. Is this a good sign for our relationship?"

It sure is! His planets in your eleventh house indicate that you have a strong foundation of friendship from which to explore your relationship. Although the eleventh house isn't overly romantic, you will likely inspire and support each other in fulfilling your greatest aspirations. Don't forget to check out where your planets fall in his houses to gain a full picture of your relationship!

Twelfth House: Your Hidden Self

The twelfth house represents the private and hidden parts of life. It governs the deepest parts of the self, including your unconscious, your dreams, and your deeper intuitions. Planets in the watery realm of the twelfth house often have a hard time expressing themselves. Ruled by romantic and fanciful Pisces, planets in your twelfth house can also indicate patterns surrounding unrequited romantic love!

Star Alert!

Planets in each other's twelfth houses can indicate that there's unfinished karmic business between you two! Depending on the signs and planets involved, you will either inspire each other to move forward and release old patterns or get caught up in old relationship issues that may have plagued you in the past.

This is the last house of your astrology chart and has much to do with unfinished business. On a symbolic level, it is where you wrap up different elements of your life so that you are free to move forward to the first house and ascendant (which represent new beginnings).

The twelfth house is associated with past lives. If you and your lover have planets in each other's twelfth houses, it indicates a very deep and even karmic or past-life connection. You probably felt an instant and intuitive connection when you met, and this powerful sense of connection will continue throughout your relationship!

Cosmic Lovers

Britain's Prince Charles and Princess Diana had some very revealing house connections. Diana's Sun in Cancer fell in Charles' twelfth house, indicating a likely karmic connection! His Scorpio Moon joins her Mars in Scorpio in Diana's eleventh house, indicating a shared desire to inspire the masses for a greater good although, as it turned out, in very different ways!.

The Least You Need to Know

◆ Each house relates to a specific area of your life.

◆ Your ascendant or rising sign is the sign on the cusp of your first house and sets up your astrology chart.

◆ Each of the houses has a ruling sign that governs the experience of the house.

◆ The more planets in a house, the more emphasis placed upon that house's experience.

◆ The placements of your planets in each other's houses indicate the areas where your relationship will play out.

◆ The most significant houses in sextrology are the first, seventh, and eighth.

Part  5

Soul Mates: Understanding Your Divine Connection

In this part, we will explore a different facet of sextrology—your soul mate connections. Soul mates are significant and life-altering relationships. Whether this means that you're meant to be together forever, however, is not always the case. To understand your soul mate connections, we look to the Moon Nodes. These astrological points represent your individual karma and destinies as well as your mutual growth experiences.

Chapter 14

Our Eyes Met Across a Crowded Room ...

In This Chapter

- ◆ Soul-mate relationships offer profound learning experiences
- ◆ Moon Nodes indicate your past *karma* and future destiny
- ◆ The South Node represents your inherent gifts and relationship comfort zones
- ◆ The North Node represents your desire for new growth and relationship opportunities
- ◆ Compare Moon Nodes to understand what you're meant to experience together

Have you ever met someone for the first time and experienced a feeling of familiarity or instant recognition? Perhaps it's a feeling that you have known this person before? Well, it's more than possible that you have! This type of deeper, intuitive reaction often indicates a soul-mate connection. Will your attraction be compelling enough that you'll want to explore a long-term relationship together? Stay tuned!

Understanding Soul Mates

Soul mates are cosmic partners who grow and evolve with each other, often through many lifetimes. Soul-mate relationships are based on agreements to come together to fulfill a commitment to each other in some way. You and your soul mate have met again—now and in this lifetime—because there continues to be karma that needs to be played out and important life lessons to be learned from each other. The cosmic glue that keeps you and your soul mate connected is the desire to explore new territory together or to release old patterns that you may have repeated in other lifetimes.

Heavenly Relations _____

Karma is based on the universal law of cause and effect. Whether it's in this lifetime or past ones, karma is defined by the choices you make and how they will impact your present and future destiny.

Debunking the Myths

The idea of a soul mate often brings to mind the image of a cosmically perfect relationship. In a sense, we are all looking for our soul mate and the deeper recognition and wholeness that this implies. The term soul mate carries a lot of expectations and also some inherent baggage and confusion. The following section describe some of the biggest myths about soul-mate connections.

Cosmic Lovers _____

In the movie *Jerry Maguire*, Jerry Maguire and Dorothy Boyd survived many challenges to come together in what could be described as a soul-mate coupling. It wasn't easy, but through many trials and tribulations, ultimately both came to realize: "You complete me!"

Myth One: Soul Mates Are Meant to Be Together Forever

Sometimes the agreement between soul mates results in a lasting, long-term relationship. In other cases, the commitment resolves itself more quickly. In the best sense, the experience between you and your soul mate—no matter the duration—frees each of you to move forward in life, whether together or separately.

Myth Two: You Only Have One Soul Mate

Not so! You will meet different soul mates throughout your lifetime, for different reasons. For example, at age 20 you may seek a relationship for emotional or financial security. As you mature, you will likely develop the need for a different or deeper kind of intimacy. Different soul mates will appear all along your journey. Your soul mates will reflect your growth, evolving needs, and desires—and the choices you make.

Star Alert!

Some soul mates offer a life-altering catalyst for each other. This kind of soul-mate connection will often invoke a spiritual and emotional crisis—both individually and with each other. Although these soul mate connections are intensely passionate, they often come in the form of short-term affairs. These relationships tend to burn out quickly and are rarely meant to last.

Myth Three: We Have a Deeper, Psychic Connection

So that means it should work, right? Soul mates connect through our psychic or sixth sense, sometimes with the feeling that you can read each other's minds! Psychic "time" does not always translate to Earth or real-world time, however. You can feel a deep, intuitive connection with someone that may be based in the experiences that you shared in past lifetimes—hence the feeling of déjà vu. Unfortunately, a psychic connection does not necessary indicate that you're meant to be together, particularly in the long term.

Myth Four: Soul Mates Are Always Lovers

Often, soul mates come to us as potential lovers and relationship partners, but soul mate connections may take many forms. You can find a soul mate in a beloved friend, teacher, or mentor or in a favorite sibling, uncle, or family member.

Myth Five: Soul Connections Are Easy

Some soul-mate relationships are easier than others! Even with the most compatible soul mates, however, there will always be challenges. After all, your soul mate is here to help you grow and evolve! The idea of a blissful, happily-ever-after future for soul mates is just that—a myth or fairy tale!

Dear Sextrologer ... _____

"I feel my best friend is my soul mate. We always seem to be in sync and
share everything from mutual likes and dislikes to a common family background.
Honestly, I don't know what I would do without him! Yet, because I'm a girl and he's
a guy, sometimes I think we should explore a romantic relationship. There's no sexual
attraction between us, however. What to do?"

It's not unusual to have a soul-mate connection with a best friend. This does not necessarily mean that you're meant to be together romantically or in a committed partnership,
though! If you were meant to have a romantic relationship, you would feel a sexual
spark. Don't confuse the situation—instead, enjoy your cosmic synchronicity and mutual
support. You're lucky to be in each other's lives!

The Nodes of the Moon: Understanding Your Destiny

Exploring your Moon Nodes will help you better understand your soul-mate connections. Moon Nodes are not planets but rather astrological points representing your
past karma and future destiny. Moon Nodes indicate the accumulation of your past
life experiences as well as what you are working toward in this lifetime. They represent the strengths and challenges that you bring with you, your soul lessons, and your
inherent gifts and potential destiny.

Whether you are already in a long-term relationship or considering a new one, comparing your Moon Nodes with your partner's will help you understand what you are
both seeking in your relationships and in your life journey. If you're not in a relationship, your Moon Nodes will help you understand your relationship patterns and what
kind of soul partner you're looking for.

North and South Nodes are based on the polarities, or the nodal axis, between the 12
signs of the zodiac: Aries/Libra, Taurus/Scorpio, and so on through each of the signs.
Ultimately, with Moon Nodes there is a need to incorporate the energies and poten-
tials of both signs to find a greater life balance.

The lessons of your North and South Nodes relate to the signs of the zodiac and also
to their placement in the astrological houses. The placement of the Moon Nodes in
the different houses corresponds to the experience of that house; they represent the
area of life where your soul lessons will play out. For example, Aries/Libra nodes also
correspond to nodes in the first and seventh houses of an astrological chart; Taurus/
Scorpio Nodes correspond to nodes in the second and eighth houses, and so on.

North and South Moon Nodes

Signs/Houses	Polarities/Balance Points
Aries/Libra 1st/7th Houses	Independence versus relationship
Taurus/Scorpio 2nd/8th Houses	Material versus spiritual security
Gemini/Sagittarius 3rd/9th Houses	Learning versus wisdom
Cancer/Capricorn 4th/10th Houses	Family versus career
Leo/Aquarius 5th/11th Houses	Creative expression versus greater humanity
Virgo/Pisces 6th/12th Houses	Intellect versus intuition

South Nodes: Past and Karma

Your South Node represents the talents and abilities that you have cultivated through many lifetimes. It symbolizes the aspects of your life that you have already mastered and are the most comfortable with. In fact, your South Node reflects the comfort zones you have the most difficulty moving away from! Your South Node reflects your inherent gifts. In the best sense, it is the wisdom that you possess and can share with others. In relationships, your South Node represents repeating cycles that you are growing out of and are seeking to release.

Dear Sextrologer ... _____

"I was at a party recently, and just as I was getting ready to leave, I noticed a guy and he noticed me—and zowie! I felt an immediate electrical connection between us. He left, I left—should I track him down to pursue?"

Sounds like this guy made quite an impression! If you feel inclined to track him down, go ahead. Often, however, what you'll find is that if you two are meant to explore your connection further, destiny—or divine synchronicity—will intervene. And you will have the opportunity to meet this potential soul mate again!

North Nodes: Future Destiny

Your North Node includes the talents of your South Node with the desire to transform these gifts into new growth and life experiences. Your North Node represents aspects of yourself and your life journey that are unexplored. These are the qualities that you have not yet mastered! In the North node, we are compelled to grow and stretch outside our comfort zones. It also indicates the type of soul partner you are seeking to help you explore new relationship growth.

Aries/Libra

The Aries/Libra polarity is the in cardinal quality. The cardinal influence represents a desire for growth and to push forward and explore new life opportunities. It also indicates a need to focus on the development of one's individual needs in balance with your relationships.

S Node Aries/N Node Libra

S Node 1st House/N Node 7th House

> **Heavenly Relations**
>
> You don't have to believe in past lives to understand your Moon Nodes or soul-mate connections. The lessons offered still stand! A helpful way to look at your Moon Nodes is that they are cosmic metaphors and examples of your inherent gifts and challenges.

This Nodal axis represents individuals who are extremely independent and used to going it alone. The Aries/Libra polarity describes innovative pioneers who are competitive risk-takers. They like to win! They also like to do things their own way: "My way or the highway!" is often a theme. In relationships, this polarity is looking for an elusive soul mate—perhaps someone who will help them to be a bit more diplomatic! This nodal axis can become caught up in the initial excitement of the chase and the new! They are great at starting relationships but have trouble following through.

Strengths: inspiring, passionate, courageous

Weaknesses: domineering, impatient, inconsiderate, fear of being vulnerable

Soul lesson: learning to put others first, cooperating, accepting help from others

S Node Libra/N Node Aries

S Node 7th House/N Node 1st House

This combination is found in individuals who are very relationship-oriented and who often put their needs on hold for others. In past lifetimes, these people needed to be taken care of and were overly dependent on the support of others. In this lifetime, these individuals will need to learn to take more "me time" so as to develop their own unique individuality and purpose in life. They are learning to be more independent and to not rely on others' approval.

In relationships, this Nodal axis is often childlike in expressing emotions or deeper sexual needs.

Strengths: giving, supportive, cooperative, optimistic

Weaknesses: indecisive, lack of self-esteem and life purpose

Soul lesson: learning to be more self-reliant, self confident, and assertive

Taurus/Scorpio

The Taurus/Scorpio Nodal axis is in the fixed quality, indicating a stubborn attitude toward life! This polarity often relies on financial or material security instead of finding personal security within. Although these individuals resist change, they have a desire for the kind of growth and transformation that will help them gain deeper meaning in life.

S Node Taurus/N Node Scorpio

S Node 2nd House/N Node 8th House

This Nodal axis represents individuals who often rely on comfort and have a deep fear of exploring unknown and new experiences. In past lifetimes, there has often been an overdependence on material possessions. These individuals are often impressed with money, which can be tied to both their self-esteem and self-worth. In this lifetime, there is a need to review their sense of value and explore their inner resources. These individuals are learning to develop their talents and abilities and to make a contribution to the world.

> **Star Alert!**
>
> Moon Nodes in fixed polarities like to do things their own way! They can be resistant to change and often get stuck in old relationship patterns.

Strengths: practical, committed, reliable, persistent

Weaknesses: lazy, materialistic, relying on the familiar

Soul lesson: to surrender material desires to a bigger perspective; to learn that money does not equal happiness

S Node Scorpio/N Node Taurus

S Node 8th House/N Node 2nd House

This polarity represents individuals who are torn between the desire for growth and the comfort of the known. They are perpetually digging deeper to find greater meaning in life. Because they have often experienced past lifetimes of great difficulty or extremes, they can be crisis-oriented—often bracing for the next disaster or unwelcome event. In this lifetime, they are learning to let go and trust in bigger spiritual perspectives: to believe that in one way or another, we're always taken care of! This polarity is here to learn to appreciate and value the things, people, and activities that bring them joy and happiness.

Strengths: efficient, intuitive, tenacious, strength in crisis

Weaknesses: vindictive, jealous, resentful

Soul lesson: learning to trust, relax, and enjoy the many ups and downs of life

Cosmic Lovers

Leo Jacqueline Kennedy Onassis had her South node in Scorpio and her North Node in Taurus. Her Scorpio South Node indicates a survivalist approach to life. Her North Node in Taurus reflects a desire for security—for herself and her children—and a tendency to seek the finer things in life.

Gemini/Sagittarius

Gemini/Sagittarius Moon Nodes are in the mutable quality. Here, the mutable quality represents a desire to evolve from past circumstances and incorporate a more diverse spiritual perspective into life. At the same time, this Nodal axis is easily distracted and has a hard time focusing on one path or relationship!

S Node Gemini/N Node Sag

S Node 3rd House/N Node 9th House

With this Nodal axis, there is a constant need to know and find out more. Logic and reason tend to dominate, and there is overdependence on the intellect. These individuals desire a more spiritual approach to life and often attract partners who will both expand and challenge their spiritual beliefs. Here, there is a need to develop one's own inner sense of wisdom instead of always relying on the facts. In relationships, they tend to challenge others with their emotional elusiveness and constant need for change and instant gratification.

Strengths: versatile, expressive, open to new experiences

Weaknesses: inconsistent, impatient, not directed

Soul lesson: to see the bigger picture rather than becoming totally immersed in the details of day-to-day life

S Node Sag/N Node Gemini

S Node 9th House/N Node 3rd House

Individuals in the Sag/Gemini polarity are adventurers with a love of travel and exploring other cultures. They are philosophers by nature and are directed toward a more expansive, spiritual viewpoint in life. At the same time, individuals in this polarity are rarely joiners and like the freedom to explore different spiritual or religious perspectives. In this lifetime, they are learning to be more diverse in their approach to life. In relationships, they will often challenge others with their strong beliefs and blunt opinions.

Strengths: honest, optimistic, adventurous

Weaknesses: blunt, inconsiderate, tactless, changeable

Soul lesson: to explore their greater meaning in life while also being open to the needs and opinions of others

Cosmic Lovers

Capricorn David Bowie has his South Node in Sagittarius and his North Node in Gemini. His Moon Nodes represent a desire for spiritual growth while also reflecting his versatility and a love of dabbling in different creative expressions: music, acting, and fashion!

Dear Sextrologer ...

"My wife and I have opposite North and South Nodes. Her North Node is in Sagittarius, and her South Node is in Gemini. My North Node is in Gemini, and my South Node is in Sagittarius. Does this have any special significance?"

It sure does! Opposite Moon Nodes indicate a deep connection and a great desire to learn from each other and grow together. Your opposite Moon Nodes are like two sides of the same cosmic coin. Although you may be approaching life and your relationship from opposite perspectives, the shared intent or spiritual purpose originates from the same place!

Cancer/Capricorn

Like Aries/Libra, this Nodal axis is in the cardinal quality. The polarity here reflects the desire to find a balance between the demands of the workplace and the demands of the heart and home. Ultimately, there is a need to find a sense of self-worth that is not based exclusively in either!

S Node Cancer/N Node Capricorn

S Node 4th House/N Node 10th House

With this polarity, there is an over-reliance on emotional security. In past lifetimes, these individuals may have sacrificed their aspirations to take care of family and home. This polarity often has many diverse talents, including business, real estate, and creative enterprises and will long to attain recognition for their abilities in the career realm. In relationships, these individuals are extreme nurturers—sometimes to their own detriment!

Strengths: sympathetic, industrious, nurturing

Weaknesses: overly emotional, argumentative, security-based

Soul lesson: to give their individual gifts to the world—without guilt about letting others down.

S Node Capricorn/N Node Cancer

S Node 10th House/N Node 4th House

This Nodal axis represents individuals who have a need to develop their inner sense of emotional security. They are extremely career-minded and tend to put too much stock in achieving their goals and getting ahead in life. In past lifetimes, these individuals have associated their careers with their personal identities. They have relied on "the rules" and played by the book. In this lifetime, they feel the desire to develop their emotional foundation and to let go of the need to always be right. They are learning to trust themselves—and others—emotionally.

Strengths: efficient, patient, persevering

Weaknesses: self-involved, pessimistic, domineering

Soul lesson: to balance their career aspirations with a deeper longing for home and family

 Heavenly Relations

With soul-mate connections, there is often a shared and even uncanny synchronicity. You both experience the same kinds of experiences at the same time!

Leo/Aquarius

Like Taurus/Scorpio, Leo/Aquarius Moon Nodes are in the fixed quality. Here, the fixed quality reflects their strong desire to develop their individuality and make a dramatic impact on the world.

S Node Leo/N Node Aquarius

S Node 5th House/N Node 11th House

This Nodal axis is extremely creative and filled with a desire to put their unique stamp on the world! These individuals are driven by a need to express themselves without restriction. Their needs can be ego-based and self-serving, however. In this lifetime, they are learning to elevate their individual desires and devote them to winning for the greater good as well as self. In past lifetimes, they have depended on friends to further their aspirations; now, they need to strike out on their own. In relationships, they are learning to let go of their need for approval and to balance their needs with the desire to support others.

Strengths: positive, ambitious, generous, cheerful

Weaknesses: self-involved, controlling, obsessive, overdramatic

Soul lesson: to balance their ego needs with their desire to make a contribution to the world

S Node Aquarius/N Node Leo

S Node 11th House/N Node 5th House

This polarity represents individuals who have avoided the spotlight. In past lifetimes, they have hidden behind the needs and aspirations of others. An accurate description is, "the power behind the throne." In this lifetime, they are learning to develop and express their own aspirations. Humanitarians by nature, in the past they may have been revolutionaries who bent or even broke the rules—often in the name of a higher purpose or goal. Here, they need to develop their individuality while at the same time honoring the paths of others. In relationships, the same applies!

Strengths: inventive, original, supportive

Weaknesses: rebellious, detached, overly eccentric, relying too heavily on the support of others

Soul lesson: to act on their desire to change the world while remembering to honor their individual needs

Dear Sextrologer ... _____

"I'm dating a man who has his South Node in Aquarius and North Node in Leo. I'm a Leo with my South Node in Gemini and my North Node in Sagittarius. Are we a good match?"

Yes, you are! Your Leo Sun aligns well with his North Node in Leo, indicating a mutual desire to explore new experiences. Your South Node in Gemini is also very compatible with his South Node in fellow Air sign Aquarius. You two have a lot in common and a strong foundation to work with!

Virgo/Pisces

The Virgo/Pisces polarity, like Gemini/Sagittarius, is in the mutable quality—here representing a changeable attitude towards life. This polarity has a tendency to be fear-based when exploring new life opportunities and can get stuck in the past.

S Node Virgo/N Node Pisces

S Node 6th House/N Node 12th House

Heavenly Relations _____

When looking at your Moon Nodes on an astrology chart or ephemeris, often only the North Node is indicated. Why? The North Node is considered to be the "higher" aspect of the two, reflecting the accumulation of your soul experiences. Your South Node is exactly opposite your North Node in sign and degree. For example, if you have a North Node in Leo at 15 degrees, your South Node will fall in Aquarius at 15 degrees.

This Nodal axis seeks to overcome limited and negative thinking in order to open up to a bigger, intuitive perspective. In past lifetimes, there has been an over reliance on the mind: "If I can't see it or touch it, it's not real!" These individuals find happiness in service. They must be careful, however, not to lose themselves in their many obligations that they become self-sacrificing. These individuals often have gifts in the healing or health-care realm but have to be careful about being over-concerned with their own health.

Strengths: analytical, helpful, supportive

Weaknesses: critical, intolerant, judgmental, fearful

Soul lesson: balancing their intellect with a greater intuitive perspective

S Node Pisces/N Node Virgo

S Node 12th House/N Node 6th House

This Nodal axis is found in individuals who in past lives have become isolated from humanity. This may have come from forced exclusion in places such as monasteries, prisons, and mental health institutions. As a result, they often feel fearful about revealing their true selves to others. These individuals are intuitive and creative by nature but tend to escape into their imaginations and fantasy worlds. Here, they are learning to balance their intuitive gifts with a more rational, discerning, and analytical approach to life. In relationships, they often keep to themselves or expect others to take care of them.

Strengths: compassionate, intuitive, imaginative, spiritual

Weaknesses: inconsistent, indecisive, overly-sensitive, overly sentimental

Soul lesson: learning to feel safe and to pursue their dreams in the world

Cosmic Lovers

Teen queen Marie Antoinette, a Scorpio, had her South node in Pisces and her North Node in Virgo. Her Pisces South Node indicates an innocent view of the real world and a love of fantasy. Yet, as she was forced into the harsh world of French royalty, her Virgo North Node—representing an exacting, rule-oriented environment—took hold. Still, her Piscean love of escapism kept her distracted for a while.

The Least You Need to Know

- ◆ Soul mates help us explore our past karma and potential destiny.

- ◆ Some soul-mate connections make for lasting relationships while others are more fleeting.

- ◆ There are many misconceptions about soul mates.

- ◆ Soul mates connect at a psychic or intuitive level.

- ◆ Your Moon Nodes will help you understand your soul lessons and life purpose.

- ◆ Comparing your Moon Nodes will help you understand your potential life experiences together.

Chapter 15

Soul Mate Connections: Your Destiny Unveiled

In This Chapter

- Moon Node connections help you understand potential destinies
- North and South Nodes in each others' houses indicate where your soul-mate connections will unfold.
- Planets near each other's South Nodes indicate past karma
- Planets near each other's North Nodes indicate a desire to explore new experiences together

Exploring your Moon Node connections will give you insight into your and your lover's potential destiny together. Your planets joining each other's Moon Nodes and the houses where they fall indicate what you are learning from each other in this lifetime!

The South/North Nodes in Each Other's Houses

The South and North Nodes are based on the polarities between the astrological signs: Aries/Libra, Taurus/Scorpio, and so on. This is also true for the houses in which they fall. If your South Node is in your lover's first house, then your North Node falls in his or her opposite, seventh house (and vice-versa). Your Moon Nodes in each other's houses represent the soul lessons you are learning together in this lifetime and the areas of life in which your relationship will teach you the most.

First, look at the placement of your South and North Nodes to gain a sense of what each of you are here to learn, particularly in respect to your soul growth. Remember, your South Node represents the areas of life that you have already mastered. Your North node represents the areas of life in which you aspire to new soul growth and experiences.

South Node Aries/North Node Libra: Overly self-reliant with a need to learn how to receive the help of others. You don't have to go it alone!

North Node Aries/South Node Libra: Overly dependent on relationships to fulfill your needs. This lifetime is meant to teach you that you can step forward and assert yourself!

South Node Taurus/North Node Scorpio: The need to feel comfortable and secure—often to the point where it impedes growth and the possibility of new opportunities.

South Node Scorpio/North Node Taurus: The desire to explore new and more spiritual forms of security; learning to trust the bigger picture.

South Node Gemini/North Node Sagittarius: A scattered approach toward life and relationships; learning commitment.

South Node Sagittarius/North Node Gemini: A need to let go of dogmatic beliefs and explore different life options; a need to be more flexible.

South Node Cancer/North Node Capricorn: An over-reliance on the familiar, especially in regards to home and family; a need to explore your career opportunities.

South Node Capricorn/North Node Cancer: An over-reliance on career and worldly aspirations; a need to allow yourself to be emotionally vulnerable and to allow others to nurture you.

Cosmic Lovers _____

Aquarius Oprah Winfrey has her North Node in Capricorn and her South Node in Cancer. Her longtime boyfriend Stedman Graham, a Pisces, has his North node in Pisces and his South Node in Virgo. Although their Suns don't have much in common, their Moon nodes in Earth and Water signs are very compatible in the long term. Marriage or not, this connection is built to last.

South Node Leo/North Node Aquarius: A need to expand out of ego-based desires and balance them with the greater good; learning to appreciate other's gifts.

South Node Aquarius/North Node Leo: A need to focus more on self and explore your own creative aspirations. It's your time to express your gifts.

South Node Virgo/North Node Pisces: An intellectual and analytical approach to life (often overly so); a need to explore your intuition and imagination.

South Node Pisces/North Node Virgo: An imaginative, fanciful, and often very intuitive approach to life; learning to ground your intuitions in reality.

Now, look to see in which houses your lover's South and North Nodes fall (and vice-versa). For more information, see Chapter 14 for a full description of the meaning of each house. Here's a brief summary of the polarities.

First and Seventh Houses

The first house is the house of self; the seventh house is the house of others. This house polarity represents the balance between self and others in your relationship.

Dear Sextrologer ... _____

"My girlfriend's Taurus South Node and Scorpio North Node fall in my first and seventh houses. What does this mean?"

Her Moon Nodes in your first and seventh houses indicate that you are learning a lot from each other about the balance between your needs and her needs in your relationship. Because her nodes are in Taurus and Scorpio, there is an added emphasis on money, personal values, and security in your connection. Be sure to look at where your Moon nodes fall in her houses for a more complete picture of your soul lessons.

Second and Eighth Houses

The second house is the house of money and security; the eighth house is the house of sex and transformation. This house polarity represents how you will relate together in regard to your deeper values, sexual intimacy, and transformative experiences.

Third and Ninth Houses

The third house is the house of communication and the mind; the ninth house is the house of philosophy and worldly affairs. This house polarity represents how you will relate together in your intellectual needs and the desire for a more adventurous and worldly approach to life.

Moon Nodes in each other's third and ninth houses usually indicate a need for lots of freedom and independence in your relationship.

Fourth and Tenth Houses

The fourth house represents emotional security, home, and family—whereas the tenth house represents outer security and career desires. This house polarity represents the balance between home and family and your career aspirations.

 Dear Sextrologer ... _____

"My Leo South node and Aquarius North node fall in my husband's fourth and tenth houses. What does this indicate that we are learning from each other?"

Your Moon nodes in your husband's fourth and tenth houses show that you are both exploring the balance between your emotional and family needs and a need for fulfilling careers. When combined in Leo and Aquarius, it indicates that both of you are creative and have a desire to make your own unique mark on the world. Here, balance is the key! You're both learning how to be supportive of each other's deepest desires.

Fifth and Eleventh Houses

The fifth house represents creativity and self-expression; the eleventh house represents friends and aspirations. In this house polarity, we learn the balance between one's individual creative needs and the desire to be supportive of your partner's aspirations.

Your Moon Nodes in each other's fifth and eleventh houses suggest that you have been friends in another life! In this lifetime, there is a shared desire to explore your creative and aspirations together.

Sixth and Twelfth Houses

The sixth house is the house of health, work, and service; the twelfth house is the house of the unconscious, intuition, and the past. This house polarity indicates how both of you relate to wholeness: body, mind, and spirit.

Your Moon Nodes and the Planets

The Sun, Moon, Venus, and Mars are the planets indicating your love, sex, and relationship needs and desires. When one of these planets joins the other's North or South Nodes, it indicates a very strong soul mate connection—for better or for worse!

When the placement of your Sun, Moon, Venus, or Mars is near each other's North Nodes, it indicates that you are here to help each other explore new experiences that reflect your soul growth. These connections are positive and life-affirming. When one or more of these planets is near each other's South Nodes, it indicates an emotional drain. This kind of connection means that there are lessons to be learned or some type of karma to be resolved in this relationship.

(For more information on how to find your South and North Nodes, see Appendix B.)

Star Alert!

The South node represents your past and karma. When planets are near each other's South Nodes, there is often a feeling of, "Haven't we done this before?"

The Sun and South/North Nodes

Your Sun sign represents your vital life force. It is your true essence, the basis for your instincts, and an indicator of how you express yourself. When your Suns are near each other's South or North Nodes, there is often a feeling of intense familiarity—and your connection is often dramatic and quite passionate! You are greatly intrigued with one other and are filled with the desire to understand each other's life purposes.

Aries Sun/South Node: You are learning how to resolve old conflicts that may have held you back in the past.

Aries Sun/North Node: You inspire each other to fully explore new life opportunities —together and separately.

Taurus Sun/South Node: You're comfortable … perhaps too comfortable? There is a tendency to get stuck in old relationship patterns.

Taurus Sun/North Node: You possess a mutual desire to explore security in new and previously unknown depths.

Gemini Sun/South Node: Your relationship is highly stimulating, yet you have a restlessness for new opportunities.

Gemini Sun/North Node: A desire exists for exploring new experiences together— especially around your intellectual pursuits.

Cancer Sun/South Node: You're both emotionally in sync, yet you have little room to break out of old relationship patterns.

Cancer Sun/North Node: You have the desire to get to know each other on a deeper, emotional, and more intimate level.

Leo Sun/South Node: Your relationship is passionate and dramatic! But there are strong personalities here that may result in large ego clashes.

Leo Sun/North Node: You root for each other to fulfill your creative aspirations in the world.

Heavenly Relations

Sun and North Node connections tend to be very inspirational and supportive of each other's needs and desires.

Virgo Sun/South Node: You're both playing it safe. You need to push forward and be willing to discover new life experiences.

Virgo Sun/North Node: You both have a mutual desire to help each other discover your life purposes.

Libra Sun/South Node: You've spent lifetimes together, yet your needs have yet to be fulfilled.

Libra Sun/North Node: You have a very strong and instinctual desire to explore your relationship and share new experiences!

Scorpio Sun/South Node: You both have had lifetimes together that have been survival-based. You're both looking for easier experiences this time around.

Scorpio Sun/North Node: Together, you support each other in exploring new levels of relationship trust.

Sagittarius Sun/South Node: You've both had lifetimes exploring the world together, but without focus or commitment.

Sagittarius Sun/North Node: You give each other the space to explore all of your interests and commitments.

Capricorn Sun/South Node: Who's in charge? This connection stimulates both of your needs to be in control of the relationship.

Capricorn Sun/North Node: You support each other in fulfilling your career aspirations.

Aquarius Sun/South Node: You're both rebels who like your freedom—which doesn't bode well for a deep relationship.

Aquarius Sun/North Node: You give each other room to grow and breathe. You're also in sync with your eccentric lifestyles.

Pisces Sun/South Node: You have a strong familiarity—especially emotionally—yet have a tendency to get stuck in the past.

Pisces Sun/North Node: You both have the desire to support each other in exploring your romantic and creative needs and desires.

Remember the aspects—conjunctions, oppositions, trines, sextiles, squares, and inconjuncts? The nearer a planet is to a Moon Node, the stronger the connection. A conjunction—within 0 to 5 degrees—is the most significant. For more information about your aspects, see Chapter 12.

Cosmic Lovers

Long-time partners Susan Sarandon and Tim Robbins, both Libras, have a significant Sun and North Node connection. His Libra Sun joins her Sun and North Node in Libra, indicating a cosmically in-sync soul mate relationship with the desire to explore new life experiences together.

The Moon and South/North Node Nodes

The moon represents your emotions, feelings, and deeper intuitions. It is also the planet that most determines your day-to-day emotional compatibility and your deeper emotional intimacy together. Your Moons near each other's South and North Nodes indicate a profound and deeply emotional connection—often bringing a sense of instant recognition!

Aries Moon/South Node: You have the desire to rescue each other. But who's rescuing whom? Two emotional heroes can be too much.

Aries Moon/North Node: You're emotionally bold and inspiring! You help each other go after what you want in life.

Taurus Moon/South Node: Your relationship is emotionally comfortable—and very lazy! You have a tendency to get stuck in old, secure patterns.

Taurus Moon/South Node: You feel emotionally in sync enough that you can expand outside your old comfort zones.

Gemini Moon/South Node: You're both emotionally fickle. You've done this relationship dance before without either of you getting what you wanted.

Gemini Moon/North Node: You give each other room to explore your different interests and emotional needs.

Cancer Moon/South Node: You're both emotionally compatible but rely too heavily on each other for emotional security.

Cancer Moon/North Node: You both have the desire to explore a lasting emotional connection.

Heavenly Relations

Water Moons—Cancer, Scorpio, and Pisces—joining each other's Moon Nodes are particularly sensitive to each other's emotional needs. These connections represent a deep and even psychic familiarity with each other!

Leo Moon/South Node: Your relationship has lots of emotional drama. Too much? It's entirely likely!

Leo Moon/North Node: Your relationship is emotionally passionate and fulfilling. You support each other's creative desires.

Virgo Moon/South Node: Emotional familiarity does not equal emotional fulfillment! You may know each other too well to allow for soul growth.

Virgo Moon/North Node: You have a mutual desire to help each other feel emotionally safe and secure in life.

Libra Moon/South Node: "Been there, done that!" It's time for new relationship experiences.

Libra Moon/North Node: You are emotionally drawn to each other with a desire to explore your destinies together!

Scorpio Moon/South Node: You have a profound connection, but in this lifetime you may hold each other back from new growth experiences. This may be a very hard obstacle to overcome.

Scorpio Moon/North Node: You are exploring new levels of emotional trust together, which is very good for your soul and karmic growth!

Sagittarius Moon/South Node: You're both great friends and lovers, yet emotional commitment has always been the big issue.

Sagittarius Moon/North Node: You're both emotionally adventurous. You give each other the space to explore your different needs.

Capricorn Moon/South Node: You have a tendency to compete emotionally and even to squash each other's desires.

Star Alert!

Moon and South Node connections can indicate that you have become emotionally merged with one another and have a hard time moving onto new life experiences.

Capricorn Moon/North Node: You have a mutual desire to explore the balance between your deeper emotional and career needs.

Aquarius Moon/South Node: Both of you love freedom, yet in the past you may have abandoned each other during moments of great emotional need.

Aquarius Moon/North Node: You have the desire to give each other room to explore greater aspirations while also being emotionally supportive.

Pisces Moon/South Node: You can read each other's minds but are too psychically and emotionally merged to allow for much growth.

Pisces Moon/North Node: You're both emotionally supportive of each other's creative dreams, desires, and fantasies.

Dear Sextrologer ...

"I'm breaking up with my boyfriend of four years. He has his Moon in Pisces within two degrees of my Pisces South Node. Even though I know that it's time for both of us to move on, I'm having a hard time letting go. Any insight?"

His Pisces Moon in your South node indicates that you have had many past lifetimes together. This karmic history has left both of you with a deep longing for one another. Yet, your feeling that it is time to move on is right. Staying together will prevent both of you from exploring new relationship experiences that will fulfill your soul's need for growth. I know it's hard, but both of you will be much happier and ultimately more fulfilled in other relationships.

Venus and South/North Nodes

Venus is the planet of love, beauty, and romance. It represents your attitude toward love and relationships. Because Venus is such a benevolent planet, when it falls on each other's South or North Node, it tends to bring out the best in both of you! Venus Moon Node connections are romantic, passionate, and very loving.

Aries Venus/South Node: You're romantically feisty and fun-loving. You adore each other's company.

Aries Venus/North Node: You are deeply intrigued with each other's fiery passion.

Taurus Venus/South Node: Your relationship is a romantic and sensual love fest but also has a tendency to become stagnant. This may get old fast.

Taurus Venus/South Node: You love spending time together exploring your mutual sensual pleasures and the emotional pleasure of your relationship, as well.

Gemini Venus/South Node: Your relationship is stimulating and lots of fun! You love to tease and explore each other.

Gemini Venus/North Node: You both have a desire to explore many different experiences together, especially socially.

Cancer Venus/South Node: You're o the same page regarding your emotional and relationship needs.

Cancer Venus/North Node: Let's nest! You want to create a loving home and family together.

Heavenly Relations

Venus on each other's South Nodes suggests that you have been lovers in past lifetimes. Venus on each other's North Nodes indicates a likely desire to become lovers in this lifetime!

Leo Venus/South Node: Your relationship is fiercely passionate and also deeply romantic! You love to make each other happy.

Leo Venus/North Node: You love to play romantic games and explore and create great passion together.

Virgo Venus/South Node: You give each other the safety net that you both need to fully explore your romantic and relationship desires.

Virgo Venus/North Node: You feel inspired enough to break out of old relationship safety zones—which is no small thing!

Libra Venus/South Node: In a word: romantic! You two meet at an art show or at a friend's dinner party—and the rest is history.

Libra Venus/North Node: You're in sync when it comes to relationship, romance, and the finer aesthetics in life.

Scorpio Venus/South Node: Your connection is passionate and intense. You really understand each other on a deep level.

Scorpio Venus/North Node: You help each other let go of old relationship fears in order to discover an entirely new level of passion.

Sagittarius Venus/South Node: You totally get each other's need for freedom and adventure. Let's have fun!

Sagittarius Venus/North Node: You both appreciate each other's worldly ways. This is a fun and romantically adventurous connection.

 Cosmic Lovers

Cancer Kevin Bacon and wife Kyra Sedgwick, a Leo, have significant Venus North Node connections. Her Libra Venus is near Kevin's North Node in Libra; his Gemini Venus is near Kyra's North Node in Gemini—indicating that these two have a very romantic and sexually exciting relationship!

Capricorn Venus/South Node: You innately understand what each other would like from your relationship.

Capricorn Venus/North Node: You bring out the best in each other, especially regarding your mutual need to feel in control.

Aquarius Venus/South Node: You're both familiar with sexual freedom, yet you also bring out each other's elusive romantic side.

Aquarius Venus/North Node: You're both very supportive of each other's intellectual pursuits. There's great relationship camaraderie in life and in love.

Pisces Venus/South Node: "Hello, lover … have we met before?" The answer is yes! You two are very romantically in sync.

Pisces Venus/North Node: You love to explore your romantic and relationship fantasies together.

Mars and South/North Nodes

Mars is the action planet. It represents your driving life force and your primal sexual needs and desires. Mars near each other's South and North Nodes indicates a very strong sexual connection! At the same time, it also tends to bring out each other's competitive natures—sometimes good, sometimes not so much.

Aries Mars/South Node: You're sexually competitive! You challenge each other around whose needs come first.

Aries Mars/North Node: You're sexually hot and adventurous! You inspire each other to go after what you want.

Taurus Mars/South Node: Sexually, you can't get enough of each other—but you may tire of constantly butting heads.

Taurus Mars/South Node: You're intrigued by each other's strength, reliability, and sexual stamina!

Gemini Mars/South Node: You're restless for new sexual opportunities. Been there, done that—now move on!

Gemini Mars/North Node: You have a desire to explore many different experiences together especially sexually.

Cancer Mars/South Node: You're both emotionally competitive. You wrangle over who's the boss in your relationship.

Cancer Mars/North Node: You push each other, but in a good way! You want the same things, especially with regard to relationship security.

Star Alert!

When Mars in a Fire sign—Aries, Leo, and Sagittarius—joins your North or South Nodes, you will almost always find great competitiveness in your connection together!

Leo Mars/South Node: You have a passionate sexual connection, yet you compete over who comes first in your relationship.

Leo Mars/North Node: Sexually passionate, you root for each other's creative aspirations.

Virgo Mars/South Node: You're both very sexual but have the tendency to nitpick each other aggressively.

Virgo Mars/North Node: This is a very sexual pairing. In addition, you are supportive of each other's relationship desires.

Libra Mars/South Node: You compete intellectually over who's right. And that's a strain on Libra's famous diplomacy!

Libra Mars/North Node: You have a very stimulating relationship. You enjoy heated debates with each other, but you're usually on the same page.

Scorpio Mars/South Node: There's a heated sexual connection here—but unfortunately, also heated power struggles!

Scorpio Mars/North Node: Here's a powerful sexual attraction. Together, you explore all of your sexual fantasies and desires.

Sagittarius Mars/South Node: Your relationship is sexually fun but usually not lasting. You're two sexual bon vivants—both of whom like their freedom.

Sagittarius Mars/North Node: You're sexually adventurous and great fun together. You will likely have many adventures!

Capricorn Mars/South Node: Who's in control? Your relationship is sexually hot, but ultimately, there are big issues surrounding who's in charge.

Dear Sextrologer …

"My girlfriend's Sun and Mars are near my North Node in Sagittarius. What does this mean for us together as a couple?"

You definitely have a strong soul connection—sexually stimulating and lots of fun! At the same time, her fiery Sun and Mars joining your Sagittarius North Node means that there will be times when you challenge each other over whose needs come first. In this lifetime, you are both learning about commitment—especially when it comes to your relationship. Yet together, you will likely give each other the space and freedom that each of you needs to explore your relationship in mutually fulfilling ways.

Capricorn Mars/North Node: You give a whole new meaning to hot sex! You may compete, but you usually want the same things.

Aquarius Mars/South Node: You're comrades in arms. Yet, you're both too independent to get much going sexually.

Aquarius Mars/North Node: You both have the desire to give each other room to explore life desires—and the sex isn't bad, either!

Pisces Mars/South Node: Hello, karma! You get stuck in old relationship patterns and struggle for completion.

Pisces Mars/North Node: Sexy, sexy, sexy! You compel each other to make your fantasies real.

The Least You Need to Know

- Your South and North Node connections represent the soul lessons you are learning together.

- The houses where each other's Moon Nodes fall indicate the areas where you are learning the most from each other.

- The Sun near each other's Moon Nodes indicates an intensely familiar connection.

- The Moon near each other's Moon Nodes indicates a deep emotional connection.

- Venus near each other's Moon Nodes indicates a romantic and loving connection.

- Mars near each other's Moon Nodes indicates a competitive connection.

Chapter 16

Is This the Relationship of Your Dreams?

In This Chapter

◆ Soul mates bring out our deepest needs and desires

◆ Soul mates offer the greatest opportunities for growth

◆ Figure out whether he or she is the relationship of your dreams

◆ Stories to illustrate various soul mate experiences

Soul mate relationships are intense, to be sure! On one hand, they are intense by necessity: a soul mate connection means that the two of you have come together in this lifetime to learn important soul lessons with one another. On the other hand, as excited as you may be to meet each other once again, intensity is not always easy!

How do you know and understand whether this is the relationship of your dreams and whether it's meant to last?

Soul Mate or Stalemate?

Soul mate relationships will usually either inspire you to move forward and explore new life dimensions together or bring to the surface the places in your life where you get stuck (and find yourselves repeating past experiences). Although there is always karma involved with soul mates, there is also choice and free will. Ultimately, it's up to you to decide whether your soul mate enhances your life and furthers your soul and relationship growth or not!

Soul Mate Checklist

To find out whether you have a soul mate or stalemate connection, review the following list and be as honest as you can!

The following are *positive* soul mate connections:

- ◆ You feel compelled to explore a connection together.

- ◆ You learn a lot from each other and give each other insight into your lives.

- ◆ You enjoy spending time together.

- ◆ Your connection unfolds in synchronistic and harmonious ways.

- ◆ You inspire each other to grow.

- ◆ You challenge each other in a positive and loving way.

- ◆ When you look in his or her eyes, there is a deep sense of recognition—of your lover and of yourself.

Star Alert!

Often, the way you will connect with a soul mate is through a strong sexual attraction, which compels both of you to further explore your connection. This sexual attraction does not, unfortunately, always indicate that you will be compatible in your soul growth!

The following are *negative* soul mate connections:

- ◆ He or she makes you feel emotionally out of control.

- ◆ You feel like you're in so deep that you can't get out.

- ◆ Your growth together usually happens through crisis.

- ◆ You constantly challenge each other through fighting and arguments.

- ◆ Intuitively, you know that he or she is not right for you—no matter how strong your attraction.

- ◆ The sex is great and even passionate, but you have little else in common.

- ◆ You find yourself constantly obsessing over your soul mate with little comfort or resolve.

If you recognize more than one of these negative indicators, you might want to consider that this relationship is probably not meant to last. Not that it can't, mind you—but it probably shouldn't.

Let Intuition Be Your Guide

Soul mates connect through intuitive and soul energies rather than through intellectual or logical ones. Intuition often comes in the form of an inner sense of knowledge: you may not know how or why, but you just know it! Intuition involves learning to listen to your inner voice. Part of the growth of a soul mate experience is learning to become more aware and trusting of our powerful intuitive sense!

Dear Sextrologer ...

"How do I really know whether someone is my soul mate? The reason I ask is because I'm dating a wonderful guy, and although we get along famously, some of my friends think he's not right for me. He's 50 years old and has never been married, and at 32, I'm almost 20 years younger with one failed marriage behind me! Yet, I just have the feeling that he's the soul mate I have been waiting for. Plus, he's kind, generous, very supportive, and we have a great sexual connection."

Trust your feelings! This man obviously treats you well and seems sincere in your relationship. True love has nothing to do with age! Although there are no guarantees, it sounds like this is a very positive soul mate connection for you both. Tell your friends not to judge a book by its cover!

What's Love Got to Do with It?

The common denominator in healthy soul mate connections is a feeling of unconditional love. It is the powerful foundation of unconditional love that allows both of you to grow, evolve, and even challenge each other! Although there will be times when you will drive each other crazy, the sense of acceptance and love will always be there.

Walking the Dark Side

Soul mates bring our deepest needs and desires to the surface. In some cases, they stimulate our darkest selves. Your dark side represents the parts of yourself that are unresolved, deeply conflicted, and often fear-based. They are the hidden parts of yourself that you are the most fearful of revealing—to others and perhaps even to yourself. In a healthy soul mate relationship, your dark sides may emerge—but with love and mutual caring, you will have the chance to work through some of your deepest fears.

In an unhealthy soul mate connection, however, your unresolved fears can lead to obsession or feeling out of control and will often bring additive tendencies to the surface. Even in these difficult circumstances, however, your soul mate connection can still offer you the opportunity to grow and evolve—no matter how painful the process may be.

Cosmic Lovers _____

Back in Hollywood's heyday, the ultimate Hollywood couple was Elizabeth Taylor and Richard Burton. Dame Elizabeth is a Pisces, and Richard Burton was a Scorpio—reflecting their very passionate and dramatic relationship! Burton's Moon in Virgo is near Elizabeth's South Node in Virgo, which also indicates an emotionally draining soul mate connection that may have been repeated in other lifetimes.

Soul Mates' Stories: Lessons Learned

The following are some examples of the difficulties, rewards, and dangers of dealing with soul mate connections. These stories come from my private practice in spiritual, relationship and astrology counseling. I want to give a heart-felt thanks to each of these individuals who were willing to generously share their experiences. Perhaps you will see a little bit of yourself in one of their stories.

Kate and Michael's Story

Kate, a Virgo, and Michael, a Libra, have been in a relationship for three years. Both are in their early thirties, and both have successful careers in the high-tech field. Both are extremely ambitious and greatly enjoy the challenges and financial opportunities that their careers offer them.

	Kate	Michael
Suns	Virgo	Libra
Ascendants	Leo	Aquarius
Moons	Leo	Sagittarius
Venus	Libra	Scorpio
Mars	Gemini	Sagittarius
South Nodes	Libra	Taurus
North Nodes	Aries	Scorpio

On the surface, Kate and Michael seem like the perfect couple. Many of their friends have remarked on how well suited they are and often gush that the two of them "are meant to be together." Kate and Michael do have a lot in common: both have their Moons in Fire signs—Kate in Leo and Michael in Sagittarius—which indicates that both are passionate individuals with strong sex drives. Furthermore, their ascendants in the opposite signs of Leo and Aquarius give their relationship a nice balance.

Kate and Michael's Suns in Virgo and Libra show that both are perfectionists. They do have a tendency to nitpick each other, although it is usually about small matters and of little consequence. In their day-to-day life, both seem very happy to be together.

Kate and Michael's Mars are in the opposite elements of Fire and Air, showing that both are very independent. So, it was quite a surprise to Michael when one day, Kate announced that she wanted to get married! Sure, Kate and Michael had joked about tying the knot—but neither had seemed very interested in marriage. Kate revealed that she had actually been thinking about marriage for some time but had been reluctant to mention it to Michael because she knew in her heart that he wasn't ready. Yet, Kate—a Virgo with her Venus in Libra—craved the security and stability that a marriage commitment would offer. She was ready to take their relationship to the next level.

Once Michael got over his shock, he realized that although he and Kate had much in common, they spent little time talking about their emotional needs or what they wanted from their relationship. Michael's Venus in Scorpio shows that he is not great at communicating his emotions and that he has some deep trust issues. Although Michael is a Libra, his Moon in Sagittarius and Aquarius rising show that he is very independent. And when it comes to relationships, he is likely to resist commitment.

Also, Kate's and Michael's Venus and Mars form an astrological sextile, showing that although sexually in sync, they have to work at keeping their sexual relationship from becoming boring. When they were honest with themselves, they realized that they both put a lot of effort into their careers but not into their sex life! In fact, their sexual relationship had become routine.

Michael's South and North Nodes in Scorpio and Taurus fall in Kate's fourth and tenth houses, indicating that he was helping Kate learn to balance her need for security and her desire for home and family with her career aspirations.

Heavenly Relations

Remember, the signs of your South and North Nodes and the houses where they fall in each other's charts indicate the soul lessons that you are teaching each other.

Kate's South and North Nodes fall in Michael's third and ninth houses in Aries and Libra, indicating that Kate and Michael are both fiery communicators. They tend to live in the heat of the moment without much foresight or attention to the bigger picture. This is something that they are learning to change. Kate is teaching Michael about commitment and is taking time to explore greater life purposes outside the work arena.

After much soul searching—and some couples counseling—Kate and Michael agreed upon a solution that worked for both of them: living together. Kate and Michael are now taking more time to talk about their emotional and sexual needs. They are also learning to respect each other's relationship needs and, most important, not to take each other for granted through an overemphasis on work. Kate and Michael recently engaged in weekend workshops in tantric yoga, which has added new zest and intimacy to their sex life.

Kate and Michael's ability to reach a compromise while still challenging each other's limits and desires is an excellent example of a positive soul mate relationship that is teaching both people to grow and evolve.

Susan's Story

Susan's deepest desire was to find her soul mate. Susan has a Cancer Sun and a Moon in Virgo, indicating that she is a nurturer and loves to help others. And in fact, she is a nurse by profession. Although her career as a nurse was very fulfilling, she wanted to settle down with a loving partner who would share her desire to start a family.

Dear Sextrologer ...

"I am happily married to my wife of six years, and I have no doubt that she is my one and true soul mate. We are rarely in sync, however, when it comes to our finances. She's a spender, and I'm a saver! Could this be because our Moon Nodes fall in each other's second and eighth houses?"

Excellent call! This Moon Node placement means that you are learning a lot from each other about money, finances, and your deeper values. Even though you are the saver—and your wife is the "spender," —keep in mind that your wife has something useful to teach you about value as well. The key is to try and find the right balance between both of your financial needs.

	Susan	Mr. X
Suns	Cancer	Leo
Ascendants	Taurus	Unknown
Moons	Virgo	Aries
Venus	Leo	Cancer
Mars	Pisces	Taurus
South Nodes	Capricorn	Gemini
North Nodes	Cancer	Sagittarius

At age 35, Susan's biological clock was ticking. Many of her friends suggested that Susan explore online dating to find a partner. She tried several dating websites, but after a few discouraging dates with men who she felt little or no connection with, Susan was beginning to wonder whether she was ever going to find her soul mate!

Susan also worked a lot. As her South Node in Capricorn and North Node in Cancer indicate, for all of her desire to find a relationship, Susan was very career driven. She logged many hours of overtime at work and had little time to herself, let alone time for a relationship! In addition to Susan's Moon in Virgo, she has her Mars in Pisces—and both of these can be overly sacrificing. Her Mars in Pisces led her to dream up many romantic fantasies, but the reality was that Susan actually had little room in her life for a partner. Yet, she told herself that would all change when she met the right man!

Dear Sextrologer ...

"Help! I've been dating a guy for six months, and initially the earth moved ... bells rang ... the whole nine yards! From the moment we met, I felt like this man was my soul mate. Yet, as we spend more time together, he's becoming a bit abusive—not physically, but emotionally. I'm wondering whether there is some karma between us that I should hang in there and resolve."

Oh, Sweetie ... remember, whatever your karmic connection, there is always free will and choice involved! This is obviously a very negative connection—soul mate or otherwise! Even though the earth may have initially moved for you two, abusiveness does not lead to growth. There is no reason to hang out with a man that doesn't respect you. Move on immediately!

One day, Susan did meet a man. Let's call him Mr. X. She was eating her lunch in the park outside the hospital and glimpsed a very attractive man sitting on the bench across from her. Susan found herself boldly staring at him—and he was staring back!

Mr. X came over and introduced himself. He was working in the building next to Susan's hospital as a real estate developer. Susan and Mr. X hit it off immediately, and they talked through her lunch hour. They exchanged numbers and agreed to meet for a real date.

Heavenly Relations

A wise man once said, "If your hearts are not in the same place, no matter what you think or aspire to become, the calling of your souls think and act differently."

At first, Susan was thrilled with Mr. X's company. A Leo, he was fun, exciting, and very romantic—which was a good match for Susan's Venus in Leo. Mr. X wined and dined her—just like a Moon in Aries—and seemed to be sensitive to Susan's emotional needs (typical of a Venus in Cancer). Susan spent many nights fantasizing about their romantic possibilities together. Mr. X said that he wanted to get to know Susan better before consummating their physical relationship. "How gallant," thought Susan. "I think I have found my soul mate!"

Fast-forward two months. Susan was starting to feel that something was very amiss in her relationship with Mr. X. Their dates, although fun and very romantic, were usually on weeknights and at the same restaurant. For all of Mr. X's resistance, Susan was more than ready to take the next step and explore their sexual relationship. She began to wonder whether Mr. X might be involved with someone else.

Finally, Susan confronted Mr. X. He confessed that he was indeed married—although he was in the process of separating from his wife, with whom he had three children. Mr. X said that he felt more connected to Susan than to any other woman he had ever met and wanted to keep seeing her. However, he could make no promises or commitments. Susan was heartbroken.

When Susan reviewed both of their charts, she found a number of astrological incompatibilities. Their Suns—hers Cancer, Mr. X's Leo—didn't have much in common. Neither did their Moons: Susan's Virgo, Mr. X's Aries. Also, Mr. X's South and North Nodes in Gemini and Sagittarius were not in sync with her South and North Nodes in Cancer and Capricorn. Ultimately, Susan realized that she and Mr. X wanted very different things in life and from a relationship. She wanted home, family, and security; he wanted a lot of relationship freedom.

After much soul-searching, Susan ended her relationship with Mr. X. She decided that she deserved much more from a relationship. What Susan learned from her experience was that she needed to take more time to nurture herself instead of always taking care of others or searching for her soul mate. By paying attention to her own needs, Susan is learning to open her heart to herself (and ultimately, to others). She is still looking for her soul mate but with a stronger foundation of her own emotional and relationship needs.

> **Star Alert!**
>
> Here's a universal truth: like energy attracts like energy. So, if you're wondering why you are attracted to a certain partner, reflect upon the situation and see what you are working on—and what you are putting out there!

Brenda and Rob's Story

When Brenda and Rob first met, they were both unhappily married. And the last thing on either of their minds was finding a prospective soul mate. Fate, however, thought otherwise! Both had careers in the entertainment industry—Rob as a television writer and producer and Brenda as an actress—and they met to work on Brenda's book about her journey as a cancer survivor. Rob was also a cancer survivor.

	Brenda	**Rob**
Suns	Aquarius	Aries
Ascendants	Gemini	Capricorn
Moons	Pisces	Cancer
Venus	Aquarius	Aquarius
Mars	Libra	Libra
South Nodes	Libra	Libra
North Nodes	Aries	Aries

Rob's first reaction to meeting Brenda was not initially positive. Rob had a long career in Hollywood and had met more than his share of ambitious and shallow blondes. Brenda—a tall, beautiful, and glamorous blonde—set off some very big red flags for Rob. Yet, Brenda was unlike any other woman he had ever met. She was not only beautiful but smart, strong, and passionate about life.

Brenda's reaction to Rob was quite different. "The moment I looked into Rob's eyes, I felt an instant sense of recognition," she remembers. Yet, Brenda was in the process of separating from her husband and was relishing her newfound independence. She had no interest in a romantic relationship with Rob—and, after all, they were both still married.

Heavenly Relations

Your first sense of recognition with a soul mate often comes from the first deep look into each other's eyes. As they say—eyes are mirrors to the soul!

In the process of working on Brenda's book, Brenda and Rob found that they had a lot in common. Both were at turning points in their lives; both were of a similar age; and both were looking for new approaches to life, relationships, and their careers. Both shared a similar spiritual approach to life and in their healing journeys.

As you can see from their astrology, Brenda and Rob have much in common. Brenda's Moon in Pisces and Rob's Moon in Cancer—both Water signs—shows that they have a strong emotional compatibility and are very in sync in their day-to-day lifestyle needs. Also, both of their Venuses are in Libra and both have Mars in Gemini—which shows a strong intellectual and stimulating sexual connection!

After some time and a lot of debating back and forth about what the other wanted and expected, Brenda and Rob finalized their divorces, left Los Angeles, and moved to Seattle. Talk about big and scary steps for both of them! Yet, both felt a very strong desire to explore their lives with each other.

Brenda now says that one of the aspects of her relationship with Rob that she particularly enjoys is that he treats her "like a girl"—in the best sense. Rob's Aries Sun loves to be the strong guy, but his Cancer Moon also reflects his nurturing side. Also, Rob's Venus in Libra shows that he appreciates beauty and celebrating the finer details of romance—which is very important to Brenda's Venus in Libra.

Perhaps most telling about this connection is that they have their Moon Nodes in the same signs, indicating that their soul lessons are the same. Their South Nodes in Libra indicate that both have been very relationship-focused in past lives, sometimes to the detriment of their own needs. Their North Nodes in Aries show that both are learning to be more independent and self-reliant. So, what's the result in this lifetime? Brenda and Rob support each other but also give each other the freedom to explore their individual needs.

Brenda's South and North Nodes fall in Rob's second and eighth houses, and her North Node in Aries is near Rob's North Node and Sun. This shows that Brenda inspires Rob to re-evaluate his values and his relationship with money and security—the second house. This polarity also indicates Rob and Brenda's mutual desire for spiritual growth and transformation—the eighth house.

Rob's Libra South Node and Aries North Node fall in Brenda's sixth and twelfth houses. His Sun and North Node also joins her North node, which is a very stimulating and growth-oriented placement. The sixth and twelfth Moon Node polarity indicates that Brenda is learning a lot in her relationship with Rob about how to balance her need to give to others—often overly so, (the sixth house)—with a need to explore her own intuitive and unconscious needs and desires (the twelfth house).

Heavenly Relations _____

Brenda and Rob had a past life reading that revealed that they have had numerous lifetimes together as lovers. As in the case of Brenda and Rob, a South node in Libra or a Venus South Node connection suggests that you have been lovers before!

Star Alert! _____

Rob's Mars is near Brenda's South node, which indicates that both are extremely ambitious—perhaps overly so. When you have Mars near your partner's Moon nodes—South or North—there can be a competitive aspect to your relationship.

Rob and Brenda have now been married for seven years and host a national radio show exploring consciousness. Although they experience their share of ups and downs in their life journey together, neither has ever doubted each other's love—the mark of true soul mates!

The Least You Need to Know

- ◆ Soul mate connections are by necessity intense!

- ◆ Your soul mate will bring to the surface your deepest needs and desires.

- ◆ You may feel a sexual connection with your soul mate, but these fireworks don't always mean that it's meant to last.

- ◆ The most important factor in a soul mate connection is unconditional love.

- ◆ Our soul mate checklist will help you know whether your lover is your soul mate or your stalemate!

- ◆ Our soul mate stories will help you understand your own soul mate connections.

Glossary

Air signs   The Air signs are Gemini, Libra, and Aquarius. Air signs are communicators and intellectual thinkers who love the abstract.

ascendant   Your ascendant (also known as your rising sign) is the sign of the zodiac that was rising over the horizon at the exact time of your birth. Your ascendant sets up your astrology chart and describes the way in which you present yourself to the world.

aspects   The aspects are the number of degrees between the signs. In sextrology, they indicate the degree of sexual heat between you and your lover.

astrology   The scientific study of the stars and planets and how they affect human behavior and your journey in life.

astrology websites   There are numerous astrology websites that can help you explore your astrology, get your astrological chart, find the current movement of the planets, compare your chart with your lover's, or get an online personal astrology reading.

astrology wheel   The universal astrology wheel shows the houses and their natural rulers. Your personal astrology wheel is based on your ascendant and shows the ruling signs for each of your houses.

birth chart   Your birth chart (also called a natal chart) shows the planets in the signs and the houses at the moment of your birth. It never changes and is a blueprint for your life's journey.

cardinal quality   The cardinal quality is active, aggressive, and forward-moving. The cardinal signs are Aries, Cancer, Libra, and Capricorn.

conjunction   Zero to five degrees between signs; one of the most sexually and emotionally intense aspects.

cusps   A cusp is the sign of the zodiac that begins and defines the experience of an astrological house.

dark side   Your dark side represents the often hidden parts of yourself that are unresolved, deeply conflicted, and often fear-based.

destiny   Your greater life purpose. Your ideal destiny is reflected in your North node.

Earth signs   The Earth signs are Taurus, Virgo, and Capricorn. Earth signs are grounded, conservative, and very sensual.

elements   The four elements are Fire, Air, Water, and Earth. The elements represent the basic sexual energies in which each astrological sign is based.

energies   Energies are male and female. Male energy represents the outgoing and aggressive parts of human nature, whereas female energy represents the receptive and nurturing aspects of human nature.

erogenous zones   Sexually sensitive body parts. Each sign of the zodiac has a particular erogenous zone.

ephemeris   A daily listing of the stars and planets in the signs of the zodiac.

fate   The idea of a predetermined life path or destiny.

Fire signs   The Fire signs are Aries, Leo, and Sagittarius. Fire signs are outgoing, passionate, and creative.

first quarter Moon   This Moon phase is a sexually active time where the lunar mood is to achieve, meet goals, and get things done.

fixed quality   The fixed quality is determined, resilient, and intense. Fixed signs are Taurus, Leo, Scorpio, and Aquarius.

free will   Fate is that which you cannot change. Free will is the exercise of choice and has a large hand in shaping your destiny.

full Moon   This Moon phase is the one during which feelings and instincts are at their most intense. The full Moon phase typically represents a desire for greater sexual fulfillment and deeper intimacy in important relationships.

houses   Each house in your chart represents a different area of your life. In sextrology, the 12 astrological houses represent the playing fields in which your relationship is likely to unfold.

inconjunct   150 degrees between signs; generally out-of-sync and highly difficult in relationships.

intercepted houses   An intercepted house occurs when the sign on the cusp of the house is in a late degree and includes the next sign (or signs) of the zodiac.

intuition   An inner, deeper sense of knowing.

karma   The universal law of cause and effect: you reap what you sow. Your karma is represented in your South node.

last quarter Moon   This moon phase reflects a need to complete things. This is a nesting period, and the lunar mood is sexually introverted and cautious.

Mars   The planet Mars represents your masculine nature. It is your driving life force, representing your primal sexual needs and desires.

Moon   The Moon influences feelings, emotions, and deeper intuitions. Your Moon sign determines how you relate at the deepest, most intimate emotional level.

Moon Nodes   There are two Moon Nodes: the South Node and the North Node. Moon Nodes are astrological points that indicate the soul lessons that you are to learn in this lifetime.

Moon phases   There are four major Moon phases: the new Moon, the first quarter Moon, the full Moon, and the last quarter Moon. Each Moon phase lasts approximately one week and shapes the emotional and sexual mood for its period.

mutable quality   The mutable quality is flexible and oriented to both exploration and growth. The mutable signs are Gemini, Virgo, Sagittarius, and Pisces.

new Moon   The new Moon is a high-energy phase where desires run strong. It is also an impulsive time, and the mood is sexually aggressive with little thought to consequences.

North Node   The North Node represents your soul's desire for new life and relationship experiences that will help you grow and evolve.

Nodal axis   A Nodal axis is the polarity between the astrological signs as they relate to the South and North Moon Nodes (*see* polarities).

opposition   180 degrees between signs. Oppositions are the most sexually stimulating of all the aspects.

orb   An orb, or orb of influence, indicates the proximity between two signs or planets. The smaller the orb, the greater the degree of influence.

past lives   The idea of past lives is based on the belief that the soul is eternal and chooses to reincarnate through a series of lifetimes in order to learn different life lessons.

planetary rulers   Each sign of the zodiac has a ruling planet. Aries is ruled by Mars, Taurus is ruled by Venus, and so on. The planetary ruler helps define the expression of each astrological sign.

polarities   Many aspects of astrology are based on the polarities, or opposite signs of the zodiac (for example: Aries-Libra, Taurus-Scorpio, and so on). The polarities represent the astrological balance point between the signs.

qualities   There are three qualities: fixed, cardinal, and mutable. Each quality has its own sexual personality and expression. Qualities are also known as modalities.

relationship astrology   A branch of astrology that specifically focuses on the compatibility between the astrological signs.

rising sign   *See* ascendant.

sextile   60 degrees between signs. In sextrology, sextiles are compatible but can become sexually boring.

sextrology   Similar in nature to relationship astrology, sextrology focuses on the romantic and sexual compatibility between the signs of the zodiac.

sextrology planets   The sextrology planets are the Sun and ascendant, Moon, Venus, and Mars. These planets are the ones that have the most to do with your sexual, emotional, romantic, and relationship needs and desires.

signs   In sextrology, the 12 signs of the zodiac become the 12 lovers of the zodiac—each with its own sexual needs and desires.

soul mates   A soul mate is a cosmic partner with whom you have made an agreement to come together in order to experience growth and soul lessons in this lifetime.

South Node   The South Node represents your past and karma. It represents what you have already mastered and the gifts you bring to this lifetime.

squares   90 degrees between signs. This aspect is very challenging in relationships.

Sun   The sun represents your vital life force. It is your true essence, the basis for your instincts, and the way in which you express yourself to the world.

synchronicity   The idea that all beings are energetically interconnected and that experiences in life do not happen by chance or coincidence—but instead are part of a greater and harmonious universal flow.

transits   The movement of the planets through the signs of the zodiac.

trines   120 degrees between signs. This is a very harmonious aspect, both sexually and emotionally.

Venus   The planet Venus represents your feminine nature. Your Venus indicates how you will relate to love, beauty, and the more romantic aspects of a sexual and romantic relationship.

waning moons   The waning Moons are the full and last quarter Moons. This Moon phase is reflective, and sexual energies become more introverted.

Water signs   The Water signs are Cancer, Scorpio, and Pisces. Water signs are intuitive, feeling-oriented, and compassionate.

waxing Moon   The waxing Moons are the new Moon and first quarter Moons. The waxing Moon phase is a time of new beginnings and the desire to explore new life and relationship possibilities.

zodiac   The zodiac represents the Earth as it revolves around the sun and passes through each of the 12 astrological signs.

Appendix B

Guide to Astrology Resources

Astrology books, websites, and software ... oh my! If you want to delve deeper into your sextrology, the following resources are some of my favorites.

Books

The following books—some new and some old favorites—will give you more information about the different components of astrology that relate well to exploring your sextrology:

Antepara, Robin. *Aspects: A New Approach to Understanding the Planetary Relationships in Your Chart*. Woodbury, MI: Llewellyn Publications, 2006.

Birkbeck, Lyn. *The Instant Astrologer: A Revolutionary New Book and Software Package for the Astrological Seeker*. New York: O Books, 2003.

Gerwick-Brodeur, Madeline, and Lisa Lenard. *The Complete Idiot's Guide to Astrology*. Indianapolis: Alpha Books, 2007.

Goodman, Linda. *Love Signs*. New York: First Harper Perennial, 1978.

Green, Liz. *Relating: An Astrological Guide to Living with Others on a Small Planet*. York Beach, ME: Samuel Weiser Inc., 1978.

Lofthus, Myrna. *A Spiritual Approach to Astrology*. Sebastopol, CA: CRCS Publications, 1983.

Macgregor, Trish. *Soul Mate Astrology*. Gloucester, MA: Fair Winds Press, 2004.

Paul, Haydn. *The Astrological Moon*. York Beach, ME: Samuel Weiser Inc., 1998.

Ronngren, Diane. *Lunar Nodes: Keys to Emotions and Life Experience*. Reno, NV: ETC Publishing, 2005.

Sasportas, Howard. *The Twelve Houses: An Introduction to the Houses in Astrological Interpretation*. Hammersmith, London: The Aquarian Press, 1985.

Online Resources

There are more than a million websites dedicated to astrology! To help you find the right one to fit your sextrology needs, we've included a few of the best and most helpful.

To get your birth chart, you can enter "astrology birth chart" in your favorite search engine. You will find websites that offer free services and others that charge a fee. To obtain your birth chart, you will need to know the day, place, and exact time of your birth. (There are, however, many services offered by these websites that don't require your full astrology chart.)

Here are some astrology websites that will give you your astrology chart for free:

♦ **www.astro.com**   The best of the best when it comes to getting your complete birth chart for free. Simple and easy to use, this site also offers in-depth interpretations of your chart for a fee with some of the best astrologers in the field.

♦ **www.alabe.com**   Another great website that will also give you your birth chart for free. It also offers a diverse menu of astrological information including travel, lifestyle, romance, career, karma, and past lives. This website will also give you information about obtaining astrology software.

After you have enjoyed the freebies, you may want to invest in an in-depth chart interpretation. The fee will depend on the length and type of interpretation but typically runs from $10 to $65.

Here are some other websites:

◆ **www.astrology.com**   The mother lode of all astrology websites! Astrology.com offers everything from daily horoscopes, romantic horoscopes, and daily astrology newsletters to celebrity profiles and astrology classes. It also includes lots of fun freebies!

◆ **www.astrologyzone.com**   Another popular website offering in-depth and interesting astrology information, including matchmaking by sign and finding your ideal mate. This site also offers a diverse menu of interesting and helpful astrology resources.

◆ **www.cafeastrology.com**   Definitely a favorite. The website is interesting and free and has lots of depth and explanation, including a soul-mate astrology section with lots of valuable information about understanding soul mate connections.

◆ **www.astrologymatch.com**   For a fee, relationship astrologer Pamela Fottrell provides love match compatibility reports, including your astrological love rating and astrological updates on your relationship!

◆ **www.astrodatabank.com**   The most inclusive list of celebrity and famous folks' birth dates on the Internet! Most of the cosmic lovers included in this book can be found in this great data bank of astrological information. This website's "Astrology Software Shop" also offers special deals on the latest astrology software programs.

◆ **www.ephemeris.com**   You can find a daily ephemeris on this website, including the different Moon phases. Or, you can plug in your birth information to find an ephemeris for a specific day and time. (To find out more about how to read an ephemeris, see Appendix C.)

Understanding an Ephemeris

You can access an online ephemeris (a daily listing of the stars and planets) by going to www.ephemeris.com.

What will appear is an ephemeris for the day, including all of the planets and their current signs and degrees. At the top of the listing, you will see "Phase of Moon" and can find the sign of the Moon in the listing under "Moon."

For a listing of the signs and planets for a certain day and time, you will be asked to fill in the year, month, and day and also the hour, minute, and second. (Because it's unlikely that you will know the exact second, leave this space blank and the ephemeris computer will still calculate the signs and degrees.)

You will also see spaces for "Longitude and Latitude," which indicate the location or place of birth. You can find longitude and latitude by going to www.astro.com/atlas, or you can leave these spaces blank and still get your geocentric positions (a listing of the planets for the day).

Here is an example of what you will find. This is a listing for the planets for October 10, 1981, in Seattle, Washington.

Date/Time: 1981.10.10 13L00L00 UTC (GMT – Delta T), JD = 2444888.041667
Sidereal Time: 14:16:10, Delta T = 52.0 seconds
Geocentric positions

Phase of Moon: 0.389 (0.000 = New; 0.25 0= First ¹/₄; 0.500 = Full; 0.750 = Last ¹/₄)

Planet	Longitude	Latitude	Right Asc.	Declination
Sun	17 Lib 08'02"	- 0°00'00"	13:03:10	- 6°43'49"
Moon	07 Psc 03'51"	- 3°08'52"	22:39:54	-11°50'21"
Moon's Node	28 Cnc 23'22"R	0°00'00"	08:02:00	20°29'05"
Apogee	23 Sco 34'52"R	4°33'11"	15:29:28	-14°15'24"
Mercury	02 Sco 45'45"R	- 3°14'55"	13:57:37	-15°28'52"
Venus	01 Sgr 44'07"	- 2°21'36"	15:56:27	-22°49'15"
Mars	23 Leo 45'57"	1°21'12"	09:46:12	14°52'36"
Jupiter	19 Lib 57'30"	1°05'11"	13:15:22	- 6°47'51"
Saturn	13 Lib 22'09"	2°12'53"	12:52:39	- 3°14'11"
Uranus	27 Sco 52'46"	0°10'53"	15:42:39	-19°30'43"
Neptune	22 Sgr 27'31"	1°17'14"	17:27:28	-21°56'27"
Pluto	23 Lib 58'57"	16°33'18"	13:53:03	6°06'35"
Chiron	21 Tau 56'58"R	- 2°36'05"	03:20:55	15°44'28"
Quaoar	13 Sco 49'11"	4°35'54"	14:51:03	-11°35'42"
Sedna	06 Tau 53'00"R	-11°30'02"	02:33:11	2°55'31"
Sgr A/GalCtr	26 Sgr 35'26"	- 5°36'21"	18:44:29	-29°00'02"

Highlighted are the sextrology planets including the Sun, Moon, Venus, and Mars. You will want to pay attention to the first listing next to the planet under "Longitude," which will give you the sign and exact degree for each planet.

Moon Nodes are indicated in "Moon's Node." What is listed is the North Node. The South Node is not listed but is exactly opposite in sign and degree. For example, if the Moon's Node (or North Node) is 28 degrees Cancer, the South Node will be 28 degrees Capricorn.

Sextrology Quiz

Now that you have explored the different facets of sextrology, here's your chance to put your knowledge to the test! Take the following quiz to see how much you have learned and to find out what you really want in love and relationships—and what it takes for a fantastic sex life!

This is a multiple choice quiz—no essay questions! Using your sextrology knowledge, choose from: a, b, c, or d. To keep things interesting, some questions have more than one right answer. Have fun!

1. After sensual lovemaking, your lover immediately begins to make the bed and straighten the bedroom! He or she is likely to have planets in:

   a. Leo

   b. Virgo

   c. Aquarius

   d. Pisces

2. Your idea of a romantic evening is staying at home with your lover, renting a DVD, and enjoying some microwave popcorn (or better yet, ice cream sundaes!) and lots of cuddling. You're looking for a lover with planets in:

   a. Cancer

   b. Aries

   c. Scorpio

   d. Capricorn

3. You are in sync around pleasure and your romantic desires. It's likely that you have compatible:

   a. Moon Nodes

   b. Mars

   c. Venus

   d. Suns

4. The phrase, "I think, therefore I am" applies to:

   a. Earth signs

   b. Water signs

   c. Fire signs

   d. Air signs

5. You like sensual massages, shared bubble baths, and taking your relationship nice and slowly. On the other hand, your lover prefers lots of excitement and wants to move forward very quickly. What two elements define your relationship?

   a. Fire and Water

   b. Air and Water

   c. Earth and Fire

   d. Fire and Air

6. Your ascendant, or rising sign, is based on:

    a. Your Moon Nodes

    b. The exact time of your birth

    c. The time of day you prefer to have sex

    d. Your relationship with your lover

7. You like fast cars, excitement, and daredevils in love. Your ideal sign is:

    a. Capricorn

    b. Cancer

    c. Libra

    d. Aries

8. Your idea of foreplay is lots of romance and being wined and dined! You're looking for a lover with a Venus in:

    a. Sagittarius

    b. Cancer

    c. Libra

    d. Aquarius

9. You want a lover who is fun-loving, who will give you lots of independence, and who possibly wants to explore the world with you. You're looking for someone with planets in (hint: Brad Pitt is this sign!):

    a. Libra

    b. Cancer

    c. Pisces

    d. Sagittarius

10. Your deepest desire is to find a lover who will tear off all of your clothes and make passionate love to you in some seriously inappropriate locations! You're looking for a Mars in a(n):

    a. Fire sign

    b. Air sign

    c. Water sign

    d. Earth sign

11. When the Moon is transiting the sign of Sagittarius, it is a good time to:

    a. Stay at home in your fuzzy slippers

    b. Hit the town and have fun

    c. Have a serious discussion with your lover about commitment

    d. Commune with your family

12. You and/or your lover's favorite movies are romantic tear-jerkers like *Beaches*, *The Wedding Singer*, or *Casablanca*. It's more than likely that you have planets in:

    a. Aries and Sagittarius

    b. Cancer and Pisces

    c. Taurus and Capricorn

    d. Virgo and Gemini

13. Sextrology is the study of the signs of the zodiac and how they relate to:

    a. Gardening

    b. Love and sex

    c. The release of endorphins

    d. Career

14. You want some real sexual kinkiness in the bedroom. You're looking for a lover with planets in:

    a. Taurus

    b. Libra

    c. Aquarius

    d. Gemini

15. You and your lover often seem to come from two different perspectives yet mirror each other's deepest relationship desires. Without a doubt, the makeup sex is very hot. An aspect between your planets is likely to be a(n):

    a. Conjunction

    b. Sextile

    c. Inconjuct

    d. Opposition

16. Your partner is extremely dramatic, likes showing off his or her sexual prowess, and enjoys lots of "bling." It's entirely likely that he or she has planets in:

    a. Taurus

    b. Aries

    c. Cancer

    d. Leo

17. You're furious with your lover and succumb to your inner rage by using his or her toothbrush to clean the sink—without telling! It could be that you have your Mars in:

    a. Pisces

    b. Libra

    c. Scorpio

    d. Sagittarius

18. Karma is:

    a. A big drag

    b. What you need to feel guilty about

    c. Cause and effect

    d. Represented in your South Node

19. You're feeling very ready to explore new love and relationship possibilities. The phase of the Moon is likely to be:

    a. New

    b. First quarter

    c. Full

    d. Fourth quarter

20. This zodiac sign is partial to the color green and emeralds:

    a. Cancer

    b. Libra

    c. Gemini

    d. Taurus

21. You feel very in sync with your lover in your emotional and deeper intimacy needs. It's likely that you have compatible:

    a. Moons

    b. Suns

    c. Mars

    d. Moon Nodes

22. You and your lover tend to squabble about finances—a lot. It could be that you have planets in each other's:

    a. First houses

    b. Third houses

    c. Second houses

    d. Sixth houses

23. Your fantasy lover has a dark and mysterious side, à la James Bond or Trinity from *The Matrix* movies. Some leather doesn't hurt, either! You're looking for someone with planets in:

    a. Virgo

    b. Sagittarius

    c. Scorpio

    d. Cancer

24. He or she fusses over your eating and spending habits and hands you a to-do list after only a few dates. It's likely that your lover has planets in:

    a. Aries

    b. Taurus

    c. Gemini

    d. Cancer

25. You're feeling spontaneous and in the mood for sex—no strings attached! Your ideal lover for the moment is a(n):

    a. Cancer

    b. Aries

    c. Virgo

    d. Gemini

26. The two planets that most define your sexual and relationship needs are:

    a. Sun and ascendant

    b. Sun and Moon

    c. South and North Nodes

    d. Venus and Mars

27. A South Node connection with your lover indicates:

    a. Your past karma together

    b. How you relate in love and romance

    c. Your future destiny together

    d. An easy relationship experience

28. Match your ideal partner with the signs of the zodiac:

    a. Passionate and independent   a. Cancer, Pisces

    b. Caring and nurturing   b. Aries, Sagittarius

    c. Stable and reliable   c. Libra, Gemini

    d. Intellectual and well-read   d. Taurus, Capricorn

29. You learn a lot from each other in regard to creativity and fulfilling your higher aspirations. It could be that you have planets in each other's:

    a. First and seventh houses

    b. Fourth and tenth houses

    c. Second and eighth houses

    d. Third and eleventh houses

30. The sign of your Venus represents how you relate to:

    a. Emotional intimacy

    b. Your mother-in-law

    c. Love and romance

    d. Primal sexual needs

31. You are sexually curious and restless for new experiences in life and in your relationships. You are likely to share a Sun sign with:

    a. Virgos Adam Sandler and Sophia Loren

    b. Geminis Angelina Jolie and Johnny Depp

    c. Scorpios Demi Moore and Leonardo DiCaprio

    d. Cancers Meryl Streep and Tom Hanks

32. The most overtly sexual signs of the zodiac fall in the elements of:

    a. Air and Water

    b. Fire and Earth

    c. Air and Fire

    d. Water and Earth

33. You live in the moment and want a lover who is as spontaneous as you are. You're looking for a(n):

    a. Capricorn

    b. Taurus

    c. Cancer

    d. Aries

34. You know that it's time to move on but are having great difficulty breaking up with your lover. It could be that you have a strong:

    a. Sun connection

    b. North Node connection

    c. South Node connection

    d. Venus and Mars connection

35. A big turn-on for you is a lover who gives you lots of space and freedom. You're looking for a lover with planets in:

    a. Virgo, Libra, Cancer

    b. Pisces, Capricorn, Leo

    c. Aries, Sagittarius, Aquarius

    d. Taurus, Leo, Scorpio

36. Have you jumped on the high-tech bandwagon to express your sexual needs? In other words, have you indulged in text sex, online dating, or spontaneous and sexy voice mails If so, you are likely to have planets in:

    a. Libra and/or Leo

    b. Taurus and/or Cancer

    c. Pisces and/or Aries

    d. Aquarius and/or Gemini

37. It's a full Moon, and you're feeling emotionally intense. It's best to:

    a. Lay low and commune with your deeper needs

    b. Try something sexually adventurous

    c. Approach your boss for the promotion you've always dreamed of

    d. Paaaaaarty!

38. "Our eyes met across a crowded room" applies to:

    a. Sun sign connections

    b. Soul mate connections

    c. Venus and Mars connections

    d. Moon sign connections

39. You approach your life from a greater spiritual, worldly, and intuitive perspective. Your best love match would be:

    a. Libra

    b. Capricorn

    c. Cancer

    d. Sagittarius

40. You enjoy the great outdoors and nature—but at a resort, thank you very much! Your ideal lover is:

    a. Aries

    b. Taurus

    c. Gemini

    d. Sagittarius

41. You tend to compete with each other regarding whose needs come first. It's likely that you have out-of-sync:

    a. Suns

    b. Moons

    c. Venus

    d. Mars

42. You want long-term security and commitment in your relationship. Your ideal lover has planets in:

    a. Taurus

    b. Aries

    c. Libra

    d. Gemini

43. Together, you are learning how to balance your home, family, and career needs. It's likely that you have your Moon Nodes in:

    a. Second and eighth houses/Taurus and Scorpio

    b. Third and ninth houses/Gemini and Sagittarius

    c. Fourth and tenth houses/Cancer and Capricorn

    d. Sixth and twelfth houses/Virgo and Pisces

44. You are planning a romantic evening with your lover where you can bring each other's sexual fantasies to life. The sign of the Moon that could work best is:

    a. Pisces

    b. Leo

    c. Aquarius

    d. Capricorn

45. "I want to stop the world and be with you!" suggests:

    a. Two Fire signs together

    b. Two Water signs together

    c. Two Earth signs together

    d. Two Air signs together

46. Relationships between the fixed signs Taurus, Leo, Scorpio, and Aquarius can mean:

    a. An easy relationship connection

    b. Lots of power struggles

    c. Codependency

    d. Blissful romance

47. You want to spice up your love and sex life with your lover. You should pay attention to your:

    a. Venus and Mars connections

    b. Moon connections

    c. Sun connections

    d. South Node connections

48. Soul mate connections offer the opportunity to:

    a. Get comfortable and relax

    b. Experience growth and learning

    c. Have a detached love affair

    d. Get married and live happily ever after

49. Your lover is completely comfortable in his or her skin and may even like to walk around buck naked! He or she probably has planets in the sign of:

    a. Virgo

    b. Libra

    c. Taurus

    d. Aquarius

50. Match the sign of the zodiac with its sexual turn-ons:

    a. Sexy lingerie   a. Virgo

    b. Whipped cream   b. Libra

    c. Erotica   c. Cancer

    d. Good hygiene   d. Leo

51. Intuition is:

    a. The latest fragrance from Jennifer Lopez

    b. What you can find through a 1-800-PSYCHIC love line

    c. Being able to read your lover's mind

    d. A deeper sense of knowing

52. Sexual fidelity is important to you. You're looking for a lover with a moon in:

    a. A Fire sign

    b. An Earth sign

    c. An Air sign

    d. A Water sign

53. Synchronicity indicates:

    a. A happy circumstance

    b. Having the same work schedules

    c. A possible soul mate connection

    d. Lots of sex together

54. Your Sun sign represents:

    a. Your deeper emotional needs

    b. How you relate to love and romance

    c. Your appropriate SPF factor

    d. How you express your true essence

55. Match each sign with its erogenous zone:

    a. Aries   a. Hips and thighs

    b. Pisces   b. Head and face

    c. Libra   c. Neck and back

    d. Sagittarius   d. Feet

56. Even though the sex may be hot initially, you constantly challenge each other and fight like crazy. It's likely that you have the following aspect between your planets:

    a. Trine

    b. Square

    c. Inconjunct

    d. Sextile

57. Match the lovemaking experience with its likely element:

    a. Slow and sensual   a. Fire signs

    b. Passionate and vigorous   b. Air signs

    c. Fun, intellectual, detached   c. Water signs

    d. Emotionally intense   d. Earth signs

58. Your lover likes to talk before, during, and after sex, which may be highly stimulating—or not! He or she likely has planets in:

    a. Gemini

    b. Taurus

    c. Aries

    d. Capricorn

59. You meet someone for the first time and … zowie! You feel an immediate connection. It is likely that you are experiencing:

    a. A soul mate connection

    b. An extremely hot guy or gal

    c. A need to have sex

    d. Similar body types

60. You're planning a fabulous party for your friends to celebrate your new promotion. The transiting Moon sign that will help it be a great success is:

    a. Scorpio or Pisces

    b. Libra or Leo

    c. Cancer or Scorpio

    d. Aquarius or Capricorn

61. The fairytale *Cinderella* is often associated with which sign of the zodiac?

    a. Capricorn

    b. Libra

    c. Leo

    d. Pisces

62. Even upon first meeting, you two just seem to bring out each other's competitive natures. It could be that you have:

    a. Sun and North Node connections

    b. Mars and South Node connections

    c. Venus and South Node connections

    d. Moon and North Node connections

63. You pride yourself in your reputation, and your career is very important to you. You're looking for a partner who will support you career desires and who will also match your highly sexual nature. It's very likely that you have planets in:

    a. Libra

    b. Aries

    c. Capricorn

    d. Pisces

64. Match the signs with their ideal date experience:

    a. An art show and a romantic dinner   a. Aquarius

    b. The heck with dinner ... let's have sex!   b. Cancer

    c. Meeting the family   c. Aries

    d. A sci-fi or *Star Trek* convention   d. Libra

65. You prefer the strong, silent type. Your ideal lover is George Clooney or Michele Pfeiffer. You're looking for someone with planets in:

    a. Libra

    b. Aries

    c. Taurus

    d. Gemini

66. The cardinal signs of the zodiac are:

    a. Taurus, Leo, Scorpio, and Aquarius

    b. Aries, Cancer, Libra, and Capricorn

    c. Gemini, Virgo, Sagittarius, and Pisces

    d. Curly, Moe, and Larry

67. The most significant houses in sextrology are:

    a. Third, ninth, and eighth

    b. Second, eighth, and ninth

    c. First, seventh, and eighth

    d. Fourth, tenth, and third

68. The most difficult aspect in relationships is:

    a. A conjunction

    b. An inconjunct

    c. A sextile

    d. A trine

69. The signs of the zodiac that are the most sensual are:

    a. Air signs

    b. Water signs

    c. Earth signs

    d. Fire signs

70. The astrological quality that is the most stubborn and needs most to feel in control is:

    a. Cardinal

    b. Fixed

    c. Pliable

    d. Mutable

71. The quote, "You have bewitched me, body and soul" is from one of the following star-crossed lovers and has strong Scorpio overtones:

    a. Romeo and Juliet

    b. Elizabeth Bennett and Mr. Darcy

    c. Bridget Jones and Mark Darcy

    d. Jerry Maguire and Dorothy Boyd

Key

1) b

2) a

3) c

4) d

5) c

6) b

7) d

8) c

9) d

10) a

11) b

12) b

13) b

14) c and d

15) d

16) d

17) c

18) c and d

19) a

20) d

21) a

22) c

23) c

24) d

25) b and d

26) d

27) a

28) a-b, b-a, c-d, and d-c

29) d

30) c

31) b

32) b

33) d

34) c

35) c

36) d

37) a

38) b

39) d

40) b

41) d

42) a

43) a

44) a

45) b

46) b

47) a

48) b

49) c

50) a-d, b-c, c-b, and d-a

51) d

52) b and d

53) d

54) d

55) a-b, b-d, c-c, and d-a

56) b

57) a-d, b-a, c-b, and d-c

58) a

59) a

60) b

61) d

62) b

63) c

64) a-d, b-c, c-b, and c-a

65) c

66) b

67) c

68) b

69) c

70) b

71) b

If you have 60 or more correct answers, congratulations! You are extremely knowledgeable about sextrology and what you really want and need in your love and sex life!

If you have 30 to 60 correct answers, good job! You're definitely on the right path toward understanding your sextrology. You may want to review your missed answers in order to find out more about what you want in your relationships.

If you have fewer than 30 right answers, don't despair! This quiz was very in-depth. To get a better handle on your sextrology, review the chapters in this book and you will be your own sextrologer in no time!

Index

D-E

Leo and Virgo
 relationships, 69
Libra and Virgo
 relationships, 73
Mars in Virgo, 133-134
Moon in Virgo, 91, 114
Pisces and Virgo
 relationships, 75
Sagittarius with Virgo
 relationships, 70
Scorpio and Virgo
 relationships, 75
sexual characteristics,
 59-60
strengths and
 weaknesses, 60
Taurus and Virgo
 relationships, 76
turn-ons, 60
Venus in Virgo, 127-128
Virgo/Pisces Nodal axis
 (soul-mate
 connections), 188-189
Virgo and Virgo
 relationships, 76
Water and Earth
 relationships, 74-75
eight essentials of Sextrology
aspects, 11-12
 hard aspects, 11
 soft aspects, 11
elements, 7-8
 Air, 8
 Earth, 8
 Fire, 8
 Water, 8
houses, 12-13
Moon signs, 10
Nodes of the Moon, 14
qualities
 cardinal, 9
 fixed, 9
 mutable, 9
Sun signs and ascendants,
 10

Venus and Mars, 10-11
eighth house (Scorpio),
 170-171
elements, 7
 Air, 8
 Air and Air relationships,
  70-71
 Air and Earth
  relationships, 72-73
 Air and Water
  relationships, 71
 Fire and Air
  relationships, 67
 Earth, 8
 Air and Earth
  relationships, 72-73
 Earth and Earth
  relationships, 75-76
 Fire and Earth
  relationships, 69-70
 Water and Earth
  relationships, 74-75
 Fire, 8
 Fire and Air
  relationships, 67
 Fire and Earth
  relationships, 69-70
 Fire and Fire
  relationships, 66-67
 Fire and Water
  relationships, 68-69
 Water, 8
 Air and Water
  relationships, 71
 Fire and Water
  relationships, 68-69
 Water and Earth
  relationships, 74-75
 Water and Water
  relationships, 73-74
eleventh house (Aquarius), 172
energies
 Aquarius, 37
 Aries, 18
 astrological houses,
  164-165

Cancer, 42
Capricorn, 60
Gemini, 30
Leo, 21
Libra, 33
Pisces, 49
Sagittarius, 24
Scorpio, 45
Taurus, 54
Virgo, 57
ephemeris, 15
erogenous zones
 Aquarius, 37
 Aries, 18
 Cancer, 42
 Capricorn, 61
 Gemini, 30
 Leo, 21
 Libra, 33
 Pisces, 49
 Sagittarius, 24
 Scorpio, 45
 Taurus, 54
 Virgo, 57

F

feminine aspects (Venus), 122
fidelity
 Gemini, 31
 Moon signs and, 83
fifth and eleventh house
 polarity, 194-195
fifth house (Leo), 168-169
Fire Moons, 83
 Aries, 84
 compatibility
  Fire and Air Moons,
   95-96
  Fire and Earth Moons,
   98-99
  Fire and Fire Moons, 94
  Fire and Water Moons,
   96-97

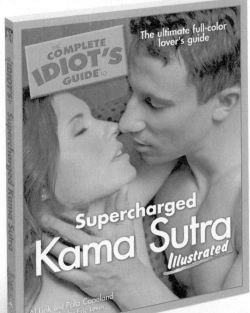